HARD TALK

HARD TALK by RAFE MAIR

Harbour Publishing

Published by
Harbour Publishing Co. Ltd.
P.O. Box 219
Madeira Park, BC
V0N 2H0
www.harbourpublishing.com

Edited by Betty Keller
Cover and text design by Anna Comfort
Cover Illustration by Peter Lynde
Printed and bound in Canada

Harbour Publishing acknowledges financial support from the Government of Canada through the Book Publishing Industry Development Program and the Canada Council for the Arts, and from the Province of British Columbia through the British Columbia Arts Council and the Book Publisher's Tax Credit through the Ministry of Provincial Revenue.

THE CANADA COUNCIL | LE CONSEIL DES ARTS
FOR THE ARTS | DU CANADA
SINCE 1957 | DEPUIS 1957

BRITISH
COLUMBIA
ARTS COUNCIL
Supported by the Province of British Columbia

Library and Archives Canada Cataloguing in Publication

Mair, Rafe, 1931-
    Hard talk / Rafe Mair.

ISBN 1-55017-374-X / 978-1-55017-374-1

    I. Title.

AC8.M315 2005   081   C2005-903200-6

Dedicated to Alexandra Morton, Captain Paul Watson and Anthony Marr, environmentalists—the highest of all callings.

CONTENTS

PART FIVE: HEALING MORAL WOUNDS IN THE CHURCH

PART SIX: VITAL SIGNS

PART SEVEN: BEEFS

PART EIGHT: A SPORTING LIFE

PART NINE: THE LIGHTER SIDE

Part One

THE AFTERMATH

Legacy of 9/11 in the United States

Early on the morning of September 11, 2001, I drove to work listening to classical music on my CD player. Just a normal ride with my thoughts centred on the editorial I would deliver at the top of the program. I came into the studio to meet a sea of thunderstruck faces. Did I not know what had happened? I had arrived just in time to see the second plane hit the World Trade Center. Along with most of the world, I watched in horror the further terrible events of that day—especially the film of the second plane—being replayed over and over.

Less than three weeks later a UBC professor, Sunera Thobani, delivered a talk at a women's conference in which she castigated the United States for its many—as she saw them—world-wide sins, saying in effect that America had only herself to blame. She was dumped on by most commentators, including me. Now, I'm not so sure that I should have. Events analyzed at the time they happen are usually analyzed incorrectly. Shock and horror produce analysis that is more a lashing out in rage than cool thought about the overall issues connected to the event. Re-reading Ms. Thobanyi's speech now, I find it hard to see what was so terrible about it. It was a typical analysis by a militant woman of the Left. The problem was the timing. We weren't yet ready for an anti-American screed. We were in shock. We were still rallying behind the victims, including the firemen and policemen who displayed such bravery that day. We were mad. Someone had to pay, didn't they? Who that should be was unclear, but, dammit, it had to be someone!

And where would Osama Bin Laden strike next? Could it be the Peace Tower in Ottawa? American authorities were pretty sure the Golden Gate Bridge in San Francisco would be a target. This was the first time most North Americans had seen war up close, and we were scared. So scared that we were prepared to accept President Bush as a latter-day Winston Churchill and follow him wherever he led. (Read now the quotes of George Bush, Donald Rumsfeld, John Ashcroft and Dick Cheney and they seem like they originated not with Churchill but with "Big Brother" in George Orwell's *Nineteen Eighty-Four*!) There were enemies out there, the president assured us, and he was going to get them "dead or alive." The United States was suddenly the sole carrier of the banner of freedom. There was a rush to judgment. The United States Congress passed the Patriot Act and other bills that gave unbelievable powers to the government to ignore the American Constitution.

But at the same time Mr. Bush was waging his war for freedom and liberty, he was not so slowly eroding at home the principles that he was, with force if necessary, foisting on nations overseas. It was just like Vietnam where "we had to destroy the village in order to save it." Now we had to eliminate free speech in order to save it. The sage words of Benjamin Franklin when his country was in peril—"They that can give up essential liberties to obtain a little temporary safety deserve neither liberty nor safety"—were forgotten in the mood of the moment. All the newspapers, including the mighty *New York Times,* were on the side of the Bush radicals as were all the TV networks. This was war and in war we must all do as we're told. I was no better than any other. I stopped thinking and thus stopped asking embarrassing questions. I went into a snooze.

President Bush cast about for enemies and the obvious one was Afghanistan, home of the Taliban and the supporters of al Qaeda, Osama Bin Laden's bunch, and of Bin Laden himself. The United States and others went into Afghanistan, beat the Taliban, didn't follow up their advantage to seek out Bin Laden when they had him cornered and wound up with a country where democracy rules—sort of—with its capital, Kabul, the only place pacified—sort of.

Most of us had little reason to doubt that Saddam Hussein was a bad man who didn't like the United States very much. My first reaction on air to 9/11 was to opine that in some way Saddam had to be the brains behind this atrocity. After all, he was the cruelest tyrant of our time and had used poison gas both in his war against Iran and in his own country against rebelling Kurds. Certainly Saddam loathed Israel, and we could all remember his sending scud missiles against that country in the first Gulf War. For me and many others the key question was simple: did Saddam Hussein possess or was he about to possess weapons of mass destruction (WMDs) that he could use on his neighbours, especially Israel?

It would take a fair-sized book to contain all the statements by the Bush administration to the effect that Hussein did possess WMDs and the capability to use them. The building of their case against him was long, thorough…and mostly bullshit. We were shown maps and photographs of the sites where WMDs were poised to go into action. We heard about intercepted phone calls. There was President Bush in his State of the Union address in January 2001 telling how Iraq had received "yellow cake," an essential ingredient in making nuclear weapons, from Niger. There was no maybe about it; it was true! Except it wasn't. There seemed to be only one man in the U.S. administration who was not too sure—Secretary of State Colin Powell. He seemed hesitant, even dovish, until February 5, 2001, when he went before the UN and made it absolutely clear that Saddam had WMDs, could use them, and must be stopped before he did use them. The man I had relied upon as the only credible person in Bush's inner circle was now 100 percent onside with the presidential position. There was only one man left to listen to, British Prime Minister Tony

Blair, who, after all, led the party that housed within it most of the nation's pacifists. He would surely tell us the truth. Well, he told us that Saddam's WMDs would be in action within 45 minutes of Saddam's orders. And that was bullshit, too.

Although there was no basis for the, to say the least, hawkish position of Blair and Bush, many of us swallowed it. The reason for attacking Iraq that they gave to the United Nations, the UN Security Council, the leaders of the world—especially those within the European Union—and the people of the world was crap. It was utterly without foundation. The US president, the vice president, the secretary of state, the secretary of defense, and all lesser officials, such as Condoleezza Rice (now, of course, secretary of state), plus British Prime Minister Blair, had not just shaded the truth or been a bit economical with it. They had lied. Most of Congress had lied, too, with one or two exceptions, such as Senator Robert C. Byrd. The press, almost without exception, had in effect lied by not seriously questioning any of the US administration's statements. The United States was now in the grip of a government that had suspended their civil rights and then been re-elected. And today there remains in the United States an atmosphere eerily reminiscent of the McCarthy reign of terror in the 1950s.

September 11, 2001 was a day of infamy. It was also the day the truth became deathly ill with little hope of recovery. Somehow we have overlooked the fact that 9/11 wasn't an elaborate plan requiring highly sophisticated weapons for its success. It was a handful of men with box cutters. And we reacted as if armies led by mad mullahs would soon be marching in our streets.

Today the America media, heavily censored by its right-wing owners, treat criticism of the administration as tantamount to treason. Members of the general public are urged to root out the bad people and report them to the FBI, to which request Americans have responded with hundreds of thousands of "tips."

The very values that had for so long set the "Great Republic" (Churchill's term) apart as a beacon of liberty are now used as truncheons by means of which dissent is muffled and, indeed, punished. The Constitution has been replaced by the Bible as interpreted by the radical Right. Evil tyrants such as Prince Abdullah of Saudi Arabia and Hosni Mubarak of Egypt are embraced as the saviours of freedom while they lead countries that don't know the meaning of the word.

The events of 9/11 did what they were intended to do as their first object: they terrorized the people of the United States such that they would quickly abandon the principles upon which their country was founded and demonize everyone, at home and abroad, who questioned the way to the future as seen by George W. Bush. It's gotten to the point where the nation is so scared that, in the words of the late, great actor Humphrey Bogart, you are suspect "if you scratch your ass during the playing of the national anthem." When he made that remark back in the 1950s, McCarthyism was rampant, and the American Constitution had in effect been suspended. If a witness before the House Committee on Un-American Activities pled the right under the Fifth Amendment not to incriminate himself, he found himself in jail for contempt of Congress! John Swinton, chief of staff of the *New York Times,* said this about where the media stood when McCarthy was terrorizing his nation:

> There is no such thing at this date in the world's history as an independent press in America...The business of the journalist is to destroy truth; to lie outright; to pervert; to vilify; to fawn at the feet of Mammon; and to sell his country and his race for his daily bread. You know it and I know it, and what folly is this toasting an independent press? We are the tools and vassals for rich men behind the scenes. We are jumping jacks; they pull

the strings and we dance. Our talents, our possibilities, and our lives are all the property of other men. We are intellectual prostitutes.

Today what the Bush administration is saying is that once again the US Constitution, that beautiful document, which along with the Declaration of Independence lays down the basis of liberty for America and acts as a beacon of hope for so many other nations, is only in effect when there is no threat to American security. In short, when you don't need rights you have them; when you need them desperately, they are snatched away by presidential edict.

The events of 9/11 demonstrated what we should have known—that judgments made in a state of fear are seldom accurate and that actions taken at such times are always excessive, often in the extreme. The Patriot Act and associated legislation in the US demonstrate that, when a government can scare people enough, they will accept having their basic and essential democratic guarantees cast aside. This is equally true in both Canada and the US. Both governments eliminated the rights of citizens of Japanese descent during World War II after claiming they posed a threat to the nation. A couple of Canadian overreactions came with the post-war banning of the Communist Party and Trudeau placing the entire country under martial law during the so-called Quebec Crisis. Even the sainted Abraham Lincoln suspended habeas corpus during the American Civil War.

If nothing else these examples should demonstrate to us that governments hate free speech because it exposes their inadequacies for all to see. Watergate was entirely about the attempt to suppress free speech and avoid accountability for a picayune little break-and-enter. Think about it! That tawdry little crime brought down the president of the United States. There were no issues of bad governance here, simply dirty politics by a dirty politician who was brought down because he refused to tell the truth or let any around him do so. But here's the rub. The Nixon lesson has not been lost on Americans or Canadians in authority, but the lesson they took from it was not that governments and leaders ought to tell the truth. It was: "For God's sake, don't get caught lying!" And it was: "Never let a president be caught lying again." This resulted in Ronald Regan, that amiable bull-shitter, getting away with the Iran-Contra scandal. Unlike poor old Tricky Dick, Reagan had no end of people prepared to run on their own swords to protect him.

But the real lesson to be learned is that governments, so afraid to be proved liars (which by definition most of them are), will do everything within their power to prevent people from using free speech as a weapon. Liars want company, not criticism. Ever since the crowds stood outside the White House shouting to an imprisoned Lyndon Johnson, "Hey, hey, LBJ, how many kids did you kill today?" authorities have done all within their power, which is considerable, to shield presidents and others in power from the hurt that comes with assembled people exercising their right of dissent. Free speech, which is hardly always accurate speech, is that which frightens authority so terribly. If you can say what you wish, authority will be forced to reply. Since the reply will often be awkward, we can't have that, now can we?

Those in authority have plenty of allies amongst the citizenry. Most people on the far Right, I'm sad to say, have such a sense of personal righteousness that they feel it's their duty to keep unpleasantness from the ears of the ignorant and the unwashed—which is to say everyone else. I have a regular caller who berates me for criticizing George W. Bush because I "simply don't know what Mr. Bush knows and Mr. Bush can't tell anyone because it would expose critical state secrets." And after I had delivered an editorial criticizing the Japanese for not apologizing to the Chinese for wartime atrocities, he dumped on me for "not supporting an ally against Red China"! The establishments have lots of allies like this man in the ranks of the general public and they know how to use them.

The worst part of what the terrible tragedy of 9/11 has proven is that the US Constitution is inadequate to the task of keeping the Bush administration from using it to trample all over the rights of people whose country used to be the beacon of liberty for the whole world.

The Legacy of 9/11 in Canada

What about Canada after 9/11? Where has the notion of liberty gone in this country? And why is it that those who truly stand for free speech in Canada are called cowards and in one form or another labeled enemies of the very freedom they are trying to uphold?

In the US since September 11, 2001, we have seen what are known as First Amendment areas blocked off so protesters can only protest well out of sight and earshot of those being protested against. But Canada pioneered that trick in Vancouver during the APEC conference of 1997, when not only were demonstrations severely restricted but the police also picked up "revolutionaries" before the event and released them only if they promised not to protest. One law student carrying banners saying "Democracy" and "Free Speech" was assaulted by the RCMP and thrown into jail. What is the point of having freedom to assemble if the assembly has to be in a place where it causes no one any discomfort or at a time when no one is listening or, both? What is the point of free speech if we cannot say what we wish, subject only to the narrowest of restraints necessary to protect the state and to the minimum constraints of defamation laws?

Today the ownership of the media is more tightly controlled than it has ever been, and the need for self-censorship by journalists in order to keep working becomes all the greater as time passes. Yet through it all, the propensity and ability of the press to self-praise and delude itself as it pretends to the public that it and it alone protects our liberties is—it would seem—limitless. Dissent is permitted so long as it is within the establishment's narrow comfort zone.

Canadians love to cluck their tongues at the clear loss of civil liberties south of the border, but what about here at home? The case of Ernst Zundel should make us all blush with shame and make us realize our own hypocrisy. Here was, unquestionably, a most disagreeable man who combined his nastiness with an unerring ability to get under everyone's skin. I don't suppose that, with the exception of anti-Semites who, like the poor, will always be with us, he had a friend in the country—perhaps not in the world. He especially offended Jews because he denied the Holocaust. So far as I'm able to determine he threatened no one with harm and incited no violence. He simply voiced an extremely unpopular notion, one that was so ridiculous that one ought to have been able to simply ignore him as half-baked cranks are ignored when they climb on soapboxes at Speakers' Corner in London's Hyde Park.

At about this time I can hear the murmur, increasing in crescendo, that Oliver Wendell Holmes Jr. said, "A man mustn't cry 'fire' in a crowded theatre." The learned justice and all who have quoted him since have ignored the fact that the man who cries "fire" in a theatre is not exercising free speech at all but committing an act of violence. If he were to pull the fire alarm, the result would be the same—panic and inevitable death. There is a very big difference between that action and free speech. The man in the theatre isn't trying to insult anyone, persuade anyone to a point of view, complain about authority, effect a political change or simply vent his anger at some issue or other; he is committing a direct act of violence.

Is there then a case for enacting laws against inciting violence? Of course there is, and always has been. And I suppose there can be times when expressing a strong opinion and inciting violence come close to being the same thing. There is a fine judgment to be made here, but expressing a disagreeable opinion is nowhere near that line. Incarcerating people who level insults is a very selective thing. Suppose I were to cross the country shouting that there was no slaughter of the Armenians? Or that Pol Pot's killing fields did not happen? Or that Joseph Stalin was a kindly old gentleman who loved kulaks? I would be regarded as a crank but no one would think of jailing me or, had I like my father been born in New Zealand, deporting me! The fact is that Armenians, Cambodians and kulaks carry no political clout and can safely be orally abused. Jews, on the other hand, are a very large, politically well-organized and strong—and I might add valuable—part of our communities. It is on this point that Jews and I have clashed ever since I got into public life. I would sue and unquestionably be successful if I were to be called anti-Semitic. I don't have an anti-Semitic bone in my body. What I do have is a strong sense that free speech to the outermost reaches should be tolerated in a free society and that lies should be countered with the truth, not jail.

Over the past few years there have emerged some pretty nasty bits of rubbish who have been clearly anti-Semitic. One of them, school teacher Jim Keegstra, became famous all over the land because he was repeatedly prosecuted for anti-Semitic statements, whereas the Red Deer school board should simply have fired him and left him to foam at the mouth in peace. The late Doug Collins, a Vancouver writer and sometime broadcaster, was more eclectic in his prejudices—he hated everyone with equal venom. Without fear or favour, he insulted everyone who wasn't his version of pure. Left alone, he was a cranky old man writing for a minor league community newspaper but, because the Canadian Jewish Congress and others chased him from one human rights tribunal to another, he became famous and to the crackpots of the world a hero and a martyr.

Do I really have to say, after all my years of fighting for the underdog and the victims of our establishment, that I detest the likes of Collins who, I might add, reserved an especially large dose of bile for me that occasionally erupted into one of his columns? Though a brave man in war, he was a moral coward who, when I once said he had been fired by a certain radio station, threatened to sue me, and my station's lawyer made me apologize. If I had said he was let go when his contract expired, which is the way one is fired in my business, it would have been okay. My point is, even if I libeled him, it was a harmless puff compared to what he did regularly to people of other races and religions that he hated. Like all cowards, he could dish it out but not take it.

So what is it about us North Americans? Are we afraid that free speech and freedom of assembly will lead to a civil war? Of course, they do indeed lead to civil wars but only where they are denied and because they are denied. Does anyone seriously contend that if someone ran down Pennsylvania Avenue shouting, "Down with Bush and hurrah for Osama Bin Laden!" that the security of America or its president would be compromised? Or if some half-baked nitwit walked down Granville Street with a sign saying, "The Holocaust Never Happened" that national security would be threatened? That such might be an actionable defamation in the civil courts is one thing, but when it is authority that decides what is an insult, and authority that is given the power to act against it, freedom of speech becomes a bad joke.

What happened on 9/11 did not come about because nasty men with beards and bombs were inciting the population to hijack airplanes and hit buildings with them. It happened because of an appalling, hugely embarrassing lack of elementary security. And the US Patriot Act was, in fact, not an act of protection but an embarrassed reaction by those who wanted to divert attention from their own inadequacies by making it appear that nothing less than the theft of all civil rights could prevent a repetition of the horrible disaster that a reasonably alert Ruritania could have averted.

Canada hasn't gone quite that far yet but it's damned close! In Canada we have confused the virtue of good manners with the right to be rude if we wish. Politeness is a quality difficult enough to define at the best of times but, even when it can be defined, should surely be a social objective and not a political imperative. There is no law—at least there shouldn't be—against bad manners. The insult must always be an acceptable verbal weapon even though it hurts, which it usually does because it is designed to do so. It is the steam from the pressure cooker. We would do well to copy American defamation law where a suit in which a public person is involved will only lie if there is demonstrable malice.

We all must learn to endure the insult and fight misinformation or exaggeration with the truth, not with arrest and punishment. The reason we must do so is elementary: If we condemn under law those who exaggerate or insult, who will know and decide what is the truth and what is not? And how long will it be before your particular truth becomes unfashionable so that it must be punished for the sake of all the rest of us?

Freedom is a very, very uncomfortable commodity. That is what makes freedom…well…freedom.

Part Two

CAN THIS COUNTRY BE SAVED?

The Cost of Appeasing Quebec

The sponsorship scandal that came to a head in the Gomery hearings in the spring of 2005 was much more serious than just a corrupt Liberal Party caught with the jam all over its fingers. It was, perhaps, the last round in the federal government's terrifyingly bankrupt policy towards Quebec. Pierre Trudeau, in spite of his vision problems with "outer" Canadian provinces such as British Columbia, understood Quebec. He had no illusions of what the fight was about. Though everyone concedes that Quebec is different socially, culturally and linguistically from the rest of Canada, he knew that to recognize it as different politically was to recognize that it was different constitutionally. As far as he was concerned, Quebec was a province of Canada with all the rights and duties that implies—no more, no less.

In 1980 when separatist premier René Lévesque staged his referendum for sovereignty-association, Trudeau took the "No" side and fought the election on its merits without bribes and won big time. When Lévesque opposed the patriation of the Constitution in 1982, especially the amending formula that did not give Quebec a veto over constitutional change, Trudeau not only stood his ground but took the matter to the Supreme Court of Canada, which unanimously supported him in spite of the three Quebec judges who sat on it. He warned time and time again that if Quebec were given special political treatment, the country would be in big trouble. Future historians will, I fear, record the breakup of Canada as starting when he stepped down.

In 1982 we had a new constitution and Quebeckers, not to say the separatists, accepted it—grudgingly in many quarters, no doubt, but at least swords were sheathed—and they, like most Canadians, needed a rest from dealing with complicated constitutional problems. A year later Brian Mulroney took over the Conservative Party and immediately made promises to Quebec that they had never asked for in order—to use Mulroney's own nauseating overstatement—"to make Canada whole again." Then to carry Quebec, he made a Faustian pact with leading Quebec separatists, and, upon the Conservatives' victory in 1984, put them into key cabinet posts and sent the country down the path to Meech Lake and, when that failed, Charlottetown. This was calamitous for national unity because it abandoned the Trudeau doctrine of no special political deals for Quebec and launched a bidding frenzy to give more goodies to Quebec that had not been asked for. Meanwhile, Meech/Charlottetown, just by happening, had established Quebec as a separate entity to be dealt with in ways different than the federal government treated the rest of the provinces. Jean Chretien, after wiping out the Tories in 1993, himself became a Quebec appeaser, damned near lost the 1995 Quebec separation referendum, then immediately fast-tracked the appeasement policy: a veto for Quebec (it's irrelevant that other provinces got one, too), a "distinct society" designation and an utter failure to object—indeed, he offered encouragement—when Quebec did its own thing on the international stage. As a result, in almost all respects Quebec now stands as a de facto sovereign entity. Much of this was done to shore up the position of Jean Charest, who, in 1998, left the federal Tories to become leader of the Quebec Liberals. I alone said, when writing for a national paper, that this would have disastrous consequences. Chretien, I told readers, would pay Quebec "tribute" in order to avoid a Parti Québécois government and would give far more special treatment to Quebec than the PQ could have ever hoped for. So it proved

Then came the sponsorship deal where the Ottawa Liberals assumed that the love and affection of Quebec could be bought with flags, lapel pins and sporting events. The fact that this has caused a scandal is less important than the fact it humiliated Quebec. This is a province that is easily humiliated, of course, but this was over the top. If Trudeau's policy toward Quebec had been maintained by Mulroney and Chretien, there would have been no need to continually pay Quebec off. But once they started paying there was no turning back. As Kipling famously said, "If once you have paid him the Danegeld, you never get rid of the Dane." Each payoff is another notch in the time-stick leading to Quebec separation. Each moves Quebec further and further away from confederation.

We fool ourselves after each crisis passes that the crisis has passed. In fact, the battle may be over but the war has been merely adjourned. Every time Ottawa pays the loser tribute, that tribute becomes part of the political fabric. The long and the short of it is that thanks to Mulroney, Chretien and now Martin, Canada stands on the threshold of witnessing yet another separation referendum in Quebec, and this time there may not be anything the rest of us can do to stop that province from seceding. It's too late to go back to the Trudeau doctrine and more bribery won't do the trick. Of course, we should be sickened, shocked and damned mad at what the Liberals did with public money in the sponsorship scandal. But the sponsorship criminals were little people with grubby paws, the kind of people that there's always been plenty of as long as there have been federal Liberal and Conservative parties to dish out slush. History will forget these grubby political hacks, but unless I badly miss my guess, they will remember Mulroney, Chretien and Martin as men who couldn't see the forest for the trees and who, to achieve their own raw, short-term political goals, changed federal policy towards Quebec and split the country asunder.

I hope to hell I'm wrong about that last point, but I don't think I am.

When the Bough Breaks...

Can Canada survive without Quebec? The short answer is no. Emphatically no. It is one of the great political ironies that Quebec is both the disruptive element in Canada and at the same time the glue that holds this country together. Those who succeeded Prime Minister Trudeau understood this, which explains their penchant for appeasement in the worst meaning of that word. Appeasement of legitimate claims is appropriate, of course, a point made by Churchill at the time of the Munich Agreement in 1938. The bad sort of appeasement is to give in to that which, in the broader sense, is unjust. Trudeau understood this distinction very well and knew it was crucial. He knew that in legal terms, in constitutional terms, Quebec had to be *une province comme les autres* and failing that, as he said at the time of the Charlottetown Accord, the country would die with a whimper.

But why must Quebec be *comme les autres*? Because if it is not, it must get powers and perks not available to other provinces—as indeed it already has. Today, in every way but legally, it is virtually in association with the rest of Canada. Its move towards greater and greater sovereignty has happened slowly but very surely, and each step taken cannot be reversed. René Lévesque, wherever he may be, must have a glowing smile as he says to his companions, "They've got to the point where one more push will get them over the top."

If Canada were like Belgium with but two cultures or even like Switzerland with three and a bit, perhaps some sort of association could be worked out, but Quebec sees association as itself on one side and the rest of Canada as a block on the other. Instinctive to the Québécois is the notion that, when push comes to shove, it will be Ontario—Upper Canada—with which it must deal and the rest of the provinces will come along for the ride. This isn't really much of a miscalculation in that, if they're wrong, the worst that will happen is Quebec will become independent with strong ties to the country of which it was once a part. "Divorce with bedroom privileges," as former BC premier Bill Bennett famously once said.

But is Quebec right to think that if Ontario were to go along with "asymmetrical federalism" (Joe Clark's phrase), would the rest of the provinces go along if only because they have no other viable choice? The question answers itself because, for at least two western provinces and perhaps two Atlantic provinces, there are alternatives. But while much has been speculated about a union of the four western provinces, this won't happen for several reasons. For one thing, how do you cobble together a country where one province, BC, has more people than Saskatchewan and Manitoba, combined? Such a country would cry out for a bicameral house, but you would soon find that BC and Alberta, so enthusiastic now for a reformed senate, would suddenly see it as taking away their legitimate power and giving it to less populous places—the same argument made by Ontario and Quebec of the present Senate. If this new country did not have an upper house, outside of BC it would be argued with accuracy that BC was the dominant player, and if BC and Alberta got along well, Saskatchewan and Manitoba would simply be satellite regions. Another vexing question would be where to put the new country's capital?

What then about a union of Alberta and British Columbia? The same arguments about an upper house would apply to the smaller union, though oddly enough with greater force. Why would British Columbia concede any power to Alberta whose people, despite the misconceptions elsewhere, are as unlike theirs as chalk and cheese? And if there were no upper house, Alberta would quite accurately see itself as vassal to Victoria.

The end result of Quebec leaving, whether legally or de facto, would be an independent BC.

Of course, a break-up of Canada would not automatically follow Quebec's secession. There would be many noble efforts made, especially by Ontario, to cobble something together. There would be conferences and conventions, both formal and informal. It would take time for the remaining federation to split but split it surely would. The plain unhappy fact is that, if Quebec goes, Ontario is virtually in charge of the country, and neither BC nor Alberta would tolerate that.

Would an independent BC then opt to join the US? I once thought not but I've changed my views on that. Joining the US would, in time, prove impossible to resist. Geography attaches us to the American Pacific Northwest and to Alaska, and whether or not as a separate state we would inherit NAFTA, our ties would become closer and closer. I don't believe that the US would annex BC. That is ancient thinking. Indeed, there would no doubt be resistance in some quarters of the US to adding a 51st state because it would add two more senators for the western half of America. But I think it would happen. Whether Alberta would also become part of the US is questionable for the political reasons given above, though by decision time those tar sands might look good enough to the Americans to muffle any who don't want Alberta in the Union.

In short, Quebec, not Ontario, is what holds Canada together, and when it goes, the great experiment will fail. Our similarities will not be enough to hold together regions where differences would divide them.

Good Neighbours?

Many years ago, sipping a mai tai with an American, I remarked, "Canadians always know that if push came to shove, the US could conquer Canada in a day."

He was horrified. "We would never ever do that," he replied.

"I'm sure you wouldn't," I said to close the subject.

Is that still true, I wonder?

I must tell you from the outset that all my life I've been pro-American. My fears have only developed fairly recently. I don't think that the US has any plans to invade us, but there are two scenarios where I can see they would take us over or, more likely, have a relationship with us similar to that of the Soviet Union with its satellites before *glasnost*. To understand this, let's look at the US as it was and as it has become. In earlier years, of course, there was the doctrine of Manifest Destiny that gave Americans the right to take over everything they could get their hands on and kill any who got in their way. This destiny was bestowed from heaven; God (In Whom America Trusted) had sent these good white folks from Europe into America to conquer it and, if time permitted, to make Christians of the savages—on penalty of death. When Thomas Jefferson negotiated the purchase of Louisiana from Napoleon in April 1803, no one quite knew what he had bought. Whether as a direct result of this purchase or simply a desire to find out what lay to the west of the Missouri River, he made this proclamation in Washington, DC, on June 20, 1803:

To Meriwether Lewis Esquire, Captain of the first regiment of Infantry of the United States of America.

The Object of your mission is to explore the Missouri River & such principal streams of it as by its course and communication with the waters of the Pacific Ocean, whether the Columbia, Oregon, Colorado or any other river, may offer the most direct & practicable water communication across this continent for the purpose of commerce.

For twenty years Jefferson had been thinking about finding a water route to the Pacific Ocean and establishing an American presence west of the United States as it then existed. But one has to assume that by the time he wrote that directive he knew that the Spaniards, from whom Napoleon had stolen Louisiana, the French and the British all had claims of some merit that had to be laid to rest by American occupation.

It can be fairly argued that the Americans, almost as soon as their republic came into existence, became one of the most militaristic, aggressive nations the world has ever seen. Most of us who have been brought up in her shadow haven't thought of our neighbours that way, but history bears out that statement. The North, the more powerful sector, couldn't tolerate the separation of the southern states and so entered into what was until that time the world's bloodiest war to prevent it happening. The Americans stole at gunpoint a huge swath of Mexico and would have taken all the Pacific Coast up to what was then Russian Alaska had cooler heads not prevailed. As it was, the acquisition of Alaska did nothing to quell the dreams of an America from Nome to Tijuana.

It was the strength of this 19th-century Manifest Destiny mood in the US that gave rise to the confederation in 1867 of the founding colonies of Upper Canada, Lower Canada, New Brunswick and Nova Scotia. It was also the force that impelled the wealthy white population in charge of affairs in Victoria—the British Columbia version of "The Family Compact"—to opt for joining Canada rather than remaining a colony or seeking its own independence or joining the United States.

The point of all this is that there has always been an unusual, semi-satellite to dominant nation relationship between the US and Canada. Canada's principal line of defence in this situation is that few Americans know much or indeed care very much about Canada. We have never fought one another, the War of 1812 having occurred before we were even thought of as a country, and we have unquestioningly accepted the role of suppliers of resources to American factories while at the same time becoming her best customer. In short, there has never in the last 150 years been a reason for the US to use force against us. They have lots of living space, they get our resources when they need them, and we consume what they produce. Moreover—and this is of critical importance though it is never, it seems, mentioned—Canada has never elected a government seriously hostile to American interests. We have always been nice and peaceful-like.

What could happen to change this pretty tranquil relationship? For one thing, a bust-up of Canada. If Quebec were to leave and the rest of the country become fragmented, there would be some ripe plums to pluck, though this might not be as attractive to the US as first appears. The Prairie provinces (I exclude Alberta), wonderful places though they are, are "have-not" places. BC, both because of its geography and its resources, might be more attractive, but the overriding problem of taking any of them on would be constitutional: Would the US want additional states? Why not simply have a bunch of dependent Puerto Ricos to the north?

The second possibility is more frightening. Countries usually take over other countries because the weaker has something the stronger wants—in our case it would be water and in the shorter term fossil fuels. For a host of reasons the US is drying up, needing more and more water for more and more people while not having that commodity in sufficient supply. There are many places in Canada that don't have enough water either, but the US need—and greed—is far greater.

As time passes, I see a Canada more and more in thrall to US interests. There will be no invasion—though if there were, Canadians would only offer vocal resistance—but just an ever-increasing demand for more of what we have and they don't. The end result will not be the slightly tongue-in-cheek solution I mentioned to my American friend over mai tais but the same result accomplished without bloodshed. If a country is unwilling or unable (and we are both) to defend itself against a larger neighbour, it must submit to the neighbour's will. And that is what Canada will eventually do—with that "eventually" being not too far off.

Giving off a Bad Odour

Canadians get very upset at corruption in places like, say, Mexico. But I suspect that a Mexican, if he were to comment, would say the only difference between your corruption and ours is that we have a price list. We know what everything costs so there is no shuffling of feet: six martini lunches, four golf games or three weekends at the cottage for the specified favour. He might also say that there is no such thing in Mexico as Canada's lay-away plan: In Mexico you pay today for what you need today, whereas in Canada you pay an indeterminate sum today for an indeterminate favour later.

At the height of Canada's sponsorship scandal CTV asked permission to come into my radio studio and record the responses of my listeners to this huge issue that was occupying the major media's time and space. But none of my listeners wanted to talk about it, not because they weren't pissed off—because they were. No, it was because it was just as their suspicions had confirmed. Isn't that the way things have always been back there? And if I asked a listener point blank, he or she would observe, "Wasn't it the same under Mulroney's Tories?"

It is true that the Tories, during Liberal regimes, did learn from them, but Diefenbaker was no good at that sort of stuff and Joe Clark didn't have time to learn. Mulroney, however, learned big time, as demonstrated in Stevie Cameron's wonderful books *On The Take* and *The Last Amigo*——neither of which, incidentally, drew a single lawsuit. And he learned well. He knew what the rules of the game were. He was once asked if he would ever give a Liberal a job and he replied, "Not as long as there's a warm Tory body left in Canada."

The Last Amigo documents the relationship between Mulroney and Karlheinz Schreiber, the fix-it man in the Airbus scandal and other big league shenanigans. Although Ms. Cameron does not allege that Mulroney was on the take, she makes it clear that no prime minister should have had that close a relationship with a crook like Schreiber who, as this is written, is still dodging German justice by fighting a first-class guerilla war against extradition from Canada. The RCMP also thought the Schreiber-Mulroney relationship might be too close to be just old pals together and started an investigation of Mulroney that took them to Switzerland with its cozy buddy system of banking. If I were to ask each of my readers what he would do if the RCMP indicated they were looking for some evidence that might get him charged, assuming he was innocent, I daresay the answer would be that he would just sit tight and await the sure exoneration that would come. If he was guilty, however, I am sure his answer would be that if he had any clout in the big leagues, he would use every bit of it to get the Horsemen off his case.

Mulroney sued because he alleged that the mere investigation of his affairs called his character into question and was thus defamatory. Now you might have thought that the RCMP would have said at that point, "Fill your boots! Since when was it defamatory for the police to carry on inquiries when investigating a case?" Instead, on the government's say-so, Mr. Mulroney and his lawyer were each paid a million dollars and the investigation was stopped before it really got started. How could this have happened? Doesn't the RCMP act independently of government? No, not since Jean Chretien took away the independent hands-off role of the commissioner of the RCMP by making him a deputy minister in the Solicitor General's office where he is subject to orders of that Solicitor General—who is appointed by none other than the prime minister himself.

Now you might wonder why a Liberal government wouldn't have been delighted to pursue a former Tory prime minister. The answer is simple. There's an unwritten code that governs this sort of thing. I first discovered it back in the early '80s after I got into radio. I learned that then deputy minister of energy—and now for his pains senator—Jack Austin had put together an international cartel to fix the price of uranium on the direct orders of his minister, Alistair Gillespie, with the full knowledge of Prime Minister Trudeau and Minister of Justice Jean Chretien. The government tried to make out that this was a matter of great national security and that deep secrecy was therefore required. This was plain, unadulterated barnyard droppings. In fact, precisely the opposite was the case.

The US, which had long relied upon Canada for its uranium, had suddenly decided that going outside US boundaries for its supply posed a security risk and that, thenceforth, it would use domestic stocks only. Atomic Energy of Canada Limited (AECL), a Crown corporation, had foolishly stockpiled a huge quantity of uranium in anticipation of the usual sales to the US, and they were now in a pickle. The law of supply and demand being what it is, with the supply the AECL had on hand, the price of uranium would plummet. What to do? Fix the price, of course, and that is what the Liberal government and the ostensibly non-partisan public servant Jack Austin did.

This was illegal as hell and, although the Combines Investigation people did spring into action, they were stonewalled by the government at every turn. Meanwhile, the minister, using the time-honoured method of buying time, appointed the highly respected Robert Bertrand to investigate the matter and report back. The Tories, in opposition, screamed for blood. Though the Bertrand Report was completed, the Liberal government wouldn't release it, and the Combines Investigation twisted and turned so much that it wound up chasing itself up its own rectum and nothing more happened. Except for an election. In the fall of 1984 Brian Mulroney sailed to victory in a huge landslide and people like me and Walter Stewart (who had written a book on the subject) waited with bated breath for the Bertrand Report to be released. Not a chance, said Brian Mulroney!

Why wouldn't the Tories release this report with glee and let the Liberals and their favourite bureaucrat, Jack Austin, twist in the wind? The answer was simple. If the Tories did that, the Liberals would do tit for tat when they got back into power, assuming there was a corruption incident during the Mulroney years—a pretty safe bet. And Mr. Mulroney rather thought there might be, so he let sleeping investigative reports lie. Jean Chretien, if nothing else, knew something about politics. And he was, perhaps next to Mulroney, the prime minister least bothered by ethical considerations. And that is why, when the Airbus affair came along, the order went out to the Solicitor General, who called off the cops and cut cheques for a million each to Mr. Mulroney and his hard-working lawyer. (To all this I must add this question: When Chretien gave Mulroney the money, do you think it might have been because Mulroney already knew that Chretien was up to his eyeballs in funny business, too? And that Chretien knew that Mulroney knew?)

None of what I've related here is any revelation. It is all documented and public—which raises the obvious point that Canadians don't care very much. But it speaks to another point that suggests why the public can perhaps be excused their casual attitude toward such matters. The main press in this country is so tightly controlled by the Establishment that, while they may not hide the facts from the public, they certainly will not investigate them too thoroughly nor make much of an issue of them.

Am I being too hard on the Aspers and Thompson and company? Let's look at the Mulroney-Schreiber connection again. By the spring of 2004 Stevie Cameron's *The Last Amigo*

CAN THIS COUNTRY BE SAVED?

had become a bestseller. Everyone who read it could detect an odour of something not quite right in the close relationship between Mulroney and Schreiber. On top of that, the buzz in Ottawa had long been—and still is—that Mulroney had come out of the sacrifices associated with public office rather well. It was at that point that the shopping bag story came out. Undisputed is the simple fact that Brian Mulroney had, shortly after leaving office, accepted from Karlheinz Schreiber a shopping bag full of envelopes stuffed with money totalling $300,000. When he realized that the *Globe and Mail* had the story, Mulroney contacted editor Edward Greenspon— this according to Greenspon's own account in his weekly column—and begged him not to print it, offering him a better one in its place. Apart from another casual mention of this event in the *Financial Post*, that was the end of the matter. Except it wasn't because in the same Greenspon editorial Stevie Cameron was accused of being a paid informer of the RCMP during the time she was researching *The Last Amigo*, a charge that Ms. Cameron stoutly denies and for which the *Globe* can't produce a scrap of evidence. The newspaper, however, chose to launch a vendetta against Cameron over allegations of conduct that—even if she had been guilty of it—was not illegal (I have no hesitation in accepting Ms. Cameron's version), rather than thoroughly investigating and reporting on the story of a former prime minister getting a bag of money from a crook! Would you not have thought that any editor worth the name, upon receiving word of that bag of money, would have charged into the newsroom yelling, "Open up the Mulroney file! Here's a hell of a story. Get on it and give it all you've got!" But the *Globe*, with gross unfairness and without any evidence, shifted attention to one of Canada's best if not *the* best journalist, Stevie Cameron, who is likely the person in the whole world Mulroney hates the most.

An old friend asked me not long ago why I didn't editorialize more favourably about politicians on the ground that no one could govern if the public believed such bad things about politicians. This took my breath away, and for once in my life I was struck dumb. But what we must always assume is that governments must be questioned no matter how credible their stories may be. Is this because governments and politicians are inherently evil or, if not evil, prone to lie? Of course they are, because we all are. We all alter the truth, whether it's about what time we got back from a poker game last night or matters with more serious social or business consequences. Ordinary decent people go into politics, but it is a system that—to use the kindest expression—forces them to dissemble. Thus, it is the very humanness of our politicians that makes them secretive and untruthful. It's their very humanness that makes them fear full disclosure and makes them lie for their political lives. And in the end it is this very humanness that makes it obligatory that we hold their feet to the fire.

In the meantime, this is Canada—a corrupt system, unpoliced, unattended to by the media and mostly accepted by a public brought up to believe that peace, order and good government mean that you go quietly about your business, never deigning to question government so long as it keeps the peace and sees that you are fed and sheltered. We're all lapdogs in this country and our governments know it.

Party Democracy

For many years now Canadians have complained that they send someone to Ottawa or their provincial capital to speak on their behalf only to have him or her return and tell them what's good for them. There is a sense of helplessness about the complaint and for good reason. While as voters we have a say in who will go to the legislature, we have no say as to what our choices will be, for the candidates are as presented to us by the political parties. This lack of involvement at the grassroots level of politics means we are really unconnected to our representative unless we are, in fact, members of the party and take part in the nomination process—in which case we are likely Indo-Canadian, a non-citizen or drunk at the time.

The nomination process for most parties is much the same. At a time so declared by the party constitution there is a convention for the purpose of naming the party's standard-bearer in the next election. If the incumbent is a shoo-in to be renominated, there will be no activity at all prior to the convention. There will be a modicum of hoopla if there is a glamorous star-quality candidate available and the party is in need of some glamour. In that case the party leader will simply parachute that bright bit of humanity into the constituency and that will end the matter. But if there is to be an actual contest, there will be a huge flurry of activity to sign up members. A deadline is usually set for new members to join in order to be eligible to vote. The exercise is then quite simple: Each contestant signs up as many new members as he can and the one who signs up the most wins. This carries with it an innate corruption of varying proportions. Even under the best of circumstances these new members hardly arrive to sign up of their own volition or express a lifelong wish to be a Liberal, a Tory or a New Democrat. No, it's not even necessary that they care a whit about politics or the party they are joining. They are there because Bloggs is running and we all want Bloggs to win, don't we? Now if good old Bloggs is a member of a large community—perhaps the Sikh or Chinese community or maybe the fundamentalist Christian community—it will be pretty easy to rally the forces behind him. It's often not necessary that the Bloggs delegates be of voting age, citizens of this country or able to speak one of the official languages. Any warm body that can read the word "Bloggs" on a piece of paper and make an "x" next to his name will do very nicely, thank you very much. This process means that in the election that follows, if there are four parties in the race, there will be four versions of Bloggs to vote for.

Not all countries have this system, of course. In Britain it is usually a committee selected by the constituency organization that interviews prospective candidates and selects the winner. Most British parliamentarians of note have had several cracks at being selected before they have been adopted by a committee in a constituency where the party has a chance of winning. Parachuting leadership favourites into "safe" ridings is common there, but in Britain no candidate is expected to live in—or indeed anywhere near—his riding. For years Churchill represented the Scottish riding of Dundee, and in Canada in our immediate post-colonial period, Sir John A. Macdonald, having lost his seat in the East, represented Esquimalt, BC, a constituency he never saw even at election time.

There is another way to select candidates, of course, and that is to allow every party member to vote for the candidate of his or her choice via a process that in the US is called a "primary election." It is the essence of simplicity and is conducted in the same manner as a general election, with people going to a polling place and voting for their favourites. All registered

Democrats and all registered Republicans in a "district"—as they call their constituencies—will, on the appointed day, troop to the polls and select their party's standard-bearer. The process varies from state to state; in some a clear majority is required and, in the event there is no clear winner, this is achieved either by a transferable vote system or a run-off vote at a later date.

Though it seems strange to Canadians, in some states one can vote in both elections, meaning that Republicans can help select the Democratic nominee and vice versa. While you might think that Democrats, for example, would try to nominate a Republican who couldn't get elected dog catcher in a one-dog town, that is not the American experience. It seems that people are more likely to select a person they can live with if their own party's candidate is defeated.

The primary system as a concept is not popular with Canadian political parties because of a fundamental flaw—it is democratic. It removes much of the power from the leader and the backroom boys because every election gives the people a chance to select the choices to be put on the slate at the general election. There is no parachuting or loading of nominating conventions because the power to select candidates moves from the leader and the constituency executive to the rank and file. This also means, of course, that once elected, the winner knows that he doesn't owe his position in any way to the party or the leader and that he must satisfy a broad base of support. A guy like Bloggs may be the darling of the leader and all who surround him, but he has to test his ability and popularity against any who want his job.

If we truly want democracy in this country and in this province of British Columbia, we must start at the beginning with the selection of the candidates. Of course, it will be a brave leader indeed who will permit this level of people participation on the ground floor of the democratic process. But if we really do wish to be in a democracy, not just think we are, this is an idea whose time has come.

Is Canada a Democracy?

The answer to the title question is clearly no if we are talking about an Athenian-style democracy. There is no such thing in the modern world, so perhaps we should invent our own definition and relate it to Canada as a federation because that status is different from, say, the United Kingdom.

What, then, would be fair criteria? We would start, I think, with the question: Is there universal suffrage in this federation after a reasonable age of majority is attained? Certainly on the face of it the answer is yes, but it gets more troubling if you consider the next question. Do most citizens have reason to feel that, if they cast their votes, those votes will have meaning? I would argue that with our first-past-the-post tradition the answer to that one is clearly no and that there is good reason why some people in this country would feel under-franchised (a term I just invented) or, for practical purposes, actually disenfranchised.

Those, of course, who accept the majority definition of what "real issues" are will feel comfortable in answering that, although they are under-franchised, they do have a voice. For example, after the rise of the Co-operative Commonwealth Federation (CCF) in 1932 poor people felt they had a voice, the choice no longer being between Tweedledee the Liberal or Tweedledum the Conservative, neither of which had paid the slightest attention to their plight, though federally the CCF never held the reins of power. But what about people who feel very strongly that there must be some constraints on abortion? To hold such a view today is certainly not fashionable with the major parties, so much so, in fact, that any who hold that view as a high priority would find it uncomfortable if not impossible to be a member of any party. Indeed, in two of those parties it would stack you against a firm party principle. What if you felt that the environment and its protection were of the highest order? Here you would be acceptable to all major parties because all, even the Tories, pay lip service to it. But to join a party that has this as a very high priority you must join one that is seen as single-issue party and, under the first-past-the-post system it will be lucky to ever win a seat in parliament. And even with a seat or two, the rules of parliament would deprive such a party of any real chance to make its supporters' views known. I would say then that there is universal suffrage in Canada, but that to a great many people it is an empty right.

Next question: Are voters throughout the country approximately the same in value?

For the reasons given above, the answer is clearly no. But even if a different system of counting votes were instituted, the power of your vote would still depend on a great many factors, such as: Do you live in the country or the city? Usually, though not always, rural votes count for more than urban ones do. Do you live in Prince Edward Island, Manitoba or Saskatchewan? If so, your vote (especially if you're from Prince Edward Island) can be worth as much as four times the votes of those in other places. Prince Edward Island has a guaranteed four members of parliament and four senators, and were it not for the small numbers involved, this would create a serious distortion. Saskatchewan and Manitoba profit from a 1978 law that says that no matter what the demographic considerations are, no province can ever lose seats because of a drop in population relative to that of other provinces. And if you live in a province with dramatic growth, you lose because the number of seats your province has depends upon the last census, which is always out of date.

The biggest problem comes about because Canada is a federation with enormous population differences and because under our system the winner takes all. About 40 percent of the popular vote elects governments who thereby get 100 percent of the power. These governments are always controlled by MPs from either Ontario or Quebec or both, meaning that British Columbians must be satisfied with the occasional cabinet minister whose appointment always depends upon him or her toeing the line drawn by the Ontario and Quebec members of caucus. Thus, the clear answer is that in Canada one vote is not even approximately equal to other votes.

Is our parliament sufficiently "democratic" that citizens have their views expressed on their behalf? The answer to this is clearly no. Our system is called "responsible government," not because it behaves responsibly but because, in theory, at least the executive, that is to say the prime minister and his cabinet, is subject to the whims of the House of Commons. The plain fact is, however, that the cart is firmly before the horse. It is not the House of Commons that tells the prime minister and cabinet what policy is and how it ought to be administered but quite the other way around. At this writing, there is talk of great parliamentary reform so that the Commons can, at least to some degree, hold the government's feet to the fire.

How come a minority (the prime minister and cabinet) can dictate to the majority (the government backbench)? There are many reasons, but to start with the prime minister is the leader of his party and, unlike other jurisdictions, can only be replaced by the party. (In Britain's Conservative Party, the party caucus can topple a prime minister and replace her, as they did Margaret Thatcher in 1991.) Being the leader in Canada gives the prime minister control of patronage, meaning that MPs might not see the promised post offices or bridges built in their ridings if they are naughty. He also controls who gets into cabinet or who goes into the cabinet-in-waiting, the parliamentary secretaries. He also controls (at this writing) who goes on which parliamentary committee, some of which get to travel to neat places in the midst of the Ottawa winter. If an MP gets unruly and talks of scuttling his prime minister, he'd better have a big majority of the caucus onside or he will be expelled from caucus and thereafter be sans party support. Indeed, the sharpest spear the PM has is the requirement under our Canada Election Act that everyone running for the party must have the party leader's signature on his or her nomination paper. This is a very sharp spear indeed as independents are almost never elected. But even when elected with the leader's blessing, MPs speaking out on issues that affect their constituencies must do so with some care. Certainly if it comes to rather mundane things like that bridge mentioned above, they can speak as freely as they wish. But Liberal MP Stephen Owen, one of BC's brighter lights, found out that it wasn't a very good idea to propose a reform that the prime minister didn't want. You may remember that Mr. Owen, seeing the unbelievably tame ethics commissioner that Jean Chretien had attached to his office, proposed that an officer of the Commons should have that job, as is done in BC. He was sent to Coventry and his obvious pending promotion to cabinet was delayed by a couple of years. There was also the Hepatitis "C" debate where, under the vicious whip system, Liberal MPs who wanted to support help for Hepatitis "C" victims were literally dragged into the Commons, some of them actually crying, to vote as the prime minister commanded. In the end I suppose the answer to this question is simply that people aren't really represented in parliament by their MPs because prime ministers don't permit it.

What about "free votes?" As long as a free vote is an open vote, this concept is a snare and a delusion because the prime minister or leader of any party can see who votes which way and mark that down for future reference—as when a cabinet shuffle is planned. If the vote were secret, it would be very different but that's not likely to happen because the public is entitled to know which way their representatives vote.

Moving on to the next criteria: is there an independent judiciary at all levels and, of equal importance, does it appear to be independent? The answer to the second part is a categorical no and it is probably the same answer for the first. Let's first deal with the lower courts, that is, the provincial Supreme Courts and their courts of appeal. Nominally, the job of making appointments to these courts belongs to the federal minister of justice, but no appointments are ever made unless the prime minister approves. This means, in effect, that the prime minister appoints all the senior judges in the country. And while the minister of justice will canvass the local bar associations before recommending an appointment, I think it's fair to say that in 99.9 percent of the cases a new judge, when appointed, is utterly unknown except to his family and friends. This means that there is no public input whatever for the selection of these very powerful people.

On the federal level, but especially for the Supreme Court of Canada, there is an appalling lack of process and input. This is the prime minister's call and what makes this so troubling is that this court, among other things, sits in judgment of federal-provincial quarrels, yet is appointed by one side of the dispute. Many Canadians are also getting a bit antsy over the ability of the Supreme Court's judges to make social policy through their interpretation of the Canadian Charter of Rights and Freedoms while being accountable to no one either for their appointments or the decisions they render.

Meanwhile, the American system is decried by the Establishment as being simply too common and degrading for the candidate. In the US prospective upper court judges and those on the Supreme Court are subjected to a hearing before the Senate Justice Committee that in turn makes its recommendations to the Senate itself. The process does get a bit rough, but some very good judges have been put through the system and survived while some bad ones have not.

Canadians, being stuffed shirts, don't seem to want a public hearing system—though I would welcome it—but if we are to have not only a fair judicial system but one that also appears to be that way, we must initiate a process whereby we the people have a chance to approve or disapprove of appointments to the highest court in the land.

Is there free speech in every real and reasonable sense of that phrase? This is a critical question that, for reasons of style, I deal with in a later chapter.

With Canada being a federation, do the provinces have equal power, or something reasonably close to it to make their influence felt on the national level? Not at all. As I have pointed out, there are imbalances built into the constitution. We can just be thankful that the Charlottetown Accord didn't pass for it would have given Quebec 25 percent of the House of Commons for all time no matter how much her population declined proportionally to other provinces. The constitutional balancing device for a federation should be an upper house that gives regions the opportunity to blunt the absolute power of a majority in the House of Commons. This is certainly the theory behind the American and Australian senates and the Bundestag in Germany. As always, the devil is in the details, for it has been unacceptable to the bigger provinces in Canada to have a senate with equal representation from each province, which would give, for example, the same power to Prince Edward Island or Newfoundland as Ontario or Quebec. Whether or not that *should* be a sticking point can be argued, but it is. As long as Ontario and Quebec have vetoes over constitutional change such a senate is a non-starter.

In 1978, as part of the debate about patriating the Constitution from London to Canada, BC put forward the concept of a five-region senate, those regions being Atlantic Canada, Quebec, Ontario, the Prairie provinces and British Columbia. At the conferences thereafter this concept was loved

51

to death and BC was constantly praised for its great ideas. Except…"Ah yes, except we don't think your senate is quite what the country needs just yet, but *do* keep studying the matter. Perhaps we can look at it again some day. In the meantime, well done, British Columbia, well done indeed!" The trouble was that, if the rest of the premiers and Prime Minister Trudeau really had been looking for good ideas, there sure as hell weren't any others that would include the notion that (to use Preston Manning's phrase) "the West wants in!"

A five-region senate would deal successfully with the Prince Edward Island situation, but leaves a few other sticking points. What about northern regions? Must there be separate representation for First Nations? And if over the years population shifts make the arrangements unfair, how would you change this senate to reflect these shifts? The ultimate sticker back in the 1980s came from Alberta's premier Peter Lougheed, whose nose was distinctly out of joint at the suggestion that BC should be a separate region while Alberta was not. Although it was clearly pique at the time, as matters have progressed, Alberta is indeed taking on a distinctness of its own. However, the real problem of arriving at a fair senate again rests with the vetoes possessed by Ontario and Quebec. You can take it as a given that neither province, but especially Quebec, will ever yield an iota of power to others without receiving a concomitant power. Thus it was that Quebec got Mulroney to stuff that bit into the Charlottetown Accord about a 25 percent share of the seats in the House of Commons as a pay-off for agreeing to a senate which constitutional expert Dr. Edward McWhinney called a "damp squib."

The alternative to having a senate in Ottawa charged with looking after provincial affairs is to give more of those powers to the provinces. This is a very attractive notion, especially to provincial rights advocates such as me. The problem is that many provinces simply cannot afford nor is it practicable for them to have many of the powers that larger provinces have the financial ability to exercise. And many federalists worry that, if more powers are devolved to the provinces, Ottawa will become less and less important and that in time we will become (in Trudeau's words) a "nation of shopping centres."

We have a vicious circle. We need change but change takes unanimous consent, which will never happen, which means we never discuss change so that we go on needing change. It would take a supreme optimist to believe that a solution can be found and the nation can be preserved.

Freedom of the Press

In November 2004 I was asked by the editor of the annual journal published by the Ryerson School of Journalism—the most or second most prestigious journalism school in the country, depending upon where you place Carleton—to contribute an article. When I submitted it, I told the nice young editor that I doubted her school would permit it to be published. I was right. Ten weeks later she phoned me to say the column had been spiked because it was "not satisfactory" and that I could either do another (one more acceptable to her dean, perhaps?) or take half my paltry fee in lieu. I politely declined and took the third option, namely, told them they could go fuck themselves. Here in part is that spiked column. I can only say that the Ryerson School of Journalism firmly verified, if it needed verification, the point of view expressed in it.

Censorship is hardly new even to countries that hold out free speech as the foundation of all freedoms. In the 1770s Thomas Paine circulated a paper he called "Common Sense," which is seen as the triggering mechanism for the American Revolution. Yet in 1798 Congress passed four laws called collectively the Alien and Sedition Acts; among other things, they made it a crime to insult the president, members of Congress and other officials. It is a lasting stain on the administration of John Adams that he neither vetoed this legislation nor came up with much of an explanation for not doing so. Lincoln suspended habeas corpus during the American Civil War, and Woodrow Wilson placed limitations on free speech under the Espionage and Sedition Acts of 1917. Until 1968 London theatres were subject to censorship by the Lord Chamberlain, and those of us of a certain age remember

Hollywood's so-called voluntary Hays Code that resulted in such film nonsense as the bride and groom, scarcely a hair out of place, clad in pajamas and awakening in separate beds the morning after the wedding night.

In a perverse sort of way, literature and the arts have profited from censorship. During Shakespeare's time, criticism of the monarch ensured that in very short order you would be in two pieces. But Scottish kings such as Macbeth were quite legitimate targets and could be criticized in lieu of the reigning monarch. Jonathan Swift's great satires, *Gulliver's Travels* and "A Modest Proposal," if written in non-satirical form, would undoubtedly have got the old Dean into the slammer, never again to emerge. Alexander Pope's wonderful spoofs of Hanoverian manners and morals and even the works of those gentle souls, the Brontës and Jane Austen, were able to tease their establishments without having to score direct hits.

Censorship of the media in recent times has been a double-edged sword in both the UK and Canada where libel actions are relatively easy to maintain as opposed to the United States where the court in the 1964 landmark Sullivan v. *The New York Times* case ruled that prominent people must show there was malice in order to make out a case of defamation. As one who has been in a couple of libel suits, I can tell you that the test facing the plaintiff in Canada is mild and the onus of proving innocence is effectively on the defendant.

But there is another form of censorship that, while it has been with us for a very long time, has become so endemic as to make it impossible for there to be a Canadian muckraker—an honourable term only made pejorative by Theodore Roosevelt after he got riled by reporters such as Upton Sinclair and Lincoln Steffens, who trolled through speeches and documents and called things what they were. Newspapers have been censored by their publishers as far back as one cares to research. Perhaps the worst of many in the UK was Lord Beaverbrook whose red pencil is now carried aloft by the likes of Rupert Murdoch and until recently by Canada's very own aristocrat, Lord Conrad Black. But newspaper censorship is seldom direct, the canning of *Ottawa Citizen* editor Russ Mills by the Asper press a few years ago being an exception. There is no need for it to be. Publishers hire editors who reflect their views. Editors hire reporters, columnists and editorial writers who are also "safe," that is, people who self-censor.

In nearly a quarter of a century in the business I have never been censored nor have I ever felt the need to self-censor, although I must say that, if I hadn't said on air that the Corus Radio Group knew the cost of everything and the value of nothing, I might still be working at their Vancouver station, where I had toiled for the previous 19 years. Interestingly enough, however, one of the most fertile areas of self-censorship is in sports departments where franchises ban reporters from the dressing rooms if they aren't suitably loyal to the team. But jocks get pretty skilled at seeing how far they can go before revenge is taken. The ones under the most pressure are those working for radio and TV outlets that broadcast the home games. When I say this, sports fans immediately point to Don Cherry as a man of great courage. I reply, "Horse shit!" When did you ever hear Cherry criticize the violence that the owners so love, especially in American cities? Listen to the man—if you can stand it—and virtually every word he utters has owners chuckling in immense satisfaction. The jocks who do call it as they see it—men like Bruce Dowbiggan—usually have to freelance and find occasional friendly or careless sports editors. One only has to look at the shameful way the hockey owners treated hockey players in the pre-union days and the disgraceful conduct of Allan Eagleson, first exposed by—are you ready for this?—not a Canadian sports writer and not by a major Canadian media outlet but by Russ Conway, a sportswriter in a hicky little paper in Lawrence, Massachusetts. And the follow-up was by Dowbiggan and two non-jocks, David Cruise and Alison Griffiths, freelance writers.

There isn't a nook, much less a cranny, in Canada where the writer is not required to self-censor, with the exception of the remaining privately owned community newspapers. In BC that means the David Black chain—for whom I write and where I feel free to say what I wish—and the estimable *Georgia Straight*, which it is feared may soon be sold. The Aspers or someone like them own most of the other community papers.

[I went on in my article to discuss the Globe and Mail's *decision to attack journalist Stevie Cameron rather than chase down the story of Mulroney receiving $300,000 from Airbus "fixer" Karlheinz Schreiber, and how their utterly independent columnists then picked up the whip and gave her a bunch of lashes of their own. When I challenged one of these writers to tell me the evidence upon which she based her charge, she replied she would have to ask her editor about that! Then I continued:]*

I offer no solution. I can't imagine what it will be like for fresh-faced graduates of this and other journalism institutions when they find that the laws of libel are the least of their worries. Oh, there is still some tough journalism left to be done but that only applies where the editor considers it safe. You'll be able to demonize the Church of England on past wrongs to Natives or slash at governments that the Establishment doesn't much like. But if I were to give you two role models, two people who spoke their minds and accurately reported what they saw, the names would be Stevie Cameron and Claire Hoy, neither of whom will ever be printed again by any of the national media in this country. And that's the sad story of the media and independence of journalism in this free democracy with its Charter of Rights and Freedoms. Freedom of speech prevails only when and as long as the boss agrees. [*end*]

After my article was spiked, I sent copies of it with an explanatory note to every journalist I knew and a few more besides. It was amazing how many well-known writers from across the county responded with "Right on!" or words to that effect. As for me, I found the situation so awfully—in the proper sense of that word—funny that I couldn't get angry. But there is censorship out there, and experienced writers know that they must stay within boundaries or they won't be printed and that they will be let go if they don't conform. Now let me be clear here: I'm hired to write political columns for the David Black papers and would expect to hear from them if I started writing columns on gardening, though a less likely subject for me to comment upon I can't imagine. And if the paper's religious writer suddenly started doing travel articles, he could expect to be told to please write about the topic he's been hired to write on. The censorship I am talking about is not offending the owner's political views, his slant on foreign affairs and matters of that sort. And if you want more proof of what I'm saying, please read Max Hastings' autobiographical book, *Editor: The Inside Story of Newspapers,* which relates the experiences of the former editor of the *London Telegraph* and the *Sunday Telegraph* as he dealt with owner Conrad Black (as he then was).

For an example closer to home, you need to ask why Andrew MacIntosh no longer writes for the Asper empire. Andrew was the bright wunderkind of Canadian print journalism working for CanWest, which owns, amongst other papers, the *National Post* and both Vancouver dailies. He was also a regular on my radio show, and things got pretty interesting as he got closer and closer to scalping Prime Minister Jean Chretien in what became known as Shawinigate. Then suddenly Andrew wasn't covering that story any more. In fact, no one was covering it in an investigative way. Andrew was, we were told, on "other assignments." Then to my astonishment he had left the *Post* and Canada to work for the *Sacramento Bee*. All I could get from him was that the *Bee* was interested in his talents as an investigative reporter. You connect the dots.

In my own experience I can tell you that, when the Charlottetown Accord was being debated and the referendum held, there was essentially no debate in the mainstream media. To the best of my knowledge I was the only person in the mainstream media who was asking any questions and arguing the "no" side. This is preposterous! To have an enormously important constitutional amendment proposed without any critical comment by any member of the nation's media! When the Accord was roundly defeated in BC, the then editor of the *Vancouver Sun*, Ian Haysom, offered a public apology for being so out of touch with his readers. But he wouldn't have been out of touch or surprised at the result if he'd been listening to my show and the voices of my callers.

In the nineties just as I was getting involved in trying to reverse the Kemano Completion Project decision, the *Vancouver Sun* took its two best environment writers off the story and the *Province* fired its long-time freelancer on environment matters, the late John Massey. After that, the coverage of this white-hot issue was so tepid in these two newspapers that, when the government tubed the project, if you had read nothing but what they printed you would have thought the decision was a bolt from the blue. Those who followed the story on my show may have been surprised at the courage of the government, but they certainly did know that it was a hot-as-hell issue.

The newspapers have a strange excuse for their behaviour. It's their duty, they proclaim, to be "responsible." Since when was it the press's duty to be unquestioning of government policy just because, in the eyes of that government, criticism would be irresponsible? This, you see, was precisely the line Mulroney took with Meech Lake and Charlottetown. To disagree with the government on those hugely important issues was just not responsible journalism. By accepting that reasoning, all major government issues that are declared by a prime minister to be in the interests of the nation would require the media to be "responsible" and follow the government line.

The absence of free speech in the media is only going to get worse if the "American disease" spreads to Canada. Until recently the best example of this disease was in the McCarthy era when even Canadians on the Left were worried about youthful connections to the Communist Party. Now in 2005 freedom of all sorts is under unremitting attack by the Bush administration, and self-censorship is being practiced by everyone working for the major networks. If you want to really dig into national policy in the US, best you forget about getting a job with NBC, ABC, CBS, CNN or Fox and buy your own network because you will not be welcome elsewhere.

If people in the media are not permitted sufficient leeway to report and indeed give honestly held opinions, free speech is essentially shut down. No one suggest that people today can't voice their opinions in the pub—although in the US that can be dangerous on some subjects. The evil to be cured is that information will be kept from citizens because it is not in the interests of the government to have that information made public. Without an independent press with the legal ability to scrutinize and comment in good faith, our apparently democratic government becomes, however softly it enforces its writ, a dictatorship.

One of the best recent examples of this is the so-called sponsorship scandal. The government would no doubt say, "See what a free press accomplished?" The answer is that the "free press" accomplished nothing. Indeed, the story would still be under the rug had not Sheila Fraser, our doughty auditor-general, uncovered the beginnings of the scam and been hot on the trail of the rest of it. There was no *New York Times* with its Pentagon Papers nor a *Washington Post* with its Watergate.

Indeed, the *Globe* and the *National Post* would have treated it all as they treated Karlheinz Schreiber's shopping bag full of money for Brian Mulroney.

There is only one answer: When consuming information on public affairs the rule is the same as when buying a used car—*caveat emptor*. The sad fact is that the mainstream media is biased as hell and must be read with that in mind. This is not to say there aren't gifted writers being published because there are. What is frightening is that you don't know what constraints they are under or, much worse, what constraints they feel they must place on themselves. I suspect it gets so that they don't themselves recognize their own self-censorship, though surely those political writers who avoided like the plague the story of Karlheinz Schreiber and the $300,000 he gave to Brian Mulroney knew they were self-censoring! No one wants the government involved in administering what the media publishes. That would make things even worse, hard though that may be to believe. Instead, readers, watchers and listeners will simply have to do their own due diligence when seeking information.

As a Canadian news junkie, I scarcely do more than "speed-read" Canadian papers, and I've gotten by without *Maclean's* magazine for years. I keep up by reading the rare independent journalists such as Barbara Yaffe in the *Vancouver Sun*, independent community newspapers and good online stuff such as John Twigg's newsletter out of Victoria and by watching the BBC World Service. And I have the added advantage of making my living by interviewing people involved in public affairs. Online news sources, such as *The Tyee* (http://www.thetyee.ca) for which I write, are gaining a considerable following. The trouble is, of course, that every day it gets harder and harder to pin facts down on the Internet because so much information is coming online every day.

In both the US and Britain there is a long tradition of "political papers," so the reader has a choice of slant. In

Canada, and especially in Vancouver where I ply my trade, the mainstream media is tightly controlled with no one truly independent. This is compounded by the practice, now all the rage, of "convergence," wherein newspapers acquire television and radio networks, a practice targeted in the Lincoln Report on the media tabled by a House of Commons committee early in 2005. The odious part of this convergence business is obvious to any who think on it: Which media owners, dollar signs always in their eyes, don't bear in mind that the political people they report on are the same people who grant or refuse TV and radio licences? Newspapers are, of course, not licensed by the government, and the people would rightly take to the streets if a government did suggest such a practice, but now they are indirectly licensed because applying for and retaining a TV licence is a political act, in spite of the CRTC's outward trappings of independence. This means that one has reason to suspect that a media company would prefer its newspapers go easy on any government that could grant or cancel their TV licence because, while the newspaper game isn't so profitable these days, the television business is a licence to make money. What do you think would happen to a columnist who, while the boss was trying for a TV licence, wrote a column calling for the end of the CRTC in no uncertain terms and pointing out that it consists of Liberal Party hacks or one who leaned too heavily on the minister responsible for the CRTC or even started to look into whether a prime minister had been behaving improperly? Do you think, perhaps, that when the Asper family's Canwest was seeking government permission to buy Global TV that their papers' coverage of the Liberal government's activities might have been affected? Especially since the late Izzy Asper and his powerful son Leonard are devoted Liberals, Izzy having once been the Manitoba Liberal leader and an MLA?

I have been privileged to have always worked for station owners and managers who knew, from a practical point of view that, if I was permitted unrestricted free speech, it would increase ratings and that would increase sales. I don't want to suggest, however, that it was only money that motivated management; I think they felt it part of their civic duty to give a muckraker a free voice.

With convergence bringing TV and radio stations into the same stables that hold our national newspapers, how can we ever have confidence in the news we hear and read? The short answer is we can't. So is there anything we can do? There is. We can demand that our government do to the media what Teddy Roosevelt did with the trust companies in the early years of the past century: simply break them up into viable pieces where there is no common ownership. That is what happened in the communications industry in the past few years with the famous bust-up of Ma Bell. Of course, Canadian governments have never had much of a stomach for a fight with the Establishment. In the past we had a Combines Investigation Act and today we have its successor organization but neither has been able to sustain action against the powerful. Somehow, the big boys always seem able to bob and weave and run out the clock until all interest has waned.

But I propose that the government do the following things:

1. Break up all electronic media/print media companies. This will be painful but the fact remains that these cartels virtually eliminate competition in the same way Microsoft did in the US and Ma Bell did in Canada.

2. Restrict media ownership to one outlet per city. I'm not talking here about music stations but those whose practice is in whole or in part driven by news coverage and public affairs.

63

3. Set up a fairness committee to deal with censorship real or apprehended. This committee must be outside both government and the media, and I would select its membership by giving each official party in the House of Commons the right to nominate someone they believe would fairly judge the media. Such a committee must have a mandate that favours free speech above all other considerations. It would have no power to penalize but simply to deal with reasonable complaints, with power to subpoena and then make periodic public reports. But let me put a bit of meat on these bones because I wouldn't want to be misunderstood. If any board, commission or what-have-you were to have the power to decide what is or is not the exercise of free speech, that in itself would deny the very thing we seek to protect. No. It must simply be a monitoring committee to which those who feel there is a problem of bias or interference with free expression can turn for a hearing and a decision. Whatever their decision, that would be the end of the matter except for whatever moral persuasion that provides and, of course, for whatever impact an adverse ruling would have on circulation or ratings.

4. Pass a law incorporating into Canadian media law the Sullivan v. *New York Times* case which only permits damages sought by public persons if malice on the part of the defendant is shown. In Britain and Canada it's far too easy for public officials to get damages for alleged defamation, the onus being on the defendant to prove that what he or she said was true or permissible as "fair comment." This is more serious than just the exposure of the media to expensive lawsuits because it also allows the government, among others, to use the "libel chill" tactic where, when the going gets a bit too rough, a thinly veiled threat of a libel suit succeeds in scaring the media off.

The disease within our media requires tough, perhaps bitter, medicine.

Hard Talk

Canada is in deep trouble and many of us saw it coming a long time ago. But the truth is that not only do Canadians not like to face their country's problems, they have a history of avoiding them. There seems to be a permanent streak of Pollyannaism about us—a belief that since it hasn't happened yet, it can't happen—rather the way many of us console ourselves about our mortality.

As the country teeters on the chasm of national disintegration, the federal government and indeed the opposition parties act as if nothing is happening for fear that simply admitting there's a problem will itself encourage a bad result. What can we do? One option is to gird up our loins for another referendum fight and do all we can to coax Quebecers to vote "no." The trouble with this is that Quebec has come to expect sweeteners. It's like trying to patch up a serious marital quarrel without roses to back up the kisses.

Another alternative would be to offer—and I can't think of an appropriate synonym—bribes. This carries two problems: 1. Bribes beget fresh demands. 2. What's left to offer? Quebec is already treated by the federal government as a "distinct society" (notwithstanding the wishes of the people as expressed in the Charlottetown Accord referendum), it has its precious veto over constitutional change, its own health, welfare and immigration programs and the tacit approval to deal as a nation with other nations. There is nothing to offer now but independence.

The only other option may disturb you, dear reader, so I ask you to pour a stiff Scotch, settle back in your favourite chair and brace yourself. What I propose is that we should embark upon an exercise like that in BC with an electoral commission, except that we should examine everything, and I do mean everything, from whether we want to continue as a constitutional monarchy to whether we should separate the executive branch from the legislative branch and become a republic. But here's the important part. We must start with this frame of reference: "This commission shall, while making its deliberations and recommendations, take as a given that whatever reforms are proposed, Canada will be made up of provinces, all equal before the law, with special privileges towards none."

That may well strike you as a slap in the face to Quebec and in some ways it is. However, to do otherwise is to concede that a special status of inferiority before the law exists for other provinces. For this is the crucial question: Do we, by giving ever increasing special privileges to some, push other provinces and regions closer to independence movements of their own? This becomes an ever more important question as world markets change so that regions become less and less dependent on a central government to care for them. In any case, as we've seen with our softwood lumber and our wild salmon, at present our federal government either cannot or will not act in our interests. This being so, since we must redefine and retool our federation if there is going to be anything left, why not do a proper job of it while we're at it?

So what are you saying, Rafe? That we actually make plans for a Quebec secession even before it happens? And won't such plans make it all the easier for the Parti Québécois to plead its case?

I concede that this argument is troubling, but equally valid—perhaps more valid—is the fact that Quebeckers have for too long felt that they could go on plumping for separation, knowing the rest of Canada would knuckle under and throw it more goodies. It would be helpful, not harmful, in my view if Quebec knew that the stakes were mortal.

But the case for my point is stronger than that because one must assume that Quebec separatism is not going away and that we must always be prepared for the eventuality of new constitutional arrangements. A Canada without Quebec will be one economically and politically controlled by Ontario. We know that BC and Alberta won't put up with that, so is there another way Canada can continue without *la belle province*? Are there structural democratic reforms that can adequately offset in part (because the majority must have its clout) the political domination of the new country by one province?

So how would a federal citizens assembly be set up? Who will be on it? Will it be strictly "rep by pop," meaning that recommendations will be essentially in Ontario's interest?

I think it's useful to look at how the Americans did this in 1787 when, with equal representation from all states, large and small, they came up with what is unquestionably the best constitution ever made. They began the exercise with the premise that each state was equal. We should proceed the same way. Since the assembly I propose is intended to be a consulting body that makes recommendations, not one whose decisions are binding, surely the bigger provinces will accept what would amount to equal rights to express opinions.

Of course, there will be much resistance to such an idea because many believe that even thinking about Quebec separating is disloyal. And since overcoming inertia is always difficult, perhaps nothing will be done. But unlikely as such leadership is in this country, let us assume that Prime Minister Martin would grasp the nettle and say, "Right. We're going to re-examine our federation from the bottom up. No idea will be too way-out. There will be no sacred cows."

I suggest that each provincial parliament select four delegates and each territory one delegate to the assembly much as we in

BC make legislative appointments; an all party committee is set up to take applications from which the committee must unanimously select four delegates who must be approved by a two-thirds majority in the House. These delegates would be paid the same salary as a member of the provincial parliament and would have all reasonable expenses paid. (One thing for sure was proved by the BC exercise: Ordinary people can indeed understand difficult issues if they are given the resources and the time.)

The terms of reference must be broad enough to examine all aspects of our federation.

But what if Quebec's provincial legislature, portentiously called the National Assembly, refuses to get involved? I frankly think they would participate in the same way the Parti Québécois participated in the discussion leading up to the patriation of the Constitution, making it clear that whatever happened they wanted out of the country. But even if they won't get involved, the assembly should meet and make its decisions. The very worst result is that we would have bottom-up recommendations on how to put a country together without Quebec. The best result, of course, would be that all provinces would be represented in recommendations that would lay out a roadmap to a better constituted country that includes Quebec.

Is this a naive notion? Many thought BC's Electoral Commission was ingenuous, but it turned out to be a very solid effort indeed. I suppose an assembly to examine the way this country operates might be likened to a person falling from the 50th story of a building all the while flapping his arms as hard as he can: maybe it won't do much good but it can't do any harm either. If BC's Premier Campbell had taken the position that he would only put together a deliberative body on electoral reform if it were guaranteed successful, it would never have happened.

I once wrote a book called *Canada: Is Anyone Listening?* The answer to that question was obviously no, and I suspect that this suggestion will meet with a similarly negative response because politicians don't like taking political risks. How sad. Because, unless I miss my guess, what we could do now at leisure and free from the panic that sets in when crises happen we will never be able to do after the separatists win a referendum.

All I am really suggesting is that we admit the country is broken and needs fixing, that our institutions have failed us and promise to fail again, and that we look for a different way to have dialogue that might, just might, keep us talking long enough to work out answers before it is too late. I fear my suggestions will be ignored because no one wants to face the inevitable, but if we don't act, and act not all that long from now, we'll be sorry we didn't at least give it try.

Federal Faces

Pierre Trudeau

I first met Pierre Trudeau at a small luncheon given for him at the Empress Hotel in Victoria in the fall of 1976. It was hosted by then premier Bill Bennett, and there were, as I recall, three more of my cabinet colleagues present. My recollection was that Trudeau was very short and soft spoken. He remained silent most of the time, which made us feel awkward as one does when one is babbling in front of someone who is quiet and dignified. As the years leading up to the patriation of the Constitution passed, I got to see a lot more of the prime minister at conferences too numerous to recall and discovered that he was the master of the putdown. He always referred to Roy Romanow, then Saskatchewan's attorney-general and later its premier, as Mr. Romanoff. I was invariably Mr. Rafe. He was magnificent to watch in action as he chaired a meeting of all first ministers; however, if the criteria of good chairmanship are one's ability to bring out the best in people and to build a consensus, he was really a lousy chairman. In fact, at the major Constitutional Conference in Ottawa in September 1980, after ministers from the provinces (I being one) and the federal government had all but reached a consensus on what the new Constitution should look like, Trudeau deliberately screwed up the meeting so he could impose his own version. On the eve of that conference a document prepared by Michael Kirby, who though supposedly an independent public servant was later rewarded with a Liberal Senate seat, was deliberately leaked to

René Lévesque. It laid out all the possible things the premiers might do and offered ways Trudeau could turn them into negatives and make them look bad. I was given the document the night before and was shocked. Indeed, I was devastated at the cynicism and the realization that I had been deluded into thinking that our committee really was important to the cause of national unity.

That Pierre Trudeau was a special person with a gigantic intellect none dare contradict. Whether he was a good leader is highly debatable, and I will, if you please, speak on the negative side of that question.

Kim Campbell

Kim Campbell is one of those I-wonder-what-might-have-happened-if people. Bright, amusing and good-looking, she ought to have made a first class prime minister and should have served for a couple of terms, but she never had a chance. Brian Mulroney, having lavishly poisoned the chalice, handed it to Ms. Campbell with the smile of the cat that had swallowed the canary. Many pundits blame Kim—we are on a first name basis—for the 1993 wipeout of the Tories, but that is unfair in the extreme. Sure, there was the odd careless remark and some bad campaign strategy, but that happens all the time to both winners and losers. The fact of the matter is that Brian Mulroney was detested, and the public, not given the chance to take a whack at him, were determined to punish the Conservatives and punish them they did.

I remember Kim Campbell for some vicious debates in my studio on constitutional matters and how we never ceased being friends on that or any other account. She deserved better, a hell of a lot better.

Joe Clark

I first met Joe Clark—it was an introduction, no more—in front of the Macdonald Hotel in Ottawa in January 1976 just before his surprise selection as Tory leader. I got to know him better in the days leading up to his short-lived term as prime minister in 1979 and better still when he was fighting back. In those days Joe had a typical western Canadian distrust of central Canada. But by the time his successor, Brian Mulroney, had him in charge of quarterbacking the Charlottetown Accord, he had become a central Canadian through and through.

Then in September 1992 when I was, virtually alone in the Canadian media, fighting the Charlottetown Accord with all the force I could summon, Joe Clark came into my studio to make his case. I couldn't believe what I saw. His face was puffy and blotched with red and white, his hands shook and he seemed almost in a state of shock. So hard had he fought for his cause that he was a badly wounded man—as was his cause. We had been friends. We became enemies. I regret that. Joe Clark is an asterisk in Canadian history but probably the most famous asterisk we have.

Preston Manning

My earliest memory of Preston Manning is in Vancouver just prior to the 1993 election. I was chairing the annual convention of the Real Estate Conference of Canada and I had persuaded them to include him on their political panel. This scholarly throwback to Mr. Peepers wowed 'em. The realtors and I were privileged to meet a man who, while his ambitions would remain unfulfilled, has had a profound effect on the politics of the nation.

I interviewed Preston many, many times over the years since

then and was always struck by his grasp of issues, even those many of us didn't yet recognize as issues. He had set himself an impossible task: He had to harness the deep displeasure many western Canadians were feeling, make a party out of that displeasure, then somehow make this party appeal to easterners, the very people western Canadians viscerally disliked. At the same time he had to suppress, if not eliminate, all the right wing nuts and fruitcakes who had been waiting eons for a party to share their bigotry with.

Preston Manning was a huge success until he had to face what I and others had long told him was an insurmountable obstacle: The more popular the Reform Party got, the more suspicious central and eastern Canadians became. And the uncomplimentary view that Quebeckers and Ontarians had of this western party was, of course, effectively fanned by the Liberals and the Tories and their captive media.

As we all know, in due course Reform became the Alliance, which became the new Conservative Party. Along the way Preston was unceremoniously dumped, but ironically when the new leaders, Stockwell Day and Stephen Harper, had trouble holding the party together, many members looked nostalgically back at him. Personally I think he could have brought the discrete factions that make up the Conservative Party together if he had stayed or even if he had come back after Stockwell Day's problems. But Preston Manning wasn't given a second chance, and all of Canada suffers as a result. When he was in politics, the Ontario-run media mostly mocked him. Now that they have helped put him back into private life, they listen to him with respect. Such, it seems, is so often the case in Canada.

Part Three

THE BIRTH AND DEATH

OF SOCIAL CREDIT

AND OTHER BC SAGAS

The Birth and Death of the
Social Credit Party in BC

The Social Credit Movement, based upon the teachings of Englishman Major Clifford Douglas, had a considerable impact on Canada—though in a strange and uneven way. By the end of the 1930s the Depression, combined with a horrible drought, had left Prairie farmers helpless in the hands of the national banks. Many were looking for a better way, and although few, if any, understood what Major Douglas's A+B=C economic theory was all about, it was a case of any port in the storm. Social Credit's major impact, however, was in Alberta under William "Bible Bill" Aberhart and later under Ernest Manning (whose son would one day form the Reform Party based upon western Canadian alienation), but it was the seepage of a bit of this Alberta movement over the Rockies that gave birth to what would become the British Columbia Social Credit Party, which was to dominate the BC political scene from 1952 to1991.

In order to understand how Social Credit took hold in BC, one has to understand BC—no mean task. As Jean Barman in her wonderful book, *The West Beyond the West,* lays out, BC did not come into being as the western states of the US did, namely via a steady migration from the east. At the time BC joined Confederation the colony was as much American as anything else, largely because of the gold rushes, and while joining Canada certainly appealed to BC's well-to-do, they formed a very small part of the population. BC was, in fact, bought more than wooed, the price including such trinkets as Canada taking over our debt and building some wharves and a transcontinental railway. And within a few years, the railway being way behind schedule, there was serious secession talk.

The obvious beginnings for the conditions conducive to Social Credit gaining a foothold in BC (this by hindsight, admittedly) came with the formation of the Liberal/Tory coalition of 1941 under Duff Pattullo who, though born and raised in Ontario, had (like so many immigrants) the zeal of a convert and soon took to quarrelling with Ottawa. (Another towering personage, Gerry McGeer—sometime mayor of Vancouver, MP and senator—once remarked that, while it was only 2,500 miles from Victoria to Ottawa, it was 25,000 miles from Ottawa to Victoria.) The Coalition—which was really a party union not a coalition—had run out of political gas by the 1950s. Despite many accomplishments, it just couldn't hold together, and it was extremely doubtful that either party could elect enough MLAs to form a government. When the election of 1952 was called, the minds of a majority of British Columbians harboured a fear of the CCF—later to morph into the NDP—exacerbated by a fear of communism. Though the CCF was scarcely communist, just a few years earlier a Russian cipher clerk named Igor Gouzenko had exposed a spy ring in Ottawa, resulting in a communist MP going to jail. It was also the start of the McCarthy era in the United States and anything to the Left raised fears of communism.

Again, with hindsight, one can see that, as neither the Liberals nor Conservatives were considered capable of keeping the "Reds" out, it was fertile ground for something else to fill the political void, and that something else turned out to be, to the surprise of all, the Social Credit Movement. In BC it was made up of various small groups, the leading one being the Social Credit League, and it was largely fractious. It was also generally at odds with the Alberta wing and sought to distance itself from William Aberhart's religious preaching. (There would be a very short period in the early 1960s when W.A.C. Bennett took an interest in the National Social Credit Party and supported national leader Robert Thompson from

Alberta, but he soon saw this was going nowhere fast. This brief flirtation is for the most part forgotten now.)

The effective death of the "movement" and its conversion to a provincial party in BC came when William Andrew Cecil Bennett was elected leader of the League after crossing the floor of the legislature from the Conservative benches to sit as an independent in 1952. But Bennett, who didn't become leader until after the election, only joined in order to use the party as a political vehicle. If he actually knew anything of Social Credit fiscal policies, he didn't betray it. Indeed, he quickly made the Socreds into a conservative populist movement. But the remake didn't become a reality until his son Bill took over in 1975 and renamed it the British Columbia Social Credit Party and pitched it to Liberals, Conservatives, old Socreds and "independents" (if such a thing exists in BC). W.A.C. Bennett won a minority government in 1952 under the Social Credit Movement label and in a gutsy move had two backbenchers resign so that Robert Bonner, a young lawyer and war hero, could be attorney-general, the old Social Credit League not being known for attracting lawyers—though that would change. Within a year he forced a new election by contriving to lose a vote in the legislature—not a difficult task when 10 of the 29 opposition members were from the old Liberal/Conservative Coalition and felt that they had been beaten by a "kook" and the other 19 were CCFers who felt they had been jobbed out of the 1952 election by a freak result.

In fact, the 1952 election had produced a result that shocked the Establishment of both the Left and the Right. Though the election was held on June 12, it wasn't until the middle of August that Lieutenant-Governor Clarence Wallace called upon Bennett to meet with him. In the interval, Harold Winch, leader of the CCF, had seen Wallace in July and argued that, while the Socreds had elected one more member, the CCF had received more votes, had more experience, and, in fact, had the tying vote in their pocket. Winch, apparently without bothering to ask, had assumed that the perennial Independent Labour Party MLA from Fernie, Tom Uphill, would support him. What he didn't know was that Bennett had Uphill's letter supporting the Socreds in his own hip pocket. He had also prepared a list of his new cabinet and Wallace had no choice but to call upon him to form a government. In 1953 he contrived to win a majority with a complicated multiple-choice voting system—a win that would be repeated in five more elections, until in August 1972 the NDP, led by the brash and personable Dave Barrett, engineered what at the time seemed like a huge upset.

The W.A.C. Bennett years saw terrific growth in BC. The coalition government that preceded him had made a deal with Alcan giving the company the right to exploit huge tracts of land in northwestern BC in exchange for building a world-class aluminum smelter in the yet-to-be-developed town of Kitimat. When one looks at that deal from today's vantage point, the rape of the environment and the callous and illegal treatment of Native people were outrageous. A river was reversed and a brand new lake created, and when Native trappers returned in the fall, they found their houses and graveyard under water. Alcan, however, had their consent on paper, obtained by having the trappers' illiterate chiefs mark "X" beside their names. Except that we now know they didn't and that all the "Xs" were made by one person, undoubtedly the Indian agent.

The coalition had also started a road-building program for which the Socreds are often given credit. In fact, the John Hart Highway connecting the Peace River area to the rest of the province, and the Hope-Princeton Highway were both Coalition achievements. That being said, however, the Socreds, led by the colourful highways minister, Phil Gaglardi, began an enormous road-, bridge- and tunnel-building exercise that permanently stamped its mark on the BC landscape. One of the results was the Massey Tunnel south of Vancouver, that made the extension of Highway 99 to the US border possible. It was pre-built then dropped into the Fraser River. "It will never work," the critics said. "It will collapse, killing everyone in it." "Deep sea ships that traditionally slow their passage from New Westminster to the sea by dragging their anchors will pull the tunnel and everybody in it out into the Strait of Georgia." Nothing of the sort happened, of course, leaving "Flying Phil" to crow that it was a "triumph of ingenuity over engineering."

Flying Phil was, of course, so named because he was often pinched for speeding, whereupon he would claim that as highways minister he had to test the curves in the roads he was building. A Pentecostal minister, he kept up his church duties by broadcasting out of Kamloops, always starting with his booming "Hello, friend o' mine!" He got into many scrapes, on one occasion using a government plane to fly to San Francisco so he could make a privately commissioned speech. Another time, the plane was used to fly his daughter-in-law to Dallas.

It was widely assumed that Gaglardi was on the take; how else could he afford that ranch near Kamloops? The fact is that no one ever laid a glove on him for any serious misbehavior, though perhaps this story will give a clue why. In 1974 I was practicing law in Kamloops and, after a term on city council, decided I wanted to go into provincial politics. After much advice and after meeting Bill Bennett, I chose to go after the Social Credit nomination, believing that they were the vehicle to beat the Barrett bunch. Phil Gaglardi had represented Kamloops since 1952, but he had been beaten in 1972 by an unknown, Gerry Anderson of the NDP. I asked Phil to come to lunch so I could determine what his plans were. I knew he couldn't win the nomination because the party organization had ballooned with Tories and Liberals who, seeing the formerly hated Social Credit Party as the way to power, had flocked to the new colours. Phil knew this as well. Over lunch he told me that he wouldn't stand in my way although he didn't like me. (Phil despised all lawyers because they—and I among them—always billed him for services rendered.) He said he would neither help me nor work against me. (In fact, he did work for one of my opponents, which I think killed the fellow's chances.) In any event he then made this breathtaking statement: "Rafe, you'll never make any money out of politics. I never did. Mind you, maybe my boys made a little through knowing where the highways were going, but I didn't make a cent." The interesting thing was that it would never have occurred to Phil that his boys shouldn't have made any money out of insider knowledge.

W.A.C. Bennett's years in power are best remembered for his "two-river system" that was intended to provide power for domestic use as well as downstream benefits. In short, he dammed both the Peace and Columbia rivers, doing enormous environmental damage but creating cheap and certain power for a long time to come. Part of the scheme—indeed the major part of it—was the public takeover of the BC Electric Company which, combined with the BC Power Commission, provided the major part of BC's power. In the election of 1960 Bennett had promised he would do no such thing, but on the first day of the next legislature—as BC Electric boss A.E. (Dal) Grauer lay dying of cancer—Bennett shocked the House by announcing the government was indeed taking over the company. This spawned one of the longest lawsuits in the history of the country, providing much employment in the legal profession and kick-starting many legal careers.

Bennett was seen as a financial genius who took BC out of debt, but he did this by creating what he called "contingent liabilities," these being Crown agencies or corporations that technically owed the debt, though it was guaranteed by the government. Then on a festive occasion in August 1959 he had all BC's debt instruments piled on a barge, soaked in kerosene, and taken out onto Okanagan Lake where he would burn them by firing a flaming arrow into their midst. He missed, of course, and an RCMP officer had to do the deed with his handy Zippo lighter. Unlike other politicians caught in such situations (Robert Stanfield dropping the football comes to mind) Bennett was unfazed and just smiled his big smile. But while the documents were destroyed, the province's debt was still intact.

Bennett is often quite wrongly seen as a man who didn't care about social issues, but it was he who first brought in hospital insurance, Medicare and landmark consumer legislation. Still, he didn't do enough to satisfy the temper of the times, which by 1972 indicated that big-ticket economic development should be taking a back seat to better social conditions. There were many things that his ministers ought to have done to appease the electorate, but by then they had all grown old together and their longevity in government had made them arrogant as hell.

How does one assess W.A.C. Bennett and his 20-year regime politically? To begin with, he was a populist, and if he had any political philosophy at all, he disguised it wonderfully. Certainly he believed in private enterprise and the general principles of capitalism—as long as it ended up in doing public good. As he demonstrated with his takeovers of the BC Electric and later the Black Ball Ferry fleet, he could be a socialist in a second if that was necessary to complete his vision. And that's what he had—a vision for the development of BC. That this vision didn't concern itself much with the environment or that it spread its bounty rather sparsely in some places couldn't be helped. Though his Peace River dam inundated millions of acres, he avoided alienating people of that area from Social Credit because he encouraged the development of the Peace's tremendous natural gas and oil resources.

The Kootenays, however, especially that part affected by the damming of the Columbia, turned against Social Credit and even today remains a tough area for free enterprise parties.

One cannot leave W.A.C. without dealing with the impression the elites in central Canada had of him and his party. Although he was called "Wacky" at home with affection, in the rest of Canada he was called that with derision. This is understandable, I suppose, since all the easterners knew were Liberals and Conservatives. What was this Social Credit stuff, anyhow? And as many of their own politicians were so conservative that they still wore spats, it was hard for them not to look down their noses at Bennett's brashness. (Oddly enough, Bennett was a very conservative dresser with three-piece suits and a Homburg hat.) They had no way to describe this BC phenomenon and his colourful band because he was a one-off—just the right man to hit the right province at just the right time.

But Bennett was also a political animal. My old, late friend Dick Lillico used to tell the story of Bennett arriving at the Phoenix Airport where nobody knew or cared who he was. They did know, however, in jig time as Bennett went through the airport, shaking hands, introducing himself and extolling the virtues of BC. He was, as well, a prudent man, though by this I don't mean a small-minded man. Quite the opposite. He loved to go to the people and tell them what wonderful things his government was doing, apparently at no cost to them as taxpayers.

But the Socred years were two strange decades. Almost no one ever admitted to voting Social Credit. I remember being at a BC Lions game one election evening when the announcer told us that Bennett and the Socreds had won another large mandate and the crowd booed lustily! Though the CCF (then the NDP) vigorously opposed him throughout his reign, oddly enough, W.A.C. is one of the sacred heroes of the present day

NDP. Were he alive and in power today, he would likely be considered a Social Democrat in the way that Tony Blair is. This may sound strange, but when you look where Blair has moved his modern Labour Party and look at its ambitions, they are not unlike that of W.A.C. Bennett's Socreds. The difference between Bennett and his Socreds and the NDP is that what Bennett did what he did competently. Moreover, he ran the ship and everyone knew it.

What about the old coalition parties during the 20-year Social Credit reign? The Conservative Party had been demolished by the 1952 election, and even when Davie Fulton, the well-known Tory MP and cabinet minister in the Diefenbaker government, took over in 1963, it didn't help. Fulton couldn't even come close to winning his own seat against Gaglardi. The Liberal Party did a little better, consistently polling about 20 percent of the vote, and by the end of the '60s it had attracted some star quality performers, such as Pat McGeer, Allan Williams and Garde Gardom, but it was never enough. In one of life's little ironies, Pat McGeer wrote a book called *Politics in Paradise*, a scathing indictment of the Social Credit government, only to become the man who led the defection of Liberal MLAs to the Socred benches in 1975! Politics does indeed make strange bedfellows!

In 1972 there was no outward indication of trouble for the Socreds, but it did show up in the campaign itself. At one point a member of the media somehow contrived to get Phil Gaglardi to hint that perhaps Bennett was a bit past it and that he, Flying Phil, was ready, willing and able to step into the breach. Bennett himself made the serious mistake of taking a limousine tour of much of the Interior, a move that didn't coincide with the image people had of a man of the people. In Kamloops towards the end of the election I made a bet— $10 a seat—with my friend the late Bryon Gardiner that the NDP would take more seats than the Socreds. I netted $280, a large part of which went back down Bryon's throat when we drowned our tears on election night in the Stockmen's Hotel bar. This was an upset, big time, but it was a funny sort of upset. It seemed to be mostly a matter of Socred constituencies all around the province just getting tired of the faces they'd seen for so many years. There was no great policy debate in that election—just provincial boredom with a government that had been around too long. W.A.C. Bennett now became leader of the Opposition, but he and his wife Mae took a long cruise, prompting the NDP to refer to him as the MLA from the Falkland Islands.

There is an old jazz standard called "T'aint What You Do but the Way that You Do It," and to some degree this applied to the NDP. Their first major thrust was to freeze all farm land sales and then bring in legislation setting up an Agricultural Land Reserve. No one seemed to notice that the Socreds had started this process a couple of years earlier and that what the NDP did was simply put meat on the bones. Had it been sold that way, much of the opposition to it would have been blunted, but the way it was done permitted the enemies of the government to make the ludicrous comparison of the NDP to the Soviet Union. Huge marches and rallies took place, but it's interesting to note that, when the Bill Bennett government arrived less than four years later, except for some minor fine-tuning, they didn't change the policy.

Some of the blame for the NDP's failure to capture voter loyalty during their short reign goes to the lack of road building and repair work by the NDP under Highways Minister Graham Lea. This was in large measure a reflection of the urban base of the NDP; you have to have lived in small-town BC to know how much the prosperity of the people with backhoes and that kind of equipment depends upon highways work. In Kamloops it was especially noticed since Phil Gaglardi, once the local MLA, had been seen as a world-famous road builder.

Another part had to do with a mining royalty that crippled the already beleaguered copper industry. In order to make money, many companies had to "high-grade" their own mines, that is, instead of mixing low, medium and high values into the milling process, they had to go for only the best stuff in order to keep their mines going. When I campaigned at the gates of the mines near Logan Lake in December 1975, the workers laughed and said, "Why the hell are you freezing your balls off standing here? We're all voting Socred!" (One of my staunchest supporters, the late Art Redman, owned a trailer park near Logan Lake that was filled with mining families and in itself constituted a polling station. On election night when the results of that station came in, it showed 34 for me, zero for the NDP and two for the Liberals. A serious Art Redman said to me, "Rafe, I'll find those two fucking Liberals if it takes me a lifetime!")

All governments do good things, things not so good and things that are terrible. The NDP was no exception, but whether they deserved the reputation of wasting taxpayer money—any more than other governments—is debatable. That they *seemed* to be wastrels cannot be denied. In 1973 the Barrett government had created the Insurance Corporation of BC (ICBC) and gave it a monopoly on car insurance. The idea was popular with many people of all political stripes who had become sick and tired of the treatment they had been receiving at the hands of the large, mostly American insurance companies. Companies such as Allstate, a subsidiary of Sears in the US, would cancel a policy after the holder had an accident (Allstate became known as "All heart"), but the worst of the lot for this kind of activity was a Canadian company, Western Union, out of Calgary. In all events, everyone had a horror story, and except for the insurance companies who lost out and the lawyers who had thrived off them (including me), most people in BC were happy to see the introduction of a "socialist" insurance company. The trouble with ICBC was that its underwriting decisions were made for political reasons, and in the first year and a half of existence—even with a monopoly— it managed to lose some $186 million dollars. Moreover, as one would expect from a very large government corporation starting from scratch, there were a lot of mistakes that caused people to ask what the difference was between the new and the old. Of course, there was plenty of rearguard action as well from the private insurance sector to keep the dissension pot a-boiling.

Early on, the NDP government bought a restaurant on Government Street in Victoria overlooking the Parliament Buildings. As there appeared to be no reason of public good for the transaction, it became known as Barrett's Beanery. Then there was the government purchase of Panco Poultry, a chicken-processing business that was in financial straits. Again, it was difficult to see why the government would be getting into the bird business and it led to the joke: "What does an NDP bird look like? All left wings and arseholes." Another NDP boondoggle—for reasons I can't for the life of me understand—didn't make the news at all. They started a potato chip plant called Swan Valley in the Kootenays. It was extensive and expensive, and it never sold a chip. When we took office, we learned that the whole project had been based upon a letter from a large retailer—Safeway, I think—that said in effect if you make good chips at a competitive price we'll look at your product. Upon this flimsy foundation many millions of tax dollars were spent. After consulting with a prominent business adviser, the late Bill McQuade, our government decided to "tube" the operation, and it was executed without a whisper from the NDP, which felt that the less said on the subject, the better.

They did good things, of course. Responding to the zest for consumerism that was then extant across the land, they brought in a Consumer Services Ministry. (It was to become my own first portfolio.) And they did something else that is hard to define—they got rid of the arrogance and chippiness that had characterized their predecessors. Landlord and tenant issues had always been a problem, but by the 1970s a new edge had developed in the issues between them, and many renters saw themselves as a persecuted group that needed help from the government. And they got it, much to the annoyance of the landlords (who remained angry at me when I refused to undo NDP initiatives and, in fact, brought in a few of my own). The NDP established the office of rentalsman to handle landlord/tenant grievances and generally behaved with an obvious sense of social responsibility. (That same ombudsman, broadcaster and former MLA Barrie Clark, came under my jurisdiction in 1975 and later we became colleagues at CKNW radio.)

The NDP also made some long overdue changes to the way the legislature worked. They implemented Hansard to record proceedings both in the House and in committee. They paid MLAs and cabinet ministers a decent wage, which many of us derided before we got into power but were delighted to have when we took office. They gave the chairmanship of the only important committee of the legislature, Public Accounts, to the Opposition. While this chair has only one vote, he does set the agenda, an important political tool since this is the only committee that ever meets (and with an Opposition chair it meets a lot) and thus gets media attention.

But they brought in one measure of reform in the legislature that came back to bite them in the ass and probably doomed their government, however unfairly. In those days, after the budget was tabled and the bill to pass it was before the legislature, the House went into what was called a "committee of the whole." This looked like an ordinary legislative sitting except it was presided over by "Mr. Chairman," usually the deputy speaker but sometimes an ordinary government backbencher. The object of the committee of the whole was to examine all the ministers' estimates that made up the budget. (Mike Harcourt's government changed the rules to allow sub-committees to do this job while the legislature proper is sitting.) One after the other, as the ministers presented their estimates, they were cross-examined by the Opposition, the latter's object being not to gain information but to wreak as much political havoc as possible. This was a wonderful time to earn brownie points, and the Opposition had great fun finding a vulnerable minister and keeping him on the griddle for weeks. On taking office, the Barrett government thought this was barbaric—since they were now the "bashees" not the "bashers"—and caused the rules to be changed so that the estimates in their entirely had to be debated within a time limit of 135 hours. Just how the NDP failed to see what was going to happen is incredible, but happen it did. The Socred Opposition dragged out debate so that the 135 hours expired just as it became the turn of the minister of finance. As a result, as each item in the finance minister's estimates came up, it was put to the vote by Speaker Dowding without debate, to the feigned outrage of the Socred Opposition. In fact, the finance minister spends very little himself so his estimates usually go by quickly, but the public didn't know this and the symbolism was important. At this point Opposition leader Bill Bennett stormed out of the House and went to the people shouting, "Not a dime without debate!" It was tricky, it was irresponsible, and it ignored the fact that with the NDP majority all estimates would have passed no matter what the Opposition did or said. But it worked. Oh, how it worked! The portrayal of the NDP as wastrels, the main Socred strategy, was hugely enhanced. And the NDP made things much worse by docking Bill Bennett's pay every day he was away, making the poor little millionaire from Kelowna into a fiscal martyr. It's beyond me just how the usually politically acute Dave Barrett failed to see that he could have ended the entire charade by simply saying, "Okay, take all the time you want." Frankly, I think it was a matter of personal animosity: Barrett hated Bennett and Bennett detested Barrett.

When the Social Credit Party came back into office in 1975, we looked at this 135-hour rule and thought that it wasn't so unreasonable after all, and Garde Gardom, our house leader, put it to NDP house leader Bill King that perhaps in the coming weeks we could limit the time of debate as the NDP had proposed. After King nearly died laughing and wiped the tears of merriment from his eyes, the pith and substance of his reply was "you have to be kidding!" In 1976 the debate on estimates dragged on interminably as the NDP used the proverbial fine-toothed comb to go over and over every estimate that looked at all sexy. They weren't finally cleared up until a couple of days before Christmas! The government could have used closure but under the circumstances didn't dare.

When Bennett toured the province with his "not a dime without debate" war cry in 1975, people flocked to the Socred banner. Although for so long it had been thought of as some kind of ill-defined goofy movement—after all, its constituency organizations met in church basements and it had been the butt of so many of the brilliant Len Norris's cartoons—suddenly it ballooned to 75,000 members (mostly ex-Liberals and ex-Tories) and growing. Kamloops alone hit 5,000 members.

But before the Social Credit Party could burst at the seams, another thing had to happen. One Sunday afternoon a number of Kamloops people, including me, met at the home of lawyer Jarl Whist, a well-known local Liberal who had twice run federally for them. Mostly because the NDP's mining legislation had angered him, Jarl had formed a one-man organization called "Stamp Out Socialism" or SOS for short. The NDP had mocked this movement, labeling it "jackboot," which implied it was like the Gestapo, something that didn't please Jarl much as he had spent his boyhood in Nazi-occupied

Norway. In any event, we hit upon the tamer name of The Majority Movement for Freedom and Private Enterprise, reflecting the increasing belief that, unless those to the right of the NDP got together, they would be divided and conquered. The idea caught on like wildfire and spread across the province. Then also like wildfire, it quickly burned out, but it did leave an excellent basis for the Socreds to work from. And work they did.

Grace McCarthy, who had been minister without portfolio in W.A.C. Bennett's government, was the leading apostle, but she shared this with others who sort of brought up the rear. People like Ken Kieran and Dan Campbell stoked the engine, and Grace went all over the province building constituency organizations. When she came to town—as she often did to Kamloops—everybody, even those who didn't necessarily agree with her approach, did what they were told and worked their buns off. It was an exciting time for those not of the left wing persuasion. Socred annual conventions became great fun, feisty and full of energy. Important people joined: Pat McGeer and Allan Williams crossed the floor to join the Socreds, and Garde Gardom soon followed. Hugh Curtis, one of two Conservatives in the legislature did likewise. People like Peter Hyndman who had run against the Socreds joined the party, as did a lot of movers and shakers who had hitherto been enemies.

I remember one incident at, I believe, the 1974 convention in the Hyatt Regency in Vancouver. Bill Bennett had put the name of the party in issue. He and most others of the "brass" wanted to call it the British Columbia Social Credit Party, but he knew that for many of the new members, including me, Social Credit conjured up bad things from past political wars. There was, therefore, a debate. At microphone number one Peter Hyndman, a staunch Conservative who had lustily if not bitterly fought the Socreds in the past, stood behind me, and

I asked him what he was going to say. He smiled seraphically and said he wasn't quite sure yet. I took the mike and said that as a new arrival from another party I thought we should look for a new name. I was lustily booed for my effort. Then came Peter, the man who had fought the hated Socreds all his adult life. While I don't remember his exact words it went something like this: "This is a grand old party whose record under W.A.C. Bennett was illustrious with one great election victory after another. It's a great and respected name, Social Credit, and I for one am proud to bear that name in the struggle ahead." He was cheered to the rafters. I learned something about politics that day.

The new party had its share of critics. Allan Fotheringham, the brilliant political writer then with the *Vancouver Sun*, called it the United Vegetable Party. Jack Webster mocked it, and Marjory Nichols of the *Sun* denigrated it by seldom concerning herself with it.

What was it, then, that won the subsequent landslide victory for Bill Bennett and his crowd, which included Rafe Mair? Was it that the electorate hated the Barrett socialists so much that they wanted to hurl them from office?

The numbers tell a strange story. The NDP lost in 1975 with exactly the same percentage of the popular vote with which they had won in 1972. The difference was that in 1972 the Conservatives and Liberals had polled 16.4 percent and 12.7 percent respectively. In 1975 they dropped to 7.2 percent and 3.9 percent with the difference going, almost to the vote, to the Socreds. So the NDP won a landslide in 1972 with 39 percent of the vote and lost a landslide in 1975 with 39 percent of the vote.

In their first term, the new Social Credit Party was beset by a scandal that was as lengthy as it was inconsequential. During the run-up to the election a couple of the "brass" at Socred headquarters had advised candidates that it might be a good plan to write letters to the editors of their local newspapers condemning the NDP and signing their letters with the names of prominent members of the NDP in that community. This came to light when a well-known NDP member in Victoria, one Gordon Townsend, blew the whistle, and we were thrown into the midst of what the media dubbed "Lettergate." Leading the charge was BCTV, and night after night for months on end they added more juicy tidbits to the story.

(In a strange irony, early in 1976 we were all sitting in the cabinet room when suddenly the door burst open and we were surrounded by shouting, sign-carrying, NDP activists. It was scary as hell though neatly defused by Bennett who took the leader to his office for a chat. And who was that leader? The one and the same Gordon Townsend. But there was an amusing sequel. Every day before the House gets down to business, members can introduce people in the gallery, and one of the NDP members introduced Gordon Townsend with some frilly remarks about what a wonderful man he was. I was able to rise in my place and also welcome Mr. Townsend as the ringleader of the bunch of rowdies who had broken into the cabinet offices.)

A couple of Socred Party staff had to resign over Lettergate, but that was about it. However, the whole affair did cause me a bit of nervous mirth because of what had happened in my Kamloops constituency. In the middle of the election I had been a guest on a CFJC radio talk show. I got hit with everything but the ring post, and when I staggered, bruised and bleeding, back into Socred headquarters, there was my campaign manager, Bud Smith (later to be our attorney general), bellowing with rage at the assembled workers. "Where the hell were you all?" he asked. Upon learning that they had all been listening but not phoning, he announced that it would be different when I went on CHNL in a few days time.

We had about 25 phone lines at headquarters, and in those days if you wanted to be sure to get on a talk show, you could dial the first six digits, wait for the last caller to hang up, then dial the seventh, and you would be immediately connected. So I went on CHNL and it worked like a charm. Soft pitch after soft pitch came over the plate and I easily swatted them out of the park. Then a lady called, apparently huffing and puffing, to say, "Oh, Mr. Mair, I was in my car and heard you and just had to rush to a pay phone to tell you what a wonderful man you are and how lucky Kamloops is to have you!" As she was talking, I suddenly thought, *That's Emily Latta, and she's in the front row at headquarters, third phone from the left!* (The next year Emily's husband, Mike, was to become the very popular, Socred-backed, mayor of Kamloops.) Then a voice I recognized as that of a strong supporter, mining engineer Bert Forster, came on line and he asked me a complicated question about the mining royalty the NDP had brought in. *Jesus, Bert,* I thought almost out loud, *you're not supposed to ask any real questions! Especially on something about which I know bugger-all!*

The NDP were livid. They stormed the office of owner John Skelly, demanding to know how come their members had been unable to get through. Skelly pled ignorance and he was telling the truth. In any event, to my relief the matter never resurfaced, and the so-called Lettergate matter eventually burned out as well and didn't cause the party any problems.

The spring of 1979 was a strange time to call an election, but less than three and a half years after the previous one, Bennett went on television and made a very long statement in which he referred to the NDP as "National Socialists," a label that was as silly as it was provocative, and then announced an election for mid-May. This was an election without issues except the usual one: Shall we throw the bastards out or not? The Socreds won a squeaker that time with the NDP increasing their share of the popular vote from 39.2 to 46.0 percent, but rather than taking votes from the Socreds, this gain seemed mostly to reflect the even further deterioration of the Liberal and Conservative parties from an aggregate of about 11 percent in 1975 and two seats to less than 6 percent and no members in 1979. But the Socreds had hardly settled back into Victoria when they were into another scandal, this time more serious.

In 1978 a former provincial court judge and ex-Socred candidate, Larry Eckhardt, had been appointed as a one-man commission to adjust constituency boundaries. Within his plan as adopted by the government was a strange new configuration to the Vancouver Little Mountain riding of Grace McCarthy. A sliver had suddenly been extended from her old riding into much friendlier political territory, and this might well have affected the result of the election. There didn't seem to be any justification for this change—what the NDP aptly called "Gracie's Finger"—other than plain gerrymandering. It didn't help when it became known that Grace had met with Eckhardt before the final draft, although it was not only common but quite proper for a boundaries commissioner to seek advice, including that of MLAs. This scandal droned on and on, and I even found myself in the middle of it when I got into a near fist fight with Frank Howard (who would have murdered me!), causing the speaker to adjourn the House. Again, as so often is the case with scandals, real or alleged, there didn't appear to be any long-term damage done. I must say, however, that we were lucky that the revelations about "Gracie's Finger" came out after the election and weren't combined with the still smoldering Lettergate affair.

However, before the 1979 election another issue had arisen that could have been much more troublesome for the Socreds than in fact it turned out to be. For what reason I'm not sure, uranium mining had become a big deal, and the NDP and others around the province accused the government of condemning BC's citizens to glowing in the dark. Dr. Bob

Woollard, a doctor in Clearwater, which was within my constituency, was particularly vocal on this subject, and I rather
intemperately called him a nasty name that had, as I recall, the
term "red-assed quack" in it. The doctor was very popular in
Clearwater, and I had to make a special trip to an open meeting
and abjectly apologize to him and take a lot of deserved abuse
in the process. I carried Clearwater in the election but suspect I
wouldn't have gotten a vote if I hadn't humbled myself.

Uranium mining was a no-winner. If we approved of
it, we were nuking our fellow citizens. If we opposed it, we
had the mining community up in arms. So, as environment
minister, I suggested the time-honoured political ploy of a
royal commission, and we appointed an eminent physician,
David Bates, giving him a wide enough mandate to take the
issue off the table. This resolved the uranium-mining problem,
but then in the midst of the campaign, the erudite Dr. Patrick
McGeer returned from China and told the assembled media
how excited he was at the prospect of "nuclear fusion." There
is a mighty big distinction between "fusion" and "fission" but
it was lost on the ladies and gentlemen of the press, and the
government was back in the business of nuking the voters! In
the end, however, the only problem for the Socreds was that
Dr. Bates, a man of great integrity and decency—and of course
international scientific credentials—didn't want to quit after
we'd won the election and were no longer much interested in
uranium mining.

There was one issue at the end of the '70s that never fully
caught on to hurt Premier Bill Bennett or his government. In
1979, Bennett, the businessman, miscalculated when he came
up with an idea that might have worked but didn't. It was called
the British Columbia Resources Investment Corporation,
though commonly known as BRIC. The idea was to take the
resource-based Crown corporations, put them all into a new
public company, give every British Columbian five shares at

$6 a share, and everyone would make lots of money. At first it looked like a brilliant idea and I, like others, also bought more stock. When it went to $9, I took my profit and gave it to the income tax people to whom I owed money. Right afterward the stock took a nose dive and stayed there. Strangely, while BRIC was certainly a bad idea or perhaps a good idea badly executed, it did no immediate damage to the Social Credit Party.

Not long after the 1979 election, Finance Minister Hugh Curtis informed cabinet that our government was headed into very tough times and things would have to be cut back. High on his list of suggested cuts was ministerial travel and accommodations, but the discovery that Hugh's own visit to Paris via Concorde out of New York and his stay at the swank George Cinque Hotel was still on, inspired a go-to-hell response from his colleagues. However, Hugh was dead right about the disintegrating economy, and it wasn't so long before other provinces and Ottawa caught on, and restraint became the order of the day. But it began to look like tough times for the Socreds as well since restraint isn't all that good an election issue.

Then in the spring of 1983 there were rumours that Bennett was going to call an election. I had left government in early 1981 to take a talk show job at Jimmy Pattison's station, then called CJOR600, so was an observer by this time, but all the feedback I was getting told me that the Socreds were going to lose—big time. I called Bud Smith, who was then working in the premier's office, and asked him if they had taken leave of their senses. He laughed and read me some poll results: people loved Barrett and didn't like Bennett, they thought that the NDP cared while the Socreds didn't, and so on. Then Bud said, "But listen to this: What is the biggest issue for you? Answer: employment. And who can best bring employment? Bill Bennett. Do you believe that restraint in government is necessary? The answer is yes." He paused and then asked, "So what do you think of an election run on restraint in the public sector and full employment?"

I wasn't convinced. When the election was called, I predicted an NDP victory, but to further my deserved reputation of making wrong election calls, Bennett, with just less than 50 percent of the vote, won a near landslide. Part of this was because Barrett had gone on television and disagreed with the need for restraint, and the public, assuming that the restraint program Bennett was pushing was all about getting rid of "fat cat" civil servants and bloated government programs, enthusiastically took his side. After the election when Bennett did what he had actually promised and brought in "restraint" legislation and policy, the BC Federation of Labour, under president Art Kube, set its hair on fire and formed "Solidarity" after the movement started by Lech Walesa in Poland. It featured marches, rallies and wildcat strikes, and it looked as if the province would be brought to a standstill. That's when Jack Munro, then president of the International Woodworkers of America (IWA), stepped in. Certainly no fan of Bill Bennett or the Socreds, he bravely and accurately stated that, in a democracy, policy was made in the legislature and not in the streets. He flew to Kelowna and made peace—mostly on Bennett's terms, putting the Socreds firmly on top in what would be Bill Bennett's last term with the Socreds. He was obviously in charge after staring down labour, leaving the NDP looking like one of those racehorses I always seem to bet on that perennially finish second.

In fact, the scene for the Socreds was deteriorating, and Bill Bennett knew it. The main issue after 1983 was Expo 86. It proved to be a huge success and without question drew a lot of favourable world attention on BC. Bill Bennett deserves the lion's share of the credit for this if only because he was the skipper and would have been the one blamed if it hadn't worked. But just after the fair opened in April 1986, he suddenly announced that he was retiring and that, as soon as a leadership convention elected his successor, he was gone. Why did he do this? The answer is simple. There was no way anyone could put a favourable spin on the polls. Bennett was very, very unpopular indeed.

It is always difficult to know why someone becomes unpopular. There are generally many explanations, but I think in Bill Bennett's case it was an accumulation of things. Certainly his fight with the trade unions over Expo had hurt him badly. He had refused to grant a closed shop and they were livid. He had ignored the fact that many—indeed I would say half the union members—had in the past voted for his dad and then for him. Now he had thoroughly pissed them off. This issue, added to all the other grievances of a long reign of power, told Bennett that it was checkout time. So we were now to witness the end of Social Credit power and, indeed, the end of the Social Credit Party. Just one thing remained—the election of Bill Vander Zalm as the new leader and thus the new premier.

It must be noted that Bill Bennett never interfered with nomination processes, taking the position that each Socred candidate had to win his own nomination, and he took the same view with the leadership race that developed after his retirement. However laudable that decision may have been morally or philosophically, it was a disaster in the result. Bill Vander Zalm was a Dutch immigrant whose father, in the bulb business, had been caught in BC when the Nazis invaded Holland. Bill, left behind with his mother and siblings in Holland, had a ghastly childhood, finally forced to eat bulbs to stay alive, but when the war ended, they all rejoined Vander Zalm senior in the Fraser Valley. Bill himself then became very successful in the gardening business and later made a name for himself as the outspoken and controversial mayor of Surrey during the early '70s. At one time he also stood for the leadership of the provincial Liberal party, although just why, given his very conservative views, remains a mystery. His sort of

Liberal wouldn't appear again until Gordon Campbell became leader of the BC Liberals in September 2002.

I first met Bill at the 1974 Socred convention and, as with all who came in contact with him, liked him very much. In the 1975 election, he ran for the Socreds in Surrey, and during the campaign he made known his displeasure with welfare recipients by announcing that he would, if he could, give them all shovels. This is not an untypical remark for a self-made person to make; such people conclude that, if they could pull themselves up by their bootstraps with hard work, everyone else could do the same. Vander Zalm won the election and was made minister of human resources, a strange choice. I suppose Bennett had to put him somewhere, if only on the theory that it would be better having him inside the tent pissing out than outside the tent pissing in. But the choice of human resources for him did seem like a poke in the eye to the less fortunate and to those sympathetic to them. Bill tried, with a special branch of his ministry, to get people who were on welfare back into the work force but failed miserably.

In the five years we were in cabinet together our relationship was cordial, and in fact, if anyone had reason to complain about the other it was he about me. On one occasion I forgot an undertaking I had made as chairman of the Environment and Land Use Committee not to sign an order that had been passed until he could talk to me about it. I had every right to criticize the public servant who was the committee secretary and who had allowed me to make this mistake, but I'm with Harry S. Truman—the buck stopped with me. My error caused a hell of a political uproar, but Bill took it well and forgave me my stupidity, as did Bob McLelland to whom I had made the same promise. It was eventually settled rather unsatisfactorily but, considering my screw-up, there was no good way out.

Bill and I sat together on the Social Services Committee of cabinet and got along well, but in all the hours I spent in cabinet meetings with him I can't remember any time that he really had much impact. What was obvious about Vander Zalm was that he was a my-way-or-the-highway sort of person. Quite unable to be part of a consensus, his instinct seemed to be to break them up when they happened. He remained in cabinet, as I see it, because it would have been politically harmful for Bennett to leave him out. The fact remains that during his time as a Bill Bennett minister from late 1975 until the spring of 1983, it's hard to find much lasting imprint of his record.

Bill Vander Zalm had sat out the 1983 election, which probably was a good thing in the sense it gave him more than three years away from the fray—sort of a political field lying fallow. But when Bennett announced his retirement, all eyes were on Vander Zalm. "Is Bill going to run?" seemed to be on everyone's lips. But Bill was very coy. One day shortly after Bennett's announcement I saw Vander Zalm on the Expo site where CKNW, with whom I then broadcast, had its talk show studio, and I asked him point blank if he was going to run. It takes a politician to know one, and his coyness didn't fool me a bit. He was going to run.

Bud Smith, who had been my campaign chairman in 1975 and again in 1979, also prepared to run. He was now fresh out of the premier's office and had recruited the very polished John Laschinger from Toronto as his campaign chair. Brian Smith (no relation), then attorney general, was given an outside chance. But the sentimental favourite—and perhaps the favourite, period— at that juncture was Grace McCarthy who, with Bill Bennett and a few others, had brought the Social Credit Party back from the dead after W.A.C. Bennett had been routed in 1972. Then there was Bill Vander Zalm, back in the limelight in which he so happily basked. It was odd to observe, as I was able to, that none of his rivals admitted that they thought he had a chance, but they all in their own ways showed fear. It was interesting, too, to see who supported whom. Bud Smith had Highways Minster Alex Fraser; Grace McCarthy had several cabinet members behind her, including the influential Pat McGeer; Brian Smith had one or two; but Bill Vander Zalm, even on the last ballot, could only count on cabinet minister Jack Davis. These were the four who had a chance to take the leadership prize at Whistler in the last days of July 1986.

It was no slam dunk. The Socred brass and cabinet ministers were betting on Grace. The pundits were divided. I wished for Bud Smith but predicted Brian Smith. Then on the night before the vote, Vander Zalm got lucky, though in fairness he may not have needed it. BCTV and the *Vancouver Sun* published polls that showed that of the four major candidates, only Bill Vander Zalm could and would beat the NDP. You could sense the excitement as this news made the rounds of the town. Just before the vote, I was a guest on Bill Good's CBC-TV show, and he asked me what I thought would happen if Vander Zalm won. Could he bring the party together? I replied, "In two years he will have destroyed the Social Credit Party." And for once, a Mair prediction—sadly for this province, I think— was right on. Bill Vander Zalm won on the third ballot and a few days later was sworn in as premier of BC.

It didn't take a sharp observer to notice that of all Vander Zalm's cabinet and caucus colleagues, only Jack Davis had supported him, but Jack had an axe to grind. He had been fired from Bill Bennett's cabinet in 1977 after it became clear he would shortly be charged with theft, his actual offence being that he took first class airfares from his ministry, downgraded them, and pocketed the difference. Davis never forgave Bennett for making him resign and saw Vander Zalm as the best way to get back into cabinet. He was right.

Vander Zalm also gave Grace McCarthy and Brian Smith cabinet posts, but even though Bud Smith had crossed to Vander Zalm in timely fashion, he was not so rewarded. (Many

103

years later Vander Zalm admitted to me and my audience that this had been the stupidest mistake he ever made in politics—which covers a lot of ground!)

Vander Zalm called an election a few months after he took office, and a landslide was predicted not just because he had received all that publicity but because the NDP leader, Bob Skelly, was really a very nice, dull sort who ought to have stayed in the school teaching profession. (When interviewed after the election was announced, Skelly got so rattled that he asked if he might start his spiel over again! It was not a promising start.) Vander Zalm and the Socreds won, again with nearly 50 percent of the popular vote, but it was generally felt that, had the campaign gone on a week or ten days more, the NDP might have closed the gap considerably.

So what happened that victory by such a popular and charismatic man could turn so sour? First of all, as I have mentioned, Bill Vander Zalm, far from being a consensus seeker, instinctively breaks them up. It wasn't that he was evil, just that he was unyielding. Second, Bill is an incurable publicity seeker and in the premier's office he was right in his element. The trouble was he just couldn't shut up. He would pronounce on any issue raised with him. In fact, it was his conservative Roman Catholic views on abortion that got him sideways with his attorney general, Brian Smith. With abortion strictly a federal matter, one has to wonder how he got into that issue at all, except that someone asked him and he couldn't resist a reporter with a pad of paper or a microphone. When Brian Smith resigned over this issue, Vander Zalm, having run out of lawyers, had to put Russ Fraser, an engineer, into the attorney general's office where fortunately he proved to be pretty competent. Vander Zalm's inability to refrain from interfering also prompted Grace McCarthy's resignation from cabinet, and his inability to command control caused four backbenchers to leave caucus. By 1988 the party was split asunder among three factions—the Vander Zalm supporters, the Vander Zalm haters and those who thought that dumping the leader would do the party in. As it turned out, Vander Zalm did survive a leadership vote at the 1988 convention in Penticton but only because the "old guard" succeeded in having the vote-to-have-a-vote declared a "voice vote," not a secret ballot.

But there was a third and overriding factor causing Vander Zalm's big victory to sour. Under W.A.C. Bennett and even more under Bill Bennett the Social Credit Party could scarcely have been called right wing. In the Bill Bennett years, for example, I passed more consumer protection legislation than had been passed before or since. Bill Bennett particularly made it clear that small "l" liberals such as me were more than welcome in the party. Grace McCarthy would have carried on that tradition. So would have Bud Smith. Brian Smith, a right winger, would have had the sense to know that the guts of the party was not of that persuasion. But Vander Zalm was of the outer Right and he had no sense at all when it came to keeping the party with him. It is a political axiom that is occasionally tested, always to be proved true that neither the far Right nor the far Left can gain even medium-term public support, and that even if, as happened with Vander Zalm, they occasionally win an election, they can't hold onto power. When Vander Zalm won, the party was split and it only needed a teeny catalyst for it to fall apart.

When Vander Zalm appointed Ted Hughes, a former Saskatchewan Supreme Court judge and BC deputy attorney general, to determine whether or not he was in a conflict of interest over the land deals he was privately conducting, it was from the outset a slam dunk decision. Just what would possess him to appoint the super-righteous Hughes to investigate conduct in which a first year law student would have found a conflict, I'll never know. Hughes, of course, did find the premier to be in a conflict, though Vander Zalm was later acquitted on the criminal charges arising from it. His departure from office left two options open to the Social Credit Party: It could select a right winger as Vander Zalm's replacement and die or move back to the centre and survive. The party selected the former route and died.

When Vander Zalm resigned in April 1991, the Socred caucus met to decide who would replace him. The critical question was whether the new premier would be an interim leader in the sense he or she would not stand for leader at the next convention or if the contest would be wide open. They were advised—badly—that there must be no strings attached to the premiership as otherwise the lieutenant-governor would be compromised. In fact, all the lieutenant-governor needed to know was whether the leader could form a government. This was a critical moment because Attorney General Russ Fraser had offered to stand in as premier and promised that he would not seek the leadership at the August convention. The caucus's decision to select Rita Johnston instead meant that she would be able to campaign for the leadership with her caucus behind her since they dared not join forces with any other candidate— which is principally to say, Grace McCarthy. It must be fairly said that Rita Johnston might have won anyway, but because of this decision, she did go into the race with a leg up. Had Russ Fraser been selected as interim leader, she would have gone into that contest on a level playing field.

By the time the 1991 election was held, the Social Credit Party was badly divided. I remember covering the leadership contest at the Convention Centre for BCTV with one of my colleagues, the late Jack Webster. (Actually, as it always was with Jack, I was his colleague, not the other way around and I always knew that!) After the vote was announced and delegates started to go, I said to him, "There they go—one half with Rita and the rest to join the Liberal Party." And so it proved.

It's interesting to speculate what might have happened if Grace McCarthy had won. Most pundits think that while she would have lost the election in 1991, she would have retained a large experienced caucus and might have recaptured power in 1995, and thus there would not have been the 10-year NDP reign that followed nor the years of Gordon Campbell that followed that. And there would still be the viable umbrella entity called the British Columbia Social Credit Party where all to the right of the NDP would feel comfortable.

For all intents and purposes the Socred Party was dead. Can something like it be revived? Only time will tell. If, once again, the NDP with their steady support can split the vote and win an election with 40 percent of the popular vote, perhaps it is possible. It is more likely that this province will institute some form of proportional representation, and there will be many parties and very little opportunity for any government to form a majority. But that's for the future. The past is gone and so is Social Credit.

How, then, can BC-style Social Credit be explained? How can other Canadians be made to understand that both Bennetts were populists when there were no others like them and that they were welcomed by voters?

British Columbia has always been Canada's "odd man out." It was born suspicious of the national government and, after 1941 at any rate, viewed national parties with considerable suspicion as well. Even members of those national parties such as Gerry McGeer and T.D. Patullo saw Ottawa as a sort of absentee landlord, and when W.A.C. Bennett declared to Ottawa, that BC was just a "goblet to be drained," most British Columbians agreed. This prejudice against national parties in BC politics remains to this day. I am convinced that, though Gordon Wilson completely divorced the provincial Liberals from the federal party, Gordon Campbell lost the 1996 election because people didn't quite believe that the two were distinct and separate entities.

This may be changing, albeit very slowly. The huge ethnic vote, much of which feels deep gratitude to the federal Liberals, is more national in outlook than many traditional voters in this province, and the arrival and near success of the Reform/ Alliance-cum-Conservative Party seems to have sufficient BC influence within it to satisfy voters as well. But before we assume that BC is settling in to the ways of other provinces (other than Quebec, that is) we must await the events of the next few years. If, as I suspect, Quebec votes for separation in three or four years, the "BC first" element will surely be resurrected.

I suppose that in the final analysis, though everything else has changed so dramatically since World War II, the Rockies remain—while not a physical barrier—a cultural and political one. BC is different (dare I say distinct?) and it shows. In fact, it probably always will.

The New Democratic Party:
A Lesson in Failure

The BC New Democratic Party is a political failure and has had to be lucky as hell to win when it did. This party, a provincial wing of the federal political party of the same name, was formed in October 1961 at a convention in Vancouver that saw the old Co-Operative Commonwealth Federation (CCF) joining forces with the labour movement. Robert Strachan, who had led the CCF since 1956, became its first leader. I remember at the time there was considerable hope that this new party would offer a home to federal Liberals who were a bit "pink" like myself. It hasn't turned out that way at all because the party became dominated by the trade unions and, what's worse, was seen as under labour's thumb. And its formation really didn't do much for the Left's election prospects; the CCF had 28 percent of the vote in 1956 and thereafter until 1979 the NDP polled in the '30s.

But they did become government in 1972 and again in 1991 and 1996. Isn't that reasonable success?

I would argue not. By 1972 a lot of things, including age, had caught up to W.A.C. Bennett's government. The Socreds had not seen the environmental and consumer movements coming and this cost them dearly. But the voters didn't necessarily mean that they wanted the NDP, which got only three percent more votes than did the Socreds. The public simply wanted change. What cost Bennett the election was the support given to right wing alternatives, the Liberals and the Tories. The vote had finally split as Liberal Premier T.D. Pattullo, back in 1941, had foreseen when he and others cobbled together the coalition of Liberals and Conservatives that held power until 1952. When the NDP only got 39 percent of the popular vote in 1972, they should have been asking themselves what they had done to send the Liberals and Tories, who used to erode the Socreds' power, back to their traditional parties and what they would have to do to get them to stay there. The fact is that they had only themselves to blame for much of the woe that descended on them during their short reign.

Barrett did, however, make many much-needed parliamentary reforms and brought in economic and social changes that weren't undone by even the most right-wing governments that followed. Some of them—such as Hansard, decent pay for MLAs and cabinet ministers, inaugurating question period, and ensuring that an Opposition member chaired the Public Accounts Committee—were all overdue reforms. The Agricultural Land Reserve, arguably the most far-reaching decision, was greeted with screams of horror from the Right, but no government since then has touched this legislation except to fine-tune it. The decision to take over car insurance was met with mixed reviews because it lost gobs of money in the first 18 months of its existence, but, again, no government has dared to abolish it.

But it was in the Barrett years that the NDP had a glorious chance to re-invent itself, though I'm bound to say it would have taken a leader of extraordinary courage and popularity to do it. The debate within the NDP at that time was not whether the party should broaden its horizons but rather whether the Barrett government had gone far enough in radical policies and legislation or, as was said then, whether they had enough eggs to make an omelet. As one of Barrett's cabinet colleagues, Graham Lea said to me, laughing, "We always assume that any moment now the Social Credit Party will shrivel up and blow away." Lea knew better but the party didn't. Their strategy was to wait until the Socreds imploded, ignoring the fact that if they did, a new right-wing political party would appear. Meanwhile, as the years of the Barrett administration passed, it became very obvious that the whipped Socreds had seen the error of their political ways and were moving towards making their party inclusive of all to the right of the NDP. Certainly, as the process sputtered to its start, any reasonably informed political junkie could see that a Socred Party without Liberal and Conservative parties snapping at its heels would stand a good chance of making a big comeback.

What is puzzling is that around this time socialist and social democratic parties were all trying to fit themselves into the new world that was so clearly developing. We had not yet reached free trade and globalization, but we could see that the silicon chip was bringing about a whole new world. In Britain the "young Turks" of the Labour Party sensed what was happening; they knew that if their party didn't change with the times it would be left behind. But the NDP did nothing by way of reform. In the same Catch-22 as other Social Democratic parties they relied upon the trade union movement for their money and workers, while their biggest "put-off factor" for voters was their close relationship to those same labour unions.

The next four elections were instructive and should have stirred the party brass to put on their thinking caps. The first time the NDP got more than 40 percent of the vote—they, in fact, polled 45 percent—was in 1979, yet that year they lost a squeaker to the Socreds in what was all but a straight two-team race. Clearly, the absence of the Liberal Party factor in that election and the virtual wipeout of the Conservatives demonstrated that for the NDP to win again they needed a facelift or a lucky break. The 1983 election saw the NDP get 44 percent of the popular vote yet lose an election they had felt sure they would win and lose it by a fairly wide margin of seats in another two-horse race. At this point Dave Barrett, having

111

lost three straight elections, had to go and did. Now here was the party's chance to look long and hard at the reasons the NDP could not get that last shove to victory.

The reason, again, was obvious. Organized labour, while it could deliver money and foot soldiers to the NDP, could not deliver the votes. It was this very fact that had galvanized the British Labour Party into major reform. The UK Labourites had, you would think, the best political target they could hope for—the very right wing and bossy Margaret Thatcher. But that lady knew what she was doing when she radically altered the labour laws; she knew that union members vote in greater numbers for the Conservative Party than for Labour and that they approved of her policy. She knew that the average British worker didn't hate the "capitalist bosses" nearly as much as union leaders did and that they felt detached from their union leaders.

All this went over the BC NDP's head as they elected the oh-so-earnest yet deadly dull schoolteacher (reminding me of Mr. Boynton in the Eve Arden sit-com, *Our Miss Brooks*) Bob Skelly, as their new leader. If ever there were a man to lead the NDP to radical changes, Bob Skelly was not that man. Then came the NDP's lucky moment in the form of Bill Vander Zalm at the head of the Socreds. Suffice it to say that Vander Zalm, as I predicted, destroyed the Social Credit party. Thus it was that BC went into the 1991 election with a dying Social Credit Party, an NDP that was doing all it could to avoid pleasing the middle-of-the-roader and a Liberal Party used to getting eight percent of the popular vote in a good year.

The NDP knew it had to change but thought it could do it with the man, not the party. Thus, Mike Harcourt, a lukewarm leftie at best, was put forward to convince the "middle" that the NDP could be trusted. It looked as if he had done that with his smiling visage and with Social Credit crumbling but, though he won 51 seats in the first-past-the-post system, he did it with a smaller percentage of the popular vote than Skelly had lost with in 1986! If that didn't get some thinking going, one might have concluded that the Liberal upsurge from near zero to 17 seats and over 30 percent of the votes would have been a pail of cold water in NDP faces. But it did nothing. Even at this point the NDP had not noticed that their popularity as a party was not moving up and that they were still relying on a split on the right to win. Perhaps if Mike Harcourt had been able to hold onto the premier's office, the party might have looked at itself more carefully, but Mike Harcourt, unable to deal with a huge scandal (of which he was not a part), resigned and the NDP went to a labour organizer Glen Clark for their next leader. Clark looked like a genius when he led the party to victory in 1996 in a stunning upset, but again it was instructive that Clark only got 39 percent of the vote in an election where once again the right-wing vote was split.

Quite to everyone's surprise, Clark was gone in the summer of 1999, having been caught up in a scandal in which he was personally involved (although he was later exonerated). And for five months, with Dan Miller as interim premier, the NDP had a chance to ponder its future. It did no such thing and instead entered a self-immolating leadership race that was won by Ujjal Dosanjh, seen as being on the left of his party. I was at that leadership convention in February 2001 and, far from being forward-looking, the entire affair was an exercise in reactionary reflection. All the candidates, even Gordon Wilson, who had left his own party after being forced out as Liberal leader, made speeches as if they had all been born into Welsh coal mining families in the early 1900s. One of the bits of entertainment was a guitarist playing—for God's sake!— "The Ballad of Joe Hill," the hero of which had been a brutal murderer who somehow became a martyr of the Left. There wasn't a constructive thought expressed; it was a throwback to times long past.

In 2001 the NDP got slaughtered at the polls, winning but two seats. Now here, surely, was the place to take some time and make some effort to re-evaluate the party's platform and make a move to modernize, but again they did little except lick their wounds and complain. In November 2003 at a convention easy to forget, Carole James, whose political experience was confined to a number of terms as head of the Victoria School Board, was made leader. No one of note ran against her, reflecting the fact that all the big kids were still in a state of shock and in no hurry to get back in the ring. Again, here was a golden opportunity to remake the party. The next election date was set for May 17, 2005, so the NDP had four years to re-tune, but the only change they made was to decide that the next time there was a leadership convention it would be one-member-one-vote, thus taking the block vote away from the trade unions.

All over the world left-wing parties have moved to the centre. This is not entirely a simple pragmatic move to gain power but much more an acknowledgement that the enemy is no longer the owner of the coal mine and that the challenge is to find a way to exist in the new world economy. The NDP across the country and particularly in BC ought to be taking the lead in making our economies work in the new world we're in. Instead, they are up to their old tricks of making up new slogans, bearing their anti-Americanism at every opportunity and brilliantly articulating problems, while they are still more than just a little short of solutions.

Until the NDP does what the British Labour Party did, namely deny special privileged status to the labour unions, it is not going to get elected. In fact, it must do more than just rely on trade unions rallying behind it; it must show that people other than trade unionists, teachers and college professors are welcome in the party. It can happen. Long ago when I was the MLA from Kamloops, one of my directors was an officer in the local union at Weyerhaeuser. In order to blunt attacks from the Left, he suggested that I make it a point to go to all local gatherings, especially those with a strong NDP flavour. I reached out and, while I didn't expect to make droves of converts, I made some, but most importantly I didn't frighten the Left. Perhaps I did no more than spike their guns and left them less willing to battle me as hard as they might have.

Carole James has tried to do this but it must be done on a broad front and it takes time. As it presently stands, James or her successor will be premier not when the NDP convinces British Columbians to vote for them but when the public gets sick and tired of the Liberals. That's reactive, not proactive, and in politics, while you must have both, proactive is by far the more important. When you see the NDP really making a move to the centre, not just faking it, then and only then will they become a viable alternative to the Liberals.

Although I've only dealt with the provincial party in BC, everything I've said applies with even greater force at the federal level—with this added wrinkle: The federal NDP have allowed the Liberals to occupy most of the Left that was once the territory of the NDP. This is because the major trade unions press all the buttons that get reactions from the NDP leader. Jack Layton almost needs the permission of Ken Georgetti and Buzz Hargrove to visit the loo. And the trouble is, the labour leaders like it this way. For the NDP to have any power in the House of Commons it must do as the Labour Party did in the UK, and that will happen in Canada over the union leaders' bodies because they would lose their own political clout with their members if they no longer had a party in the Commons, however small, to dictate to.

The NDP will have a chance to win power in non-industrialized provinces such as Saskatchewan and Manitoba, occasionally in BC, and seldom in Ontario. Why? Because, paradoxically, where union membership is highest, the chance of success is lowest for the very good reason that more than one half of the electorate, union and non-union alike, see the NDP as dominated by union leaders. Interestingly, that one-half-plus includes a substantial number of working people, union and non union.

As a place for ideas on social reform, the federal NDP has played an important role. To implement those ideas, it has no role at all except as a national scold.

The Citizens' Assembly on Electoral Reform

Instituting the Citizens' Assembly on Electoral Reform was one of the most courageous steps ever taken by a political leader. To give a commission the opportunity to investigate the fundament of democracy—which is, of course, how we vote—knowing that the status quo is not likely to be an option, was a very gutsy move, and Premier Gordon Campbell is very much to be congratulated.

It's not my purpose here to give a history of that commission; that must be done either by the chair, Jack Blaney, or the author of its procedure, Gordon Gibson. The notion of the Single Transferable Ballot, though not Gordon's idea, became an issue for the commission, thanks to the efforts of former MLA Nick Loenen, who was tireless in bringing it to the fore and who wrote his master's thesis on the subject. Instead I would like to record how the Commission itself became the idea picked up and acted upon by Premier Campbell. It's possible, of course, though very unlikely, that the premier or his advisers came up with this notion out of the blue. Assuming that didn't happen, here's what did.

I have long been interested in constitutional affairs and for some years during the Bill Bennett government was the cabinet minister in charge of constitutional matters and had an active role in the run-up to the patriation of the Constitution in 1982. One of the things I remember most about that time was being among the ministers and officials led by BC's Mel Smith, deputy minister of constitutional affairs, who recommended the so-called "Vancouver Charter" that became the "Amending Formula" for the new constitution. I knew the issues. Quebec, in one of those great political ironies that pop up from time to time, actually would have preferred to see the Constitution stay in London. Why? Because separatist Premier René Lévesque believed that London wouldn't permit an amendment to the old British North America Act of 1867, a law passed by the British Parliament, without Quebec's consent. He would, as he saw it, have a de facto veto if the Constitution stayed in London. From Lévesque's point of view Quebec would soon separate, then the rest of Canada could do as it pleased. In the meantime, better the Constitution stay in London rather than come to Ottawa.

In the negotiations leading up to the Constitution Act, the question of the amending formula was the sticking point. It had been that way ever since the notion of a home-grown constitution began to take hold. How to amend it? All previous suggestions had contained some sort of veto process, the most famous being the Victoria Charter of 1971, which would have given a veto to each of four regions—the Maritimes, Quebec, Ontario and "the West."

In the fall of 1976 then Prime Minister Trudeau wrote all the premiers asking that they help him find a way to have a home-grown constitution, and from that time Mel Smith, the greatest constitutional expert in the country, and I teamed up. The one very clear instruction Premier Bill Bennett gave us was that we would not go back to the Victoria Charter, which—because BC had been lumped in with "the West"—had caused much offence. Whether he also took issue with the notion of vetoes—and I rather think he did—or whether this was a result of Mel's and my views, I cannot say. At any rate, by the time Mel and I had visited and examined the West German system, we could see clearly that vetoes resulted in constitutional constipation, and in Canada this would mean that there would never be any substantial changes to the way we governed ourselves unless Ontario and Quebec agreed, and that wasn't ever likely to happen.

In December 1995 after the "yes" vote nearly carried the day in Quebec's separation referendum, Prime Minister Chretien put forward a resolution that would have effectively given federal approval to the 1971 Victoria Charter. After an outpouring of anger from BC, we were given our own veto so that five regions of Canada could veto any proposed constitutional change. I along with many others was outraged at this. None of the changes many of us across the country saw as fundamental to any new working agreement could ever happen because Quebec had been given the power to veto what it didn't like. The proposed veto also had a side effect, seen in the Charlottetown Accord as well, that Quebec would only agree to a reformed senate if for all time she was given—no matter what population changes might occur—25 percent of the seats in the House of Commons. However, BC and most provinces outside Quebec and Ontario wanted changes, not the ability to prevent them.

All this explanation is by way of background for a speech I gave at the inauguration of the Mel Smith Chair for Constitutional Studies at Trinity Western University in 1977. It was a great honour to give this address and I thought long and hard about what I would say. It dawned on me that although the Chretien Resolution made it impossible to have any sort of meaningful discussion or reform, much less actual reform at the federal level, there was no reason why British Columbia could not reform its own manner of governance. Here is what I said, in part:

> There is one more matter of great consequence I must refer to before I answer, as best I can, the question posed: I speak here of the electoral system that sees the first-past-the-post win, often with a third of the

vote or less. I haven't the time today to set out all the problems with this system or to offer all the solutions, but suffice it to say that our system invariably provides a majority government based upon a minority of the votes. Sometimes, as here in 1996, a party can gain power with fewer votes than the leading opposition party.

Nick Loenen...has written a very useful book about proportional representation (or PR), which in its pure form elects MPs based upon the percentage of the popular vote achieved by each party. In most jurisdictions with PR there is a threshold—often five percent—that must be reached before a member is elected. Some countries, Germany and New Zealand to name two, have a mixed system of some first-past-the-post, some off the list. I must say that I'm not as big a fan of PR as many and would prefer to have a first-past-the-post with a preferential ballot system, but for many brighter and more learned than I, that's not sufficient reform. (Just by way of an aside, my concerns about PR can be seen in New Zealand where the first-past-the-post MPs are almost universally thought better parliamentarians than the "listers" who are usually party hacks chosen more for their ability to raise money than to legislate.)

A couple of years ago I had an idea that I expressed to the provincial government that, if nothing else, got me a tax-paid lunch with the Intergovernmental Affairs minister, Andrew Petter, a man I like and respect. I suggested that British Columbia ought to move within its own constitution to make changes. It is in a position... to make any or all of the changes I have suggested above and can do so by a simple amendment to BC's Constitution Act or by adding new legislation.

And this brings me to my point: Why not put together a permanent Constitution Committee to examine [the situation] and make suitable recommendations for changes to how British Columbia governs itself? It must be a serious exercise. It must have as its chair a man or woman of considerable stature in the community...

The terms of reference should be extremely broad, though not vague. Some of the issues should be spelled out, not so as to direct a finding but to make it clear to the committee and the public alike that everything is on the table. The expense would surely not be great, especially when one thinks of what governments spend our money on these days. I would envisage that at the end of the exercise it might well be time to convoke a constituent assembly to debate and make final recommendations to the people who would ultimately deal with the recommendations by referendum.

No one wants to say it but many will think how can the public—which is, after all, pretty stupid and ill-informed—to be trusted to make decisions like this? That thought betrays a fundamental distrust of the thing we boast about so much—democracy. Mel Smith and I both fought in the trenches of the Charlottetown Accord battle, and I suspect he would join me in praising the ability of the average person—*like the average juror in a court case* [my emphasis]—to get to the meat of the matter and make an intelligent decision. Even if they're wrong, that's what democracy is all about. But I don't think they will be wrong. Moreover, after the recommendations are in, the legislature must do what the parliament of New Zealand did—make the changes and select a time, say, ten years hence, to revisit what has been done....

The country cries out for reform. We are in danger

of splitting and not just at the Quebec border either. We have lost all respect for our politicians because we can no longer relate to them. They don't do our bidding but that of their leader. We must change but we think that there is little if anything we can do because no one will listen to us. Very well then, they must be made to listen. And I can assure you that if we proceed as I suggest and begin our reform here in British Columbia, there will be curiosity. And with curiosity will come the slow grinding of brain cells in other parts of the country. We will—though not immediately—become beacons for reform not just for Canada but other countries as well.

At this writing there are at least four other provinces looking carefully at the process of an electoral commission based upon BC's example. And why not? Looking at our troubles in this wonderful country, have we any right not to try to set an example? And when all is said and done, what do we have to lose?

I do apologize for my wordiness but I feel entitled to state my case that I was at least one of the fathers of the electoral commission that was to come. But I went further and called upon Gordon Gibson, a constitutional warrior in the same trenches that Mel and I served in, and suggested that we form the very steering committee I had suggested in my speech. He agreed and we invited Nick Loenen and former NDP cabinet minister Gary Lauk to join us. Mel, by this time stricken by the cancer that would take him from us, was a member but made his interventions by phone. He was, of course, the spirit of the movement. However, it must also be emphasized that Gordon Gibson had been pushing for a national constituent assembly for years and pointing out similar exercises in Australia and Germany.

At the end our group filed a report. We had each concentrated on a different aspect of the problem. Nick, for example,
was very much for a change in the electoral system, supporting
the Single Transferable Vote (STV) that was later put to the
public, while I examined the benefits of separating the executive
from the legislative. We all agreed, however, with the notion of
a "constituent assembly," although ours would not be precisely
in the form it finally took. It was the premier who in the fall of
2000, as leader of the Opposition, committed to his party that
he would empanel a "jury" of British Columbians. From this
point the story belongs to others. Premier Campbell, having
decided on using a jury system, turned the matter over to
Gordon Gibson to put the necessary flesh on the bones. To
Jack Blaney, former president of Simon Fraser University, fell
the task of chairing the assembly of 160 British Columbians, a
duty he discharged with great distinction. Nick Loenen was the
man who persuaded the assembly to adopt as its resolution the
Single Transferable Ballot system. The spirit behind it all was,
of course, Melvin H. Smith, QC.

The government, in promising a referendum on electoral
change, first of all showed considerable courage since any
recommendation other than the status quo would make it more
difficult for them to be re-elected as a majority government.

There are many who criticized the process because they were
not asked whether they wanted reform in the first place. That
this issue was not often raised during the assembly's deliberations
or again when the referendum was called is strong testimony to
the notion that British Columbians did want change. Perhaps
a more valid argument was that there should have been more
options than the status quo and STV. That is what happened
when New Zealand changed their first-past-the-post system
to a mixed member proportional system many years ago. I'm
personally satisfied that because the assembly examined all
systems, but especially Mixed Member Proportional (MMP)

with such care, it was fair to simply put forward only STV or the status quo. Part of my opinion comes from the fact that since half of MMP members would be first-past-the-post, it was no reform. The other part is that, as the other half of the MLAs would be selected off the party list, the voters would have no say in who they elected when they marked their favourite party, and this would simply be "not on" for those voters who wanted less party politics.

On May 17, 2005 the voters in 77 of 79 ridings endorsed STV with a 57.4 majority. However, a 60 percent majority was required to put the reforms into effect, and at this writing it is unclear what the government is going to do. The "no" side is claiming victory, while the "yes" side is complaining that the threshold placed on the vote by the government was too high. They point out that the 1944 conscription referendum, the Quebec separation referenda and the Charlottetown Accord (which proposed massive constitutional change) all merely required a simple majority. The two parties in the legislature must now deal with it because it won't go away. As for me, I would prefer that the matter be referred to the legislature in a "free vote" and let the chips fall where they may.

Playing the Polls

I don't trust polls. I think people lie a lot to pollsters if only because they are annoyed at being bothered. Also, many people don't want to tell anyone else what their real issue is for fear of it being seen "out of the ordinary." It is easier to say, "I want good health care" than I to admit you want lots of money in your pocket and to hell with all those sick people. In fact, I don't think many voters are thinking of the issues as defined by office seekers at all but actually vote on their overall feeling on a number of matters. Of the people who vote in BC, roughly 35 percent will vote NDP and 35 percent Liberal no matter what the issues are. They are party loyal. It's the middle that matters.

Let's look at elections past. In 1972 BC didn't vote NDP because of any specific policy; they voted against W.A.C. Bennett's government because it had become old and tired. In fact, only 39 percent of them voted NDP. Many voted either Liberal or Conservative because they didn't want the Socreds back but were afraid of the NDP. In 1975 the election was less about the NDP record than it was about the ability of Bill Bennett and Grace McCarthy to get the right all under one tent. Once again the NDP got 39 percent but this time they lost.

Until 1976 it was against the law to publish polls during an election campaign, but an enterprising restaurateur began naming his hamburgers after each candidate so that the purchase of a burger showed support for one's favourite. When I ran in 1975, I ate so damned many Mr. Mike's burgers I began to look like one! But it was remarkable how accurate these unofficial polls were. However, the best way to find out how you were doing in those days was to poll a Grade 6 or 7 class because the kids could be counted upon to reflect the views of the family dinner table.

The election of 1983 was a strange election because Dave Barrett blew it in a nano-second when he denounced the restraint program that was popular with most British Columbians. If he'd stuck to the theme that it was time to throw the Socreds out, he would have won. On the other hand, Bill Bennett and his advisers knew where they and the NDP were vulnerable, avoided the first and concentrated on the second. Another strange year was 1986 because it was one of those rare times, like Trudeaumania in 1968, that a flashy leader, Bill Vander Zalm, carried the province on charisma, not policy. At that, most experts thought that if the election had gone on for two more weeks the public would have tired of Vander Zalm, and the NDP might have thrown the Socreds out. Here, the front runner's numbers ran considerably ahead of his actual support, which showed that even a day or so delay between poll-taking and the publication of the poll numbers can make a huge difference.

In 1991 everyone knew that Mike Harcourt and the NDP would win, but it certainly wasn't because of traditional issues. The public, fed up with Vander Zalm and unwilling to judge Rita Johnston on her own merits, simply wanted to see the back of the Socreds. Once again, many people were afraid of the NDP and unwilling to vote Socred, and as a result they vaulted the Liberals from nowhere to official opposition. But if you had checked on what the polls were saying about how the Liberals were doing a week before the televised debate in which Wilson got off his winning zinger, or even a week before the election, you could have gotten odds on Wilson that would have paid off handsomely when the real votes were counted.

In 1996 the NDP win wasn't a matter of the big issues that we are told are important to us. In this case Gordon Campbell simply bungled the campaign. The pre-election polls showed him and his Liberals ahead, which they undoubtedly were, but you couldn't have taken from those numbers that they would poll more than the NDP and lose! In 2001 there was no conversion to Liberals policy; there was only one issue—toss the NDP out on their ears.

The Charlottetown Accord referendum was another interesting example of the accuracy of polls. On the eve of the short campaign the polls showed British Columbians in favour of it, but with a week to go before the vote, a poll published by the *Vancouver Sun* showed, to their surprise and horror, 58 percent of British Columbians opposed. A few days later they voted a full 68 percent against. A much more accurate poll was my audience—not just the numbers who expressed themselves as being against it but the voices I recognized who were opposed. Brian Mulroney would have been wiser to listen to my radio show than hire pollsters.

Most polls taken before an election, especially if they are well before it, are inaccurate, a waste of money and an insult to the public's intelligence. I believe that polls taken on the eve of an election are reasonably accurate. But apart from the actual vote, the most accurate predicters are "exit polls" where questions are put to the voters just after they have cast their ballots. At this point people are focused and no longer "parking" their votes as they watch the political landscape.

Probably the most famous election polls of all time were uncannily accurate and utterly ignored. Winston Churchill's Tories were behind Labour for the entire 1945 campaign, but the Labour win was considered an upset. It was an upset, however, only in the sense that the polls had not included the servicemen and women overseas who, in the actual event, voted much more solidly Labour than the folks back home. They had been fighting for something and it sure as hell wasn't the return of the party of the aristocracy, even when led by the hugely popular Churchill.

The other famous poll that was both accurate and ignored was the one showing Harry S. Truman with a slight lead over Thomas Dewey in the final days of the 1948 US presidential election. So sure was the *Chicago Daily Tribune* that the poll was wrong that in the early hours they printed a special edition shouting "DEWEY DEFEATS TRUMAN!" a headline seen again in the following days splashed all over the front pages of other papers carrying a photo of a grinning Harry Truman holding the *Tribune* aloft.

I've raised many concerns about polls, but I have no answers for you. Pollsters claim they are scientists and one contradicts that claim with ease but offers alternatives with reluctance. I wish it were as simple as saying, "Look, folks, pay polls no mind," but publicized polls that tell us what we're supposed to think are only one part of the problem. Private polls which tell us what we think without us knowing about them are a bit more scary. Even then, I suppose not much harm is done if, based upon polls, Colgate sends too much plain toothpaste one place and too much flavoured stuff elsewhere. What is more worrisome is when governments plan policy upon the voiced opinions of a tiny fraction of the people to be affected, basing that policy on polls.

Political Profiles

Grace McCarthy

Grace McCarthy is another one of those I-wonder-what-might-have-happened people in politics. In July 1991 the reigning bit of the tottering Social Credit Party was in the midst of a leadership campaign. Rita Johnston, who had taken over for the somewhat disgraced Bill Vander Zalm as premier a few months before, was definitely in the race along with a few others who left no reason to be remembered. But Grace dithered until it was too late before throwing her hat in the ring and in the end lost a close race to Johnston.

Her hesitation puzzles me to this day. Although her very keen political nose told her that far from being the darling of the party she had once been, having thoroughly pissed off the right wing who saw her as disloyal to Bill Vander Zalm and in part responsible for his downfall, she still had a lot of political capital with the party and even more with the public. As far as bringing down Vander Zalm, this was, of course, nonsense. He needed no help whatsoever. From the beginning of his premiership Vander Zalm had been determined to commit political hara-kiri.

I believe all political pundits watching the BC scene in 1991 would agree that, had Grace become Socred leader, while she might not have avoided defeat in the next election, at the very least she would have survived it with a caucus and party intact. She might even have won against the underwhelming NDP leader Bob Skelly.

I don't blame the Socred demise on Grace. Far from it. It was the party that abandoned her. If key and influential members of the Social Credit Party had put aside their petty dreams of revenge and put their party first, Grace would have won the leadership and the Social Credit Party would not only be alive and well today but would probably be the government.

Grace McCarthy is a wonderful lady who performed and indeed is still performing sterling service to her province and community. Unfortunately, the only time this usually sure-footed politician hesitated, it cost her, her province and her party dearly.

Bill Bennett

Bill Bennett was one of the best premiers BC has ever had. He, his father and one or two others stand head and shoulders above the rest.

When the Socreds came to power in 1975, the NDP was sure that the caucus would split because, after all, wasn't Bennett just Daddy's boy? He wasn't. We who worked with Bill Bennett would have crawled a mile on bare hands and feet over broken glass for the man. Unfortunately he had a Richard Nixon look about him. He seldom smiled, and if the media didn't actively dislike him, they didn't like him either. While he could be vicious in debate, he was never funny. Oddly enough, in private life he was extremely witty and, as he warmed up to his cabinet colleagues (many of whom he hadn't known before and several of whom had opposed him), we began to see his fast and often wicked wit.

He was bright as hell and his words demanded respectful attention. And he was a hell of a good politician. I well remember when Finance Minister Evan Wolfe was ready to present his first budget, and he came to cabinet to give us a briefing. As he went down the list of proposed revenues, he said that liquor prices would go up—the old "sin tax" ploy that ministers of finance always employ. Rye would go up, so would gin, scotch, vodka and beer. Bennett's face tightened in that expression we all came to know as disapproval, to say the least. "Don't touch the workingman's beer, Evan. Do you want every British Columbian sitting in his pub over a beer cursing this government until the next election?" Bad logic but bloody good politics.

Bill Bennett was responsible for steering BC through some rocky periods and won three elections in a row, something only one premier has bettered—his father. But he was a leader on the national stage as well, much more recognized for that leadership elsewhere than at home, thanks to our eastern-owned local press who, when the government put forward its superb Constitutional Papers in 1978, refused my request to invite the premier to appear before their editorial boards. It was this more than anything that hardened my dislike of the two Vancouver dailies into hatred.

This province and country owe a great deal to Bill Bennett, and one day, if the whole story is told, including his problems with the securities people, that will finally be recognized. He gave me a lot of responsibility in the five years I was with him and I'm deeply in his debt—as a colleague and a friend.

David Barrett

As premiers of BC, Dave Barrett and Bill Bennett provide an interesting contrast. Barrett was outgoing, ebullient, sometimes witty, at other times outrageously funny, and he fully fitted the picture of the showman. In surveys he was always much more popular than Bennett, but he lost out to Bennett in one crucial matter—he looked like he was doing everything off the top of his head and by the seat of his pants—and he was. Bennett looked sharp and businesslike and people respected him, and that's what counted. They fought three elections—1975, 1979, and 1983—and Bennett won all three.

Barrett, the first Jewish premier in Canada (for whatever that's supposed to matter), came to power when he derailed the mighty W.A.C. Bennett machine in August 1972, thus launching a 40-month government that, if nothing else, was interesting. While Bennett Sr. had seen the legislature for what it was—a game which if properly played got done what a strong premier wanted done with a minimum of interference—Barrett had a love of British parliamentary traditions that he wanted to see adopted and maintained in our legislature, and he brought reforms like Hansard and question period that were long overdue.

However, the two lasting legacies of the Barrett government were the "land freeze" and the Insurance Corporation of British Columbia (ICBC). The fuss made about bringing in the land freeze looks almost comical now, but at the time the Right acted as if Stalin had moved into the parliament buildings. ICBC has also turned out to be popular, although the cries of the right about socialism and expropriation of property without adequate compensation rang truer with it than they did with the land freeze. But once the Socreds got back onto power, it was clear that ICBC was one omelet that could never be put back in its shell, and despite occasional mumblings about privatization, it will probably remain.

Why did the Barrett government get tossed out just as unceremoniously as it was tossed in? I think it was lack of government experience. The Opposition is not government and being in the Opposition trains its members to do little but oppose and embarrass. I think this led to a push-pull that Barrett couldn't control. On the one hand there were moderates who wanted to lay the basis for a long NDP reign and on the other a very strong, intellectual group that wanted to make as many dramatic dents on the status quo as they could in that first term. One of the wittier members of the NDP government of the day was Gary Lauk who opined, tongue ever so slightly in cheek, that this division in the government was best exemplified when they took forever to decide whether the province should go on daylight savings time or not!

However, Dave Barrett, much loved and bitterly hated, left his mark on this province—which is all any political leader can hope for.

Patrick McGeer

Dr. Patrick L. McGeer, nephew of one of Vancouver's most famous mayors, Gerry McGeer, is a remarkable man. A doctor of medicine and a PhD, he and his brilliant wife, Edie, are world-renowned medical researchers at the University of British Columbia. I know him better as a politician.

Pat entered the legislature in the 1960s and soon became the Liberal Party leader. In 1975 he crossed the floor to the hitherto despised Socreds along with Allan Williams and followed by Garde Gardom. When Bill Bennett became premier on December 22, 1975, Pat became the minister responsible for the Insurance Corporation of BC (ICBC), which had managed in 16 months as a monopoly to lose some $180 million. It was Pat's job to turn this around, which he did with a healthy increase in premiums. He also founded the Open University and the Knowledge Network and did a superb job as education minister and then as the first minister of higher education.

Pat had one infuriating habit—he commuted to Victoria from his home in Vancouver every day and was thus almost always an hour late for cabinet meetings and when he did arrive would want to be brought up to date before we went on. It must be admitted, however, that cabinet without Pat was missing a lot of spark and good ideas. The trouble was that, like Churchill, if he had ten ideas, one would be absolutely brilliant and the others were crap. As Bill Bennett recalled to me recently over dinner, "The trouble with Pat was he argued his terrible ideas with the same passion and oratory as he did his good ones, so it was often difficult to tell them apart!"

It was Pat who spearheaded the research into a fixed link across the Strait of Georgia, an idea that brought howls of protest from environmentalists because it would mean that one of the Gulf Islands would be scalped in the process. Flying over to Victoria with Pat one day, I saw him look down at the island in question. "I can't see what the fuss is all about," he said. "That's just MacBlo timber." It would never have occurred to Pat that the environmentalists weren't interested in who owned the land, that they just didn't want the island wrecked.

If there were a hall of fame for politicians, Pat McGeer would be immediately voted in without the usual five-year waiting period for these things. An unbelievably brilliant and accomplished man, he was and remains an enormous asset of his beloved province and his country.

Gordon Gibson

Gordon Gibson, son of Gordon Senior (a man better known as the "Bull of the Woods"), is the political image of his dad but with the rough edges sanded off. His father was the Liberal MLA who, back in the early '60s, said "money talks" in the Socred government's granting of timber licences and who, when the smoke cleared, was proved right. Several men, including a cabinet minister and a judge's brother, went to jail.

In 1973 Gordon Jr. became the leader of that same BC Liberal Party, though by the time I got to the legislature in late 1975 he was not only leader but his party's entire caucus as well. It was at that same time that I became the cabinet minister in Bill Bennett's government responsible for constitutional matters with the emphasis on the run-up to the patriation of the Constitution. It seemed to our government that BC should play a full role, and to that end we sought help and input from everyone in the House. Gordon Gibson was the only member of the opposition parties who showed any interest in the matter and he showed a lot. I became a great admirer and we became friends. At this time we both got to know Melvin H. Smith, the deputy minister of constitutional affairs and arguably the foremost expert on that subject in Canada.

Fast forward to 1986 when Brian Mulroney was pushing Meech Lake, which failed without BC having to do anything except provide a lot of moral support to Premier Clyde Wells of Newfoundland and Labrador who, upon taking power, had rescinded his province's support and promised that it would be debated in his legislature. As it turned out, there was no need for a vote in Newfoundland because Meech was sent down the tube in Manitoba by an aboriginal NDP backbencher, Elijah Harper. In 1992 Mulroney tried again with a deal he called (to his Quebec audiences) "Meech Plus! Plus! Plus!" At the time I was hosting a very popular talk show at Vancouver's CKNW and was implacably opposed to this deal for a number of reasons, all of which were better articulated by Gordon and Mel. We formed an unofficial triumvirate, and it was these two with their superior knowledge of constitutional affairs who encouraged me, especially after I began to hear things like "Canada's most dangerous man" and "traitor" hurled at me. To the extent that I had any influence in the matter, I wish to say here and now that it was because of the knowledge and courage of Gordon and Mel.

Gordon is currently one of the foremost experts on public policy in Canada, having contributed many, many papers and books on the subject, and remains my own resident expert on constitutional affairs, especially since Mel died in 2000. We came together again in laying the basis for BC's Commission for Electoral Reform.

Witty, brilliant and articulate, Gordon has served his province and country grandly, but don't hold your breath to see him get the Order of BC or the Order of Canada. The Establishment doesn't hand out these baubles to those who oppose them. But as Cato the Elder said, "I would rather have people ask why there is no monument to me than why there is." It is the same line I used to explain Mel Smith's lack of an OC or OBC when I delivered his eulogy, but it is equally true of Gordon. The Establishment reserves its baubles for its own.

Part Four

PRESSING QUESTIONS

What Should Canada's Role Be in World Affairs?

Until I was a grown-up, Canada's role in world affairs was pretty well summed up in the older version of "O Canada" which declared "at Britain's side whate'er betide unflinchingly we'll stand." Even after we became a self-governing dominion in 1867, we were at Britain's side, and no one argued when Canada was simply absorbed into the Allied effort in World War I. Having said that, it must be noted that I'm talking about official Canada, not French Canadians who, for the most part, wanted nothing to do with slogging about in the muddy trenches of Belgium. This attitude stunned many Anglos who thought that Quebec would feel some attachment to France. They didn't. As far as most Quebeckers were concerned, France had deserted them in 1763 and that was that.

Under the Statute of Westminster of 1931, the "dominions" became part of the British Commonwealth of Nations (later the "British" was dropped) and were free to do as they wished. Thus, in 1939 while others felt bound by Britain's declaration of war against Germany, Canada waited a week and, as a symbol of its independence, gave its own declaration on September 10. Once again, the war wasn't accepted nearly so much amongst French Canadians as amongst Anglos, and though there was fairly high recruitment in Quebec and many valorous French Canadians served in the armed forces, the prime minister, W.L. Mackenzie King, felt it necessary to have a referendum on conscription, a vote that split the country. The question was so convoluted that one wag asked, "Why didn't they just ask if French or English was your mother tongue?" In World War II Canadians did fight as Canadians under

Canadian officers, and this certainly added to our sense of Canadianism. There was, however, a colonial putdown yet to come: when planning the formation of the United Nations, Roosevelt and Churchill agreed to allow representation from several Soviet republics on the grounds that Britain's satellite dominions—Canada, for example—were to be allowed representation at the table.

It's fair to say, I think, that since the war in Korea, to which Canada sent armed forces, we have been looking for more than just a role in NORAD and NATO. This search has been urged on by the fact that NATO, of which Canada was a founding and active member, has changed; where once it was a force to offset eastern European communism, it now embraces formerly despised countries as comrades-in-arms. We feel the need now, probably to show we are not American puppets, to play some sort of special part on the world stage. Though we have distinguished ourselves at times as peacekeepers, at other times we've not been so distinguished. Worse, we can't even get our act together on North American defence. The left wing of the Liberals plus the NDP are against anything America does, while to the right there is almost total obedience to Washington. At the same time, we have allowed our armed forces and their equipment to become badly outdated. We have been consistent in only one thing—our inconsistency in letting our military know what we expect of them and in providing them with what they need to do it. The truth is we really don't know what we want to do.

Of course, playing a role on the world stage involves more than just having a military presence. For many years Canada was seen as the honest broker between American and British interests. We were British yet not British, American yet not American, so we could be trusted. That job has all but disappeared with Canada's deepening commitment to NAFTA on this side of the Atlantic and Britain's commitment to the

European Union on its side of the pond, while the United States has become committed to unilateralism, an our-way-or-the-highway policy. Britain's position is still as US politician Dean Acheson described it after the war: "Britain has lost an empire and is looking for a role." Margaret Thatcher saw that role as Churchill had seen it—a special relationship with the US. But the closer the EU comes to being one large integrated state, the more difficult it is for the UK to have that special relationship, especially since the two real powers in the EU, France and Germany and especially the former, show a growing inclination to tug on Uncle Sam's beard whenever the opportunity arises. At this writing, the proposed European Union constitution has been rejected by referenda in France and Holland, leading the UK to decide not to hold a vote in the spring of 2006 as planned. These serendipitous rejections of the constitution will, for a time at least, save Britons from deciding whether or not to transfer their right to set foreign policy to the EU where the general love of the US—and the need for its goodwill—is considerably less than it is in Britain.

In this country, I believe the problem is that Canadians have magnified their sense of their importance to western defence. We are a small country with a limited ability to do anything, but paradoxically, we take the view that we should be consulted on all issues yet not bound by any solution, especially if it is American-inspired. There is, however, one role that Canada has been playing effectively if unevenly, and that is trying to help third world countries. In this, our Canadian International Development Agency has done good work, and plenty of private agencies have done invaluable service. But let's get back to that word "uneven" for that is what characterizes all help from the wealthy nations to the poor. "Uneven" means that help is uncoordinated and often last-minute or rather well past the last minute. It means that there has been profiteering off aid that is given, eroding the

141

desire of citizens in better-off places to help. But I see no reason why Canada cannot seek the support of the G7 (or G8, sometimes) and other economic arrangements to take the lead in assessing the needs of Third World economies and quarterbacking the efforts. This would mean bringing together not only nations but also such institutions as the World Bank and the International Monetary Fund. It would be a huge and complicated endeavour, but surely that shouldn't stop us from lobbying other nations to get them to see the problems as ongoing, not just events to be dealt with when a famine or epidemic gets out of hand.

This is where most of our military budget should be going. We have to stop kidding ourselves that we are a player in the international politics of the day because we are not. Much of the time we are at best a nag, at worst a nuisance. We have only one natural enemy and that is America and we couldn't begin to defend ourselves against the Americans if we wanted to. We do have a need for a much strengthened Coast Guard, but all our other efforts should be focused on preventing brush-fire wars (though certainly they are only brush fires to us, not to the innocents caught in the middle of them) and helping to remove the causes of war, which usually can be summed up in one word—poverty.

If Canada has a role to play on the world stage, let it be as a relatively wealthy, kind and decent country that wants to work towards the elimination of the grinding poverty that always brings with it political unrest unto civil war and famine. Let us not do what some, out of jingoistic pride, want us to do but that which we can actually do and do well.

Can Japan Afford to Be Unrepentant?

In the spring of 2005 many were surprised to note that the Chinese government did not step in to stop anti-Japanese student demonstrations. In fact, the Chinese government pointedly refused to apologize to Japan for the damage done to Japanese property. While the official reason for the Chinese student protest was Japan's application to become a permanent member of the Security Council, the *casus belli* is the latest Japanese school history text that the Chinese say glosses lightly over what Japan did to China during World War II. The unpleasantness between the two countries has been smoldering a long time, and I'm surprised that it has taken so long to manifest itself. Add to that mix the antipathy—to put it mildly—of Koreans toward Japan and there are the makings of serious issues in that region. My readers should be well aware that I have always drawn a line between Canadians and Americans of Japanese descent and the people of the nation of Japan. However, when I made a recent public comment on the causes of the growing tension in the Far East, I was taken to task by Japanese Canadians who said that I was not providing balance and they pointed out the loyalty and bravery of Canadians and Americans of Japanese descent in World War II. They cannot have it both ways. If they are going to complain that, when they were interned and their property stolen during World War II, they were Canadians and Americans and not Japanese, they cannot then be offended as Japanese people when Japan is criticized. They are either Canadians and Americans or they are Japanese.

I have done a number of radio editorials and printed articles about the disgraceful treatment of Japanese Canadians during World War II, have consistently fought off those who tried to equate our treatment of them with the way Japan behaved, always making the point I just made. Ergo, that these were not Japanese we were mistreating but Canadians. I have confessed my personal shame at the fact that my upbringing and schooling was financed by my father buying, at 10 cents on the dollar, a paper box factory from the so-called Trustee of Japanese-Canadian goods. No, I'm not talking about North Americans at all but about the citizens of the Empire of Japan during World War II. The activities of the Japanese in Korea during the time it was a Japanese colony (1910-1945) were atrocities. The Koreans became slaves and, in the case of many of Korea's women, sex slaves for the Japanese armed forces. And the bitterness is still very strong. Years ago when in Japan just before making a trip to Seoul, I had business cards printed in both Japanese and Korean. In Seoul, I mistakenly handed a Korean official a business card in Japanese instead of Korean, and no amount of apologizing would make it right. The interview was over. Afterwards I took the time to re-read my history and could well understand the insult I had conferred. The Japanese attacked China without provocation in 1931 and annexed Manchuria, changed the name to Manchukuo and put a puppet king on the throne. Japan's aggression then continued and in 1937 its forces took China's ancient capital, Nanjing (or Nanking as it was known in the west). No one knows how many adults and innocent children were summarily executed in that unfortunate city, but 300,000 seems to be an accepted figure, about the same number as the bombs on Hiroshima and Nagasaki killed. Adults were decapitated. Babies were thrown in the air then speared with bayonets. Thousands and thousands of women of all ages were brutally raped. Iris Chang, who sadly died by her own hand not long ago, wrote the essential book on these atrocities, *The Rape of Nanking,* and any today who think I exaggerate need only read that book.

But Nanjing is only part of the story. Though the Chinese came in for special brutality, the Japanese military behaved with calculated cruelty everywhere they went, and in some parts of Asia where the people had initially welcomed the Japanese as liberators from the European colonial powers, they swiftly came to hate the invader. Japanese prisoner of war camps were horror stories.

The Bataan Death March, a cruel chapter in military history, began at Mariveles, at the southern tip of Bataan Peninsula on April 10, 1942. Lacking enough trucks to move their captives, the Japanese forced the prisoners of war to march about 100 kilometers north to a prison camp at San Fernando. Japanese troops beat their captives with no provocation and denied the POWs food and water. Malnourished and dehydrated, those who fell behind were executed. Troops were tortured by "sun treatment"—forced to sit in the intense heat and humidity of the Philippines in April without protection from the sun or water. When the prisoners were allowed to rest for a few hours, they were packed so tight that they could barely move. The final distance was covered by train, with prisoners so tightly packed into suffocating boxcars that many men perished. It took the POWs over a week to reach their destination. Of the 70,000 soldiers that set out from Mariveles, only 54,000 reached the prison camp.

One of the memorable pictures shown in the news at the end of the war was that of American General Jonathan Wainright, who had surrendered the Wake Island garrison to Japanese forces in December 1941. At war's end he was so emaciated that it was a miracle he survived. If that was how the class-conscious Japanese treated a general, you can imagine what it was like for the ranks. Pictures of prisoners of lower ranks emerging from Japanese camps were eerily similar to pictures of the Jews who survived the holocaust. I can hear people saying that this is what war is all about and I betcha that we were no better. Well, that is not what war is all about, and yes, we were a hell of a lot better. To suggest what the Japanese did by comparing it to anything other than what the Germans did in their concentration camps condemns as trivial the memories of millions who suffered and died. But why bring this all up now? For the very good reason that, unlike Germany, Japan never formally and properly apologized for its inhuman behaviour or paid compensation. Japan was allowed to remain silent in order to make it easier for General MacArthur to govern. Had all the people experienced in governing been excluded from posts in the post-war government because of their complicity in atrocities, there would have been almost no one left to do MacArthur's bidding. (The Coalition in Iraq faced the same problem because most of the middle and upper level civil servants were members of the Ba'ath Party and supporters of Saddam Hussein.) Nazi Germany, on the other hand, was held to account at Nuremberg and in other similar trials, and the horrors of the holocaust were widely publicized. In Canada every kid I knew was forced by their parents—and properly so—to see the atrocity films that hit all the theatres in 1945-46. And not only did Germany admit responsibility, she also paid compensation to Jews and continues to do so. No one suggests that Japanese and German people of today who were alive when those atrocities were being committed bear responsibility for them. They were, after all, kids at the time. How much the ordinary adult citizen could have done is also pretty speculative. You have to ask yourself what you would have done. But there is a matter of national culpability and admission of fault and, of course, compensation, something that the Canadians captured by Japanese forces in Hong Kong on Christmas Day 1941 are still seeking. And this should lead to an ongoing acknowledgement of what really happened. And the very least the millions of victims of Japanese wartime cruelty should have a right to expect is that the Japanese people be taught what their military forces really did.

The wounds run deep, very deep, as recent events demonstrate.

Is it Time to Abolish Remembrance Day?

Every year on Remembrance Day the memory dims for those born back when major wars were fought. Every year we notice, as the bugle plays "Taps" again, that the ranks are fewer. Those who remain seem—and indeed are—very old. After all, if they were 18 at the time World War II started, they are in their mid-80s today. Even those who were 18 at the start of the Korean War are today in their 70s. It seems so strange to think that these old people in their navy blue blazers and bright medals were once kids in high school. Now it won't be long before the last of them is gone. We're almost out of World War I veterans—a few centenarians, that's all. When the last vet goes, will the need for the November 11 parades, the ceremonies at cenotaphs and those minutes of silence go with them?

I think not. Indeed, I think the very opposite will be the case.

For all recorded history, man has fought his fellow man over one thing or another. Perhaps it was for land upon which to hunt or plant grain. Perhaps it was in defence of family. Sometimes it was for a great religious principle, though more often for the kind so brilliantly satirized by Jonathan Swift in *Gulliver's Travels* in which a war is fought between a country that breaks the egg at the big end and another that selects the smaller end. Sometimes it has almost seemed as if war was fought just for the hell of it—which it probably literally was.

Sometimes, however, wars have been fought to stop a great tyranny, a force that was truly evil and bent on destroying civilization as we know it. And sometimes that fight was carried on a long, long way from home.

This is what I think we often forget about the Canadian men and women who fought and died overseas—they did it as much, in fact even more, for others than they did it for themselves. I remember my feelings upon seeing the Canadian cemeteries in Normandy, one for the veterans of Dieppe and one for those killed on D-Day and beyond, and the British cemetery at El Alamein in Egypt where so many young New Zealanders—many of whom were Maoris—rest. All these young people were thousands of miles from home. They had left mothers and fathers, sisters and brothers, sweethearts and husbands and wives behind in order to face death—not for the land they died on but for a cause they believed to be that of their own country so very far away.

They did so, for the most part, as volunteers. Without any sort of compulsion, they decided to leave the comfort of their homes, jobs or education and risk death in a foreign land. Those not old enough to have been there must think about that in the context of their own lives. They must think about when they graduated from high school, ready to face life, probably in love, the best part of youth staring them in the face, the prospect of their lives to come and families-to-be. Can they imagine what it would have been like to put all those dreams away for another day (as the song goes) and head down to the local recruiting office because that was the thing to do? Not every one of those long-ago recruits died or was wounded or taken prisoner—and thank God for that. Some never left home. But all of them took the risk that they would die long before their time, fighting someone from another country who, but for the language they spoke, was just like them.

War wasn't just for the armed forces either. I have long felt that we have overlooked most unfairly those who fought the fires, drove the ambulances and braved the bombs in cities all over the world. And not just those doing official things, either. There were millions of ordinary everyday people and their frightened children who went about their business under severe and constant attack because ever since man devised efficient ways to lob bombs at one another, it's been the civilian who has taken the worst hits.

But we all know this. Why make a fuss about it every year?

That is not as easy to answer as one might think. Some think that days like Remembrance Day glorify war. We hear the great speeches of Winston Churchill and Franklin Roosevelt, the cheery songs. We absorb the patriotic fervor that moves its way into church sermons. If we're not careful it can seem like a great adventure, a game, hard-fought yet fun to remember with a beer or two and a song. But when that does seem to be the message, it's the wrong one. War, as General Sherman said, is hell. It was hell then, it is hell now and it will always be hell.

No. Remembrance Day is more than just remembering while trying to blot out the bad stuff with the good. It's about today and tomorrow. For there is still more than enough evil in the world to challenge those who value the same things these old men and women fought for. And as in the past it won't go away by wishing it away. Britain and France tried to wish away Hitler, and the US tried to wish away Tojo and Hirohito. But inherently evil people and the forces they lead just can't be wished away.

Remembrance Day reminds us, I think, not just of the sacrifices made and the rewards those sacrifices brought to all of us, but also of where we are today. It reminds us that past generations of our countrymen responded when the principles for which their country stood were threatened and that those threats are always with us and must always be met. Remembrance Day is of the past and very much so, but it is also of the present and the future, too. As long as man remains surrounded by evil and that evil threatens what we all hold dear, it is best we remember what our duty is.

That's what John McRae meant when he wrote:

Take up our quarrel with the foe:
To you from failing hands we throw
The torch; be yours to hold it high.
If ye break faith with us who die
We shall not sleep, though poppies grow
In Flanders fields.

Where Have All the Fishes Gone?

Ever wondered what the woodsman would do if there were only a few acres of trees left on the planet or what the fisherman would do if the runs he fishes were approaching extinction? The answer is that the woodsman would cut down the remaining trees and the fisherman would take the fish that are left. This is no knock on fishermen or loggers; they are only human. For many years we humans have paid lip service to saving the environment, never thinking that we would run out of time. Well, I have news for you: we have already run out of time in too many areas to count, and I think it important that we all understand that we can quite easily get past the point of no return in many more areas and are approaching environmental catastrophe.

In years gone by when reading and listening were our only options, citizens read and listened and pondered. Then came the age of television and now, unless we can actually see something happen, we don't accept it. We assume that if we can't see a problem, it isn't there. Fish demonstrate my point. Both the orange roughy and the John Dory are luxury items at the dinner table, and since the southern oceans abounded in them they were caught and sold in the thousands. We saw the water they lived in, saw fishermen catching them, and assumed that, because we couldn't actually see anything worrying about all this, these fish would always be there in great quantity. Then as their numbers dwindled, it was discovered that they live a very long time, 20 years or more, and it is many years before they are mature enough to breed, so that fish caught are not quickly replaced. Now, I believe, catching these two fish is forbidden. But it was a case of acting first and asking questions later—when it was too late.

This, alas, has been a salient feature of fisheries management all over the world. The loss of cod on the Atlantic coast had nothing to do with seals but everything to do with overfishing, and even after the approaching catastrophe was obvious, fishermen insisted on being able to fish anyway and the authorities permitted it. When at last a moratorium was placed on cod fishing because there were almost no cod left, the fishermen screamed and demonstrated for their right to pursue their ancient trade. That there were no fish or very few fish left didn't alter their position. And now every year, as the cod stocks slowly, very slowly, recover, fishermen demand to fish again.

We have two forces at work here. On the one hand we have globalization, which has made corporations so strong that wherever they can't control governments, they disobey them with impunity. On the other hand we have a dramatic decrease in our natural resources such that industries are prepared to cut down the last grove of trees or catch the last fish. But when hitherto renewable natural resources are as imperiled as ours are, they are no longer renewable. Once you pass a certain point, you are harvesting that which can no longer sustain itself. You are "mining the environment," to use author Jarred Diamond's term in his book, *Collapse,* a term that doesn't just refer to the extraction of what we've come to think of as non-renewable resources like minerals and coal but also to those resources that might be renewable if we gave them the chance to renew but no longer are. It is of critical importance that we understand this because BC is, in fact, mining its environment, especially its fish resource. We in BC have been brought up to believe that, no matter what we do, our fish stocks can be replenished. In fact, they cannot. Once a fish run is depleted to the point it cannot regenerate itself to former numbers, that run is lost. And that loss means that all else in nature that relied upon it is lost, too; the bears, the gulls, the eagles, the insect life, the resident fish and even the trees near the river suffer. Even the best of fish hatcheries can't replace that lost gene pool.

We all tend to comfort ourselves and one another with the thought that since it hasn't happened so far, it never will. It is a nonsensical approach, of course, but we all follow it. What we are ignoring is that it *has* happened in the oceans and on land and that the hour is late, very late. Some years ago my wife Wendy and I were in Tahiti and took a trip with a fish biologist to see the famous "spinner" dolphins that jump out of the water and, as the name implies, spin like skaters doing triple axels. As we watched them, our host asked the dozen of us a question. "Two years ago this pod was about 100 in number. It is now about 135. Is that good news or bad news?" We were all puzzled and to a person said that it was good. "No," our host said, "it's bad news. You see, after dark these dolphins go out across the reef to open water to feed. They then become prey to a shark species, but because this species is rare and its bones are considered great aids to erections for Chinese gentlemen, they have been fished very hard. The fishermen catch them, cut off their fins, then throw them back still alive. Of course, they die and as a result the dolphins are not predated upon. Thus their numbers have increased, creating greater competition for a limited food source, which means that the dolphins will flourish until there is no food left for them and they will die out. That's what happens when man doesn't understand the food chain." It was a very sobering moment, especially when our guide went on to tell us that already Polynesian fishermen throughout the islands were finding their livelihoods disappearing.

You may wonder why I so badly want all of us to make the environment into an ongoing issue for all political parties whether in elections or in between. It is because individuals commit all sorts of environmental sins but, because they see their own contribution to the problem as miniscule, they continue their practices. The trouble is that governments now behave exactly the same way. In BC we have the rare opportunity to actually do something about the problem if the people in our government have the will to act. But they will only have the courage to do so if we make it clear over and over again that we care enough to make some sacrifices of our own to avoid cutting the last forest grove or taking the last seine full of fish.

Has Science Gone to Hell?

One of the things scientists—like politicians—must do is assess the unintended consequences of any act or decision. Both groups are very bad at this. Thalidomide, for example, was great in preventing morning sickness in pregnant women. That it might have enormously adverse effects on fetuses didn't occur to anyone until those women, being the guinea pigs in the scientific experiment, began having terribly deformed babies.

No one could deny the capacity of DDT to kill insects we don't like or its efficiency in delousing people. Its other consequences, exposed in Rachel Carson's 1962 book, *Silent Spring,* never occurred to the men in white coats holding the test tubes. DDT was a miracle drug and that was that.

Industrial science, which gives us things to stick into ourselves—breast implants and contraceptive devices—that have never been tested outside the industrial laboratory, is not, by definition, all that self-critical. And US and Canadian authorities do very little testing, relying instead upon the findings of these same scientists, who are being paid for developing things their bosses can sell. While I don't say that industrial scientists deliberately set out to hurt anyone, they are like any other worker in wanting the boss's approval.

We can credit scientists with creating the wonder of the whole new cyber world out there, but as a society we haven't begun to assess its unintended consequences. Thomas L. Friedman in his latest book, *The World Is Flat,* does a brilliant job of telling us what we now have the capabilities to do—and it's scary. What he can't tell us is what all this outsourcing, in-sourcing, instant worldwide communication and so on is going to mean for societies and members of those societies. Thanks to scientific development we now have a communications system that is brilliant but utterly out of control in the sense that nothing but one's innermost thoughts (and who knows about them one day) is private anymore. Everywhere we go we're on "Candid Camera." We have no secrets. At one time, statistics were just numbers; now they are us. Information that we would in the past have been too horrified to disclose to a government, a bank or just a store, we are now routinely required to fill into the blank spaces in our online requests for goods or services. And if we don't divulge this personal information, we are denied the goods or services we need.

Science has given us genetically modified foods, some of them including "foreign" genes. We had better hope these scientists are right about their new seeds having no adverse effects because, as a consequence of their introduction and the copyright owners insistence that farmers cannot use their own seed, old varieties are disappearing. Thus, if the scientists have not thought out all the consequences, we are in for a worldwide irreversible catastrophe. But the fact is that they can't test for all the consequences without laboratory rats and so we, dear reader, have become those rats.

There is a way that we can look at this whole process in slow motion just by examining the salmon farming industry in BC. It tells us exactly what happens when the unintended consequences are bad. Though aquaculture is as old as time, when it came to BC back in the late 1970s, the federal and provincial governments saw it as a brand spanking new technology that would be good for everybody. With it they could take the pressure off BC's wild salmon populations. From the get-go this meant that fishers of the wild had best take care that the scientists were right because if farmed fish were to dominate the market, who would buy wild fish? But it turned out that the fishers didn't have to worry about that problem because, far from reducing the impact of the fishing industry on wild salmon, the introduction of salmon farming threatened to wipe the wild fish out. I don't know if the fish farmers knew what the consequences of their act would be but it wouldn't have mattered if they did. It was a disaster.

Let's start with the filth that fish farms dump on the ocean floor. This includes not only fish excrement but unconsumed food, antibiotics, colourants and anti-lice compounds. (This last item, generally marketed as the hugely expensive "SLICE," is formulated to kill crustaceans, which is what sea lice are. But crabs, shrimp and prawns are crustaceans, too.) Meanwhile, the provincial government says it has the toughest regulations in the world to keep the ocean clean. This may be true, but since they have never enforced any of them, one will never know. In fact, the BC Liberal government actually repaid fish farmers their past fines levied for contaminating the ocean, and the fisheries minister has been known to advise a farm when a rare inspection is about to take place.

There is the question of disease. Farmed fish are more likely to become sick because they don't have the immunities wild salmon do, and they are farmed in such densities that when disease does come, the number of sick fish is enormous and the farms become one large plague unit. And this unit is infectious for every wild fish that passes by.

There is the problem of escapes. Salmon escape from fish farms in massive numbers and for a variety of reasons, and when they do they pose huge problems. The first of these comes about because, when fish cages first arrived on this coast, the Department of Fisheries and Oceans (DFO) proclaimed that the fish couldn't escape; that if they did escape, they couldn't survive in the wild; that if they did escape *and* survive they would never get into our rivers and spawn; that if they did escape, survive, *and* get in our rivers and spawn, why the DFO would destroy them. Given the ability of the DFO to destroy wild salmon runs, I'm inclined to believe they were capable of the last part of that statement, but of course, when farmed salmon did escape, survive and spawn in our rivers, the DFO did nothing. The second problem came about in the early 1990s when most BC fish farmers switched to raising Atlantic salmon, a species foreign to Pacific waters. Today there is no longer any question that escaped Atlantic salmon have established themselves in many, many BC rivers and streams, and new evidence seems to indicate that they have spawned and returned, thus displacing wild salmon on the spawning beds. Would it have been okay if all the caged fish on this coast were Pacific salmon? Unfortunately not, for while it is doubtful that Atlantic salmon can cross-breed with Pacific salmon, escaped Pacific farmed salmon can and do cross-breed with wild Pacific salmon, and what this does (forgive my scientific language) is bugger up the gene pool. And throughout this entire exercise, BC's ministers of fisheries have all denied it was happening.

Lastly, let me touch on the sea-lice problem. Every ocean in the world has sea lice, tiny parasitic crustaceans. They become a serious problem, however, when you cage hundreds of thousands of fish. The best example of this happening is in the Broughton Archipelago. If you lay both of your hands on the table with your fingers outspread, that is much like the Broughton Archipelago with dozens of islands in close proximity and separated only by narrow waterways. Now imagine each of those waterways clogged with fish cages containing hundreds of thousands of fish and each cage host to millions of sea lice. Now imagine it is time for the exodus from nearby streams of several million two- or three-inch-long pink and chum salmon smolts and for them to journey past those fish farms on their way to the open sea. They don't have a chance. They are slaughtered. We have already had two wipeouts of pink salmon in this region and, as I write this, another is predicted for the fall of 2005. But fish farmers continue to deny this is happening, which proves the point the Nazis made: the bigger and more preposterous the lie, the more it will be swallowed.

What is so insane about all this is that the same thing has happened in Norway, Scotland and Ireland. A couple of years ago my wife Wendy and I were guests of Dr. Patrick Gargan of Galway, Republic of Ireland, the world's foremost expert on the sea lice problem as it relates to wild salmonids. I had interviewed Paddy a few months before, and so when we found ourselves in Galway, we accepted his offer to take us for a bit of a fish on the famous Lough Corrib. But before we went out, Paddy took us down to his station near the mouth of the Corrib River where I met his technicians. One of them asked me in a delightful brogue that I won't try to put on paper, "What's the matter with you people out there in British Columbia? Can't ye read? Don't ye know what has happened in Norway? In Scotland? And here?" I had no answer!

The sea lice situation in the Broughton Archipelago has been brilliantly researched by Alexandra Morton, a very plucky lady indeed, about whom I have written more fully in my last book. But here's where you will begin to wonder if we're not with Alice in a Wonderland ruled by the Red Queen. Alex is a biologist, though her specialty is whales not fish, yet her findings concerning sea lice killing migrating smolts was peer-reviewed, published, and validated by Dr. Gargan, Dr. John Volpe (who did the research on escaped Atlantics in BC's rivers), and no less a scientist than Dr. Dan Pawley, lauded by *Time* magazine as one of the fifty top scientists in the world. Even with all this corroboration, the industry remains in denial. Maybe, they say, the loss was due to sun spots or El Nino or the phases of the moon, but the sea lice killing all those pink salmon smolts couldn't possibly have come from those lice-infested cages that the little buggers had to pass! Then a study was done by a partnership of scientists from the universities of Alberta and

British Columbia, the results being released in March 2005 and published in the journal of the Royal Society—and you don't get much better validation than that. One of the lead researchers on that study, Dr. John Volpe, told me and my radio audience that the cause of the pink salmon wipe-out was now more than just a "smoking gun." His team had, in fact, traced the lice on the smolts directly to the fish cages responsible. And there it sits. There is not a single independent scientist in the world that doesn't accept the findings of biologist Alexandra Morton and those of the researchers from the universities of Alberta and British Columbia, yet if you question John Van Dongen, BC's minister of agriculture, food and fisheries (an especially dense man) or indeed Premier Campbell, they will still tell you that "science is on our side." It is the big lie technique. Meanwhile, they are preparing to license new farms on the North Coast.

The question often arises why governments would permit this to happen. The answers are simple—and have much to do with the money the farmed fish industry puts into politician's re-election coffers. First, responsibility for the health of wild Pacific salmon belongs to the federal DFO, but back in the 1970s DFO staff were also given a directive from on high to promote aquaculture. Hold on! you say. Isn't that a conflict of interest? How can they protect wild salmon while they have the obligation to put them in harm's way? Of course, they can't and they don't. Second, because of the peculiar division of federal and provincial jurisdictions, the actual licensing of fish farms has always been the prerogative of the provincial government. Therefore, the minister of agriculture, food and fisheries has both a mandate to promote aquaculture—as it has to promote any industry in this province—and a mandate to grant licences to fish farmers.

Finally hear this. The University of British Columbia, my old alma mater, has an Aquaculture Centre that funds research into fish farming. Doesn't that sound like wonderful news?

At least, you say, now we will bring the independent mind of university researchers to the problem. But you might want to know who funds this Aquaculture Centre. One of them is the DFO, another is the provincial Ministry of agriculture, fisheries and food, John Van Dongen, proprietor. And—are you ready for this? The fish farmers! Thus, if you have a bright youngster with a desire to do independent aquaculture projects, the Centre should be the first place but in fact is the last place he should go for funding.

So I say, "To hell with science!" Gone are the days when it carried with it a moral imperative. Now it is money, huge soulless corporations, greedy, ignorant governments, toady industry researchers and a hapless, passive population that constitute our modern society. Science is no longer a search for the truth but an exercise in making money—lots of it and quickly. The fact that the environment suffers big time is of no consequence. We have become a society that knows in its soul that the oceans all around the world are crippled, that more and more animals are on the verge of extinction, and that the price will soon have to be paid.

Science, perverted by greedy corporations and mindless governments has brought us all to where we are content to let the rest of the environment go. There is no longer any point to doing anything to save it. Our legacy to our kids is a world for the servile who, if they keep their noses clean, will be able to drive huge air-conditioned SUVs up and down immense highways and for whom the out-of-doors will mean sitting on the banks of fishless rivers, the quiet unspoiled by the sound of birds. The bears will be long gone as will the gulls and the eagles. It will turn the land God made into a world of man's science. If I'm lucky, I won't live to see it. My grandchildren will not be so lucky.

So Where the Hell Are We Then?

As we said as kids, we're up Shit Creek without a paddle. Humans are now way past what the doomers and gloomers of the 1960s had to say. We have arrived at the place where they have been proved right except in those areas where they have turned out to be optimists.

Of course, all of us are in denial. It's human nature to accept any sliver of good news no matter who brings it rather than face up to truth and reality. We on the West Coast of Canada, seeing the ocean but never having been able to see what's in it, comfort ourselves that all must be well out there. But if I were to parade before you the world's top ten experts on ocean biology, they would tell you, chapter and verse, how bad it is in the world's oceans. They would tell you that the oceans have lost 90 percent of their predators, mostly due to man. We kill salmon by destroying their habitat, by permitting poaching and overfishing and by permitting disgraceful polluters such as fish farmers to sell our politicians on the idea, George Orwell-style, that in order to save the salmon we must first destroy them. We pay no mind to what happens when we extinguish species. Rivers in the Broughton Archipelago, having lost their fish, have lost their bears, too, and their eagles and gulls, and their insect life and all that depend upon it, and the plant life that depends on the nutrients from salmon corpses…and on it goes.

We are losing our sea mammals at an alarming rate. If it weren't for people like Paul Watson and the Sea Shepherd Society we would have lost a hell of a lot more. We are losing seals and sea lions because we have taken away their prey, the salmon and other fishes. We poison our seals with our untreated sewage and they in turn poison the killer whales. Global warming threatens our polar bears while the ravaging of krill off Antarctica threatens several species of penguin. Oceans are sturdy things and can, given time and care, replenish themselves. But not only are we not giving them time and care to do so but we make it worse every day.

The world has never been so divided between rich and poor as it is today. The rich get richer and the poor get poorer. Whenever I speak on the outrageous poverty of the Third World and urge that we help more, I can count on someone calling in to my show to say, "We should look after our poor at home first," without considering that the poorest Canadian is rich compared to the poor of sub-Saharan Africa. I hear them say, "Don't give money to those places! It will just fall into the hands of tin pot dictators." Instead of that being a reason to find better ways to deliver help, it becomes a reason not to help at all. "They shouldn't have all those babies" is often the complaint. This doesn't recognize that the only way these people can expect to have help when they're old and sick is if they have children to support them. And to have one child survive it is necessary to have, perhaps, five children who die of starvation. This, coupled with the Roman Catholic Church's refusal to consider birth control methods for those of that faith, and you have a big time problem that can't be cured simply by preaching birth control from the comfort of the local pub.

Even if one is not touched by humanitarian concerns, we must learn to think of the practical. How on earth are we to establish peaceful, decent, democratic regimes where there is such grinding poverty and no will within the populace to rise toward it because they can hardly rise from their beds for want of food? And if you want yet more practical reasons, how can we expect countries to trade with us if they haven't got the ability to create anything to sell? And how do you tell people to look after their endangered wild fauna and flora when in order to maintain life they must destroy it, often to satisfy the greed of those who live in the "have" nations?

The world has never been more dangerous. At least the Cold War had its "mutually assured destruction" and only two real combatants. But today weapons of mass destruction are in the hands of—or soon will be in the hands of—a dozen or more countries. India faces down Pakistan; China faces down Taiwan; North Korea faces down South Korea, Japan and—in some ways—China and Russia with whom they share borders, as well as the US.

The US, led by those who think they are doing God's work, stands for liberty and democracy, except, of course, when President Bush is on the White House lawn holding hands with Crown Prince Abdullah of Saudi Arabia, a country that doesn't even permit women to drive cars much less take part in public affairs, stones adulteresses to death (not adulterers, you'll note), cuts off thieves' hands and permits no vestige of democracy.

Perhaps worst of all—because solutions to the world's problems so depend upon it—we have lost free speech, especially in the US where the concept first occurred to modern civilized people. To express opinions contrary to the world according to Bush is to court condemnation as a traitor. Nothing is private anymore, though one could say that modern computer science is to blame for that, but to blame computer science for providing the wherewithal is like blaming the Derringer people for Lincoln's assassination. Governments, especially that in the US, instead of doing everything possible to protect the civil rights of its citizens, almost seem to take pride if not pleasure in denying rights. Not that this is new, as a quick look at a biography of former FBI chief J. Edgar Hoover would demonstrate. The difference is that in Hoover's day the elite at least paid lip service to the belief that what he was doing was wrong. Now if you protest that personal liberties are being violated because a handful of terrorists are on the loose, you are cast in their camp. It seems to catch no one's attention that the prisoners in Guantanamo Bay are being held without any rights whatsoever and have been for nearly three years. Only a traitor, it would seem, would demand rights for those the state deems it convenient to hold without rights and incommunicado.

Governments—especially in that cradle of democracy, the US—are not elected so much as bought. President Bush owed his first presidency not to more votes but a Republican Supreme Court that tossed two centuries of precedents out the window by taking away the state's right to hold its own elections.

The US seems to live by the creed that a huge deficit, a large trade deficit and a national debt beyond the ability of most to comprehend represent fiscal responsibility. China intends to dominate the economy of the world and someday will succeed. The European Union looks more and more like the National Hockey League as it takes in more and more countries, seemingly for no better reason than taking them in. This spells expansion, which by definition means prosperity.

Is there no ray of hope? Don't ask me. I'm just a passenger, not the bus driver. But it does seem to me that a false assumption is now spreading to many areas—an assumption Canadians often apply to secession by Quebec—that it hasn't happened so far so it probably won't. All I, as an observer, can hope is that their assumption is right (which, of course, it is not) or that we can still get our collective acts together (which is most unlikely).

Worst of all, time is short, very short indeed.

Part Five

HEALING MORAL WOUNDS

IN THE CHURCH

A Not So Gay Church

I am sickened by the split in the Anglican Church over the issue of asking God to bless homosexual unions. I have slowly come to the realization that, now when I say the Creed, my heart isn't in it and that I am perhaps that worst of all non-violent sinners, the hypocrite. That I am at present considering other religious options for myself, however, has nothing to do with my feelings on the issue of asking God's blessing on homosexual unions, except for this connection: I do not believe the Bible to be a divine book and thus infallible. At the Council of Nicea in 325 when the bishops selected and rejected books to make up the Bible, they were careful to leave out anything that challenged the notion of the Trinity, the virginity of Mary or the divinity of Christ, and those who didn't agree—the Arians and the Gnostics—were excommunicated and often put to death. I raise this point because some of my correspondents go to great lengths to demonstrate that homosexuality is against God's Law. One went to extremes of work and logic to demonstrate that Jesus—who uttered not a word on the subject despite its prevalence in the society of his day—was also against the practice. Another line of correspondence says that homosexuality is an unnatural thing, that it is unhygienic and can be cured. One of my correspondents quotes a long passage from a psychiatrist who holds this view.

On the religious point, I believe communicants in a church can hold whatever views they wish and can, like the Catholic and fundamentalist strains reject gays, or like the United Church accept and ordain them, or like the Anglicans debate the issue unto the destruction of their own faith. Whatever view a church has, it is irrelevant to the civil matters of criminal law and social law such as marriage. However, it would seem to me, as still a member of the Anglican community, that Christians might accept the fact that the judgment is God's and not theirs— "judge not lest ye be judged." If I'm wrong on that subject, I believe that there are lots of other sins these good Christians ought to root out, such as greed, lust, adultery, theft (corporate and otherwise), at the same time as they deal with one aspect of homosexuality, sodomy between males, which *is* proscribed by parts of the Bible. But it is interesting that the Good Book doesn't deal with oral sex, anal sex between male and female or lesbianism, although it approves, of course, of slavery, brutality, bloody wars, human sacrifice and the degradation of women.

The second group of my correspondents really bothers me. Several of them have asked why I don't present the "other side," namely the uncleanliness of homosexuality and the "fact" that it can be "cured"? If homosexuality is unclean and curable, what do they care? Why is it their business? Is it a matter of fear? Do they suppose that, if allowed to marry, gays will adopt and/or create little sex perverts to poison the minds of their innocent young? That the gay agenda, presumably headed by the Great Gay himself, will slowly but surely convert us all, thus relieving earth of its overpopulation if nothing else? The uncleanliness issue interests me. I'm not sure that many who find oral sex to be gratifying and lots of fun are overburdened with hygienic concerns any more than are those who enjoy French kissing are likely to seek the advice of their dentist before so indulging.

In the meantime, while we are dealing with the sin and uncleanliness of homosexuals, why don't we poke our noses into the private notions of other well-known groups of non-fundamentalist Christians. Why, we could even deal with other "deviants" like Buddhists, Muslims and Jews. And while we're curing people of unapproved sexual habits, why don't we take on those who don't believe in our Bible or even—may the saints preserve us—Jesus Christ himself. The field is unlimited. There are Sikhs, Buddhists, Muslims, Jews, agnostics, atheists—the list of those whom we must cure of their ignorance is never ending.

Perhaps we should start by curing the Jews of their Jewishness and their propensity to eat certain foods and refuse others. We could enlist that hero of the Christian Right, the Reverend Jerry Falwell, whose anti-homosexual obsession is only matched by his strong strain of anti-Semitism. As he claims he can "cure" homosexuals and convert heathens, he would be perfect for the role. I could do a show on it, inviting all who hold the view that Jesus Christ is their saviour to join in and beat the crap out of those who don't. What fun we could have!

Well, I won't. Sorry about that. Quite apart from the fact I would obviously offend Jews (as homophobes consistently offend homosexuals) it would be none of your business or mine. And that is the point. It is simply none of your business or mine how people pray, whom they pray to or—dare I say it—how they demonstrate their love or, for that matter, to whom they demonstrate it, as long as they are consenting adults. We are a secular, not clerical, state and have been since the beginning of our country.

Here I simply address the bigots of the land who are determined to bring scorn or worse on a group of people simply because their sexual habits don't meet with their approval. They are right when they say that there is a sickness abroad in the land, but happily it is confined to this minority of bigots. Their sickness is called intolerance. I don't ask these people to embrace anything or anyone they don't care for, whatever the reason. I only say they should learn to mind their own bloody business and get on with life.

Catholicism and the Third World

The election of a new pope on April 19, 2005, had worldwide connotations that none can ignore. It is not surprising that the conclave of cardinals elected an old, conservative successor to Pope John Paul II since he selected all but three of the cardinals himself. When he died, out of respect for Catholic listeners, the media around the world muted their criticisms of his papacy as they stressed the positive parts of his rule. There is a time and a place for everything and that was not the time or place to speak ill of the recently deceased. But after a decent interval, especially since the Church has elected to fast-track John Paul II to sainthood, all who are affected by the papacy are entitled to express their views

I must also say that I really don't care what beliefs any religion holds dear, however ridiculous they may seem to me. I part from my own church, the Anglican Church of Canada, on a number of beliefs, some of which are the same as Catholic beliefs. Both churches rely upon interpretation of the Bible for their dogma, and in the Catholic Church the beliefs are either time-honoured or the result of councils, such as the Vatican Council in 1870, which confirmed the infallibility of the pope on doctrinal matters. Where I part company with the Catholics is in areas where they don't rely upon direct injunctions from Jesus but upon interpretations by other biblical figures. To say that all words in the Bible are God's word and that when those words are interpreted by popes they are being interpreted by a man invested by God to do so is to me, with respect, dangerous nonsense. (Upon reflection I submit that I ought not to categorize anyone's beliefs as nonsense, but the word "dangerous" is perhaps a fair comment.) That Catholics have every right to their beliefs I don't contest. When, however, those beliefs contribute to the suffering and death of others or to the denial of civil liberties, I must protest—as indeed many Catholics do.

In this context, as far as the homosexual issue is concerned, I must point out that in order to justify making this a sin, you will not find help from Jesus but must trawl through St. Paul and Old Testament stuff. If Catholics want to call homosexuals sinners, that is their affair, but when they enjoin against the use of condoms, male on male or male on female, to prevent the transfer of AIDS, that is quite a different story because they are in effect passing death sentences.

If Catholics wish to believe that birth control is a sin, again they have to look long and hard for support in the Bible and to stretch such sayings as "go forth and multiply" and injunctions against "spilling seed on the ground." But there are Catholics all over the world, especially in its western parts, who now pay little or no attention to the papal injunction against birth control. Within my lifetime we have virtually seen the last of the big Catholic families in western countries. But birth control is still considered a sin in Catholic Third World countries, and this rule condemns hundreds of thousands of children and their overburdened mothers to starvation and death. This may not be the Church's intent but it is clearly the result.

The Catholic Church, in common with many Protestant churches, makes the point that you can't allow the passage of time or changing of fashions to alter basic truths. I don't argue with that, but I ask what these truths are. Lawyers have two Latin phrases for the point I wish to make here. Some things are *malum in se*, that is, inherently bad, while others are *malum prohibitum*, which is to say not in themselves evil but made so by authority. Clearly some of the sins—or perhaps all—listed in the Ten Commandments are *malum in se;* it is wrong to murder, commit adultery and so on. But male-only clerics,

clerics forbidden to marry, birth control and matters of that sort are merely *malum prohibitum*. They are not in themselves evil, merely prohibited by church authorities for small "p" political reasons.

All of what I've said here undoubtedly offends the Catholic Church, but my views are shared by a hell of a lot of other people, including many Catholics around the world. There are, in fact, active groups within the church trying to get equality for women, acceptance of birth control, absence of discrimination against homosexuals, and marriage for priests, brothers and sisters. What the Catholic Church ought to regard with both sadness and alarm is the number of Catholics who refuse to accept the church's prohibitions. Even more the Church should be lamenting the loss of many who don't want to be hypocritical by appearing to accept that with which they don't agree, seeing hypocrisy as a greater sin than birth control, women priests, priests forbidden to marry (unless, of course, they are married Anglican priests who have converted) and homosexuality.

I want to make it clear that, while I think many of the doctrines of the Catholic Church make no sense, my only concern is when insistence upon the practice of these doctrines brings in its wake the evil of destitution and death as seen in much of the Catholic world, especially in Third World countries, however unintentional these consequences may be. Then the dogma of Rome becomes the affair of all people of all persuasions or lack of them who want to stop the spread of AIDS, put an end to the plight of children born into families that can't support them, support full rights for women and full civil rights for gays.

Why the Church of England Will Never Reconcile with Rome

The death of Pope John Paul II reminded many Anglicans of early efforts by this pope and several archbishops of Canterbury to repair the breach that occurred in 1534 when Henry VIII was refused an annulment of his marriage to Catherine of Aragon and established the Church of England. During the pontificate of Paul VI (1963-1978) an ongoing commission called the Anglican Roman Catholic International Commission (ARCIC) was put in place to examine those areas where agreement might be found. Unfortunately for the fate of ecumenism, few were found though many areas of profound difference were identified. However, efforts made during the pontificate of John Paul II (1978-2005) seemed at times to be making headway, especially when in 1982 he and the then Archbishop of Canterbury knelt and prayed together near the site of the murder of St. Thomas à Becket (1118-1170) at Canterbury Cathedral. Over the years there have been several other efforts made to reunite, but certainly in retrospect they look pretty tepid.

There are a number of large stumbling blocks to reunification, starting with the doctrine of the supremacy of the papacy, though strangely enough, at one point it appeared as if some clever wording might be found to satisfy both Canterbury and the Holy See on this matter. That didn't happen. The issue of female priests provided a double whammy for the Anglican side; not only did the Catholics reject such a notion but some 50 Church of England priests also rejected it and defected to Catholicism. Priestly celibacy was a lesser problem, and one suspects that if the marriage issue could have been settled, the celibacy issue would have solved itself.

The question of same-sex marrying or seeking the blessing of God on their relationships has in itself, I think, poisoned reunion possibilities for a long time to come. Again, this issue has been doubled up for the Anglicans because, while many of the flock are quite prepared to see such unions blessed, many are not and little schisms have occurred within the church all over the world. I am bewildered by the Anglican Communion's handling of this issue. As far as I can detect, there is no desire within the church, priesthood or laity to have Anglican clergy allowed to perform same-sex marriages, but many, perhaps a majority, would have little trouble with a priest asking God's blessing on such unions. And here is where I puzzle. Since the Reformation, Protestant priests have not been able to bless anything—at least that's how I read the banning of indulgences, which is how blessing got started. What they can do is simply ask God to bless, which is a very different thing. And if the Anglican faithful have no problem with a priest asking God to bless a warship bristling with weapons of mass destruction and all who sail in her, I find it breathtakingly amazing that they would object to a priest asking God to bless two people in love.

There is also the problem of history, and there is a hell of a lot of it behind and backing up the split ecumenism wishes to heal. Catholic utterances and writings on ecumenism still seem quite unable to avoid some tut-tutting over Henry VIII and all that. But Protestantism really had a double start in England, first over the issue of Henry's annulment, then again after the death of Mary I—who tried to restore Catholicism—and the reassertion of Protestantism under Elizabeth I, a reassertion made all the stronger by the impact of the Reformation on England and very much on Scotland. Anglicanism also had to survive Oliver Cromwell and was threatened again by the

Catholicism of James II, from whose ousting flowed the Act of Succession that required each British monarch thereafter to be an Anglican as well as head of the Church of England. But the bitterness has hardly been one-sided. Many Roman Catholics suffered greatly under Protestant kings and, indeed, the last vestige of anti-Romism—the requirement that the monarch be Anglican—remains.

I believe that the foregoing are petty issues, however, compared to the basic doctrinal ones. The first and most obvious of these is the doctrine of transubstantiation, which holds that the wine and bread of communion does in fact become the flesh and blood of Christ upon its ingestion. Oddly enough, the father of the Reformation, Martin Luther, accepted this doctrine, though it became such an obvious dividing line thereafter. Lesser doctrines—the rise of Marianism (the near worship of Mary, mother of Jesus) and the intercession and indeed creation of saints—have also divided the two communities, but transubstantiation remains, I believe, an unbridgeable gap.

The second basic doctrinal difference is more subtle. Although England was the first Protestant state and thus the first heretic state, this didn't mean that England rejected all things Catholic. Far from it. A visitor just here from Mars would find a High Anglican service and a Catholic one very similar. As well, the Anglican Church, without presuming to name any saints itself, retained the existing Catholic ones, as the names of most Anglican parishes would demonstrate. What did happen over the centuries was a relaxing of discipline within Anglicanism that did not occur either in the Catholic Church or most other Protestant faiths. Once Anglicans got past burning recusants at the stake, strains of liberalism, mostly unofficial, crept in. Archbishops, if they tried at all, were not especially effective in bringing the flock back to ancient truths. Popes, on the other hand, have been pretty good at this. A good example is the issue of divorce. Once the church in England lost the sole power to divorce and civil divorces became common, the Anglican Church found itself with a lot of divorced members who weren't the slightest bit interested in what the vicar thought about it. So the Anglican Church sort of slid into the practice of butting out of such matters and gradually into marrying divorced people. Certainly by the late 19th century, the Church of England found itself without the doctrinal severity of the Roman Catholic Church and unwilling to "shun" naughty parishioners as other Protestant faiths did.

As this is not intended as a history of the Church of England, permit me to jump ahead to the times of Bishop James Pike of California, the inspiration behind the erection of Grace Cathedral in San Francisco where my wife Wendy and I sometimes attend services. Bishop Pike, who went from being a Catholic to an agnostic to the Episcopalian (Anglican) Church, was—in my estimation—the most famous heretic of the 20th century. Though his life was marred by tragedy, his trial in 1966 for heresy being the least of them, he started an unofficial thoughtfulness in the Anglican community that obviously has not gone away. Far from it. Probably the best known of Pike's descendants—though he might deny it—is Canada's own Tom Harpur, a former Anglican priest who holds that if there was a Jesus—a fact he no longer concedes—he was one of 13 Jesuses to have preached as a prophet or messiah over the centuries. Another Anglican priest I interviewed about a decade ago had written a book about the crucifixion. Afterwards I asked him if it was essential to being a Christian that one believed in the literal resurrection of Jesus. "Of course not," he replied emphatically. And far from being a "young Turk," my guest was well into his 70s.

Many Anglicans have asked and continue to ask similar questions. And for ecumenism here's the rub: These "heretics"— far from being excommunicated—are being listened to in open debate without fear of priestly reprisal. Many, like me, want to re-examine heresies like Arianism and Gnosticism with an open mind, and when I speak to my priest on these matters, instead of smiling pontifically as he urges appropriate biblical passages on me, his favourite heretic, he urges me to keep right on thinking. But alas, I think a new wave of Puritanism has seeped into if not enveloped the Anglican community in its moment of dire peril. I doubt that the book of Leviticus was as much read in its first 2,500 years as it has been in the past dozen when it has become the basis for denying homosexuals rights. This modern Puritanism, though so far devoid of violence, is no less intense for all that because the survival of the church itself is in issue.

I suppose it might be argued that the Anglican Church, even rent asunder, is worth the trouble it would take to bring it back to the Catholic fold. One reason why this won't happen is that the Roman Catholic Church simply hasn't had its own internal revolution—yet. John Paul II managed to paper over some of the cracks, but there are perhaps more of them that he widened. The issues of female priests, homosexuality and questionable dogma hit the Anglican Church because its fundamental indiscipline made them acceptable discussion topics. The Catholic Church will only avoid them becoming issues that strike at the roots of the Catholic faith if it maintains its discipline. But it won't maintain its discipline because it can't. Such is the closeness of modern society and such is the state of information dissemination that the Roman Catholic Church will either go through a revival process based upon modern introspection or it too will fragment. We all tend to think that because something hasn't happened for a long, long time it never will. It is a fatal assumption.

Perhaps, sometime in the not too distant future a pope will re-read Mark 12: 30-31 and conclude that perhaps it would be a good idea if all Christian faiths took it from there and started all over again. This is not likely, of course, as and for the same reason that Canterbury won't agree with Rome or vice versa. And, I must confess, I will lose no sleep nor waste any energy trying to unite doctrines rather than Christians.

Part Six

VITAL SIGNS

Some Thoughts on Health Care

Many years ago (1979-80) I was minister of health for British Columbia and, while that certainly does not of itself guarantee wisdom, the experience did provide me with a sound basis for watching and understanding the health care system in this country. And now that the Supreme Court of Canada has ruled that it is unconstitutional to forbid a person to go outside the Medicare system to get private treatment, it is useful, I think, to survey what's happened to that system in the intervening years. Back when I held the BC health portfolio, Emmet Hall was doing the national tour that led to the recommendations on which the Canada Health Act was based. By its terms, Ottawa, which under the constitution has no jurisdiction for health, can still exercise its clout by making the provinces obey the rules contained in the act or forgo tax dollars. But as those dollars have declined over the years, so has respect for the act by rich provinces such as Alberta.

There are, therefore, some facts about health care in Canada that we should ponder. When Judge Hall made his recommendations, the huge baby boomer bulge was young, healthy and full of pee-and-vinegar. No one had heard of AIDS. There were no successful heart transplants. We had only just started to use those hugely expensive scanners, and MRIs were still in the future. The drug industry had not yet taken off with its never-ending cost increases, and most wages throughout the system, except for those paid to doctors, were pitifully low compared to the present. I remember my provincial health budget being just over a billion dollars; it's now probably four times that (using constant dollars).

The cold, hard fact is, with all the changes that have

occurred in the last 25 years, our health system is now broke and getting more broke every day, and it's time we stopped letting the sainted but very late Tommy Douglas rule from beyond the grave. Though he didn't introduce Medicare to Canada—his successor Woodrow Lloyd did that—Douglas is seen as the father of the scheme, and whenever anyone suggests any changes should be made, virtually the entire Left screams blue bloody murder that no changes can ever be permitted. This generally seems to mean that we must not involve any private money in our health system, even if it could be demonstrated that giving people the right to buy insurance that would provide them with prompter care would reduce the strain on the public purse and get faster care for the people on the public system. If we let that happen, they say, we'll have the American system and everyone knows that means millions of poor people dying in the streets for want of the money to buy care. In fact, not even the right-wing Fraser Institute proposes that we adopt the American system, and I sure as hell don't. But that is the best argument the Left can raise against change. Unfortunately, what this shrill cry from the Left has done is stifle debate so that, when the Supreme Court brought down its decision, our governments had no plans in place. They had to know that things were permanently out of hand. Advances in medical science mean that more and more people are living longer and longer. This translates into uncontainable costs that are being covered by reducing services because there is simply no more money to be had. How many studies have been done on Medicare and how many wonderful recommendations have emerged from them, none of which worked? Money has been added to the kitty here, money has been added there, and the line-ups have only lengthened. All this in order to postpone the dreaded two-tiered health care in which, so the hysterical argument went, a private tier would get all the best doctors and the government would ignore public healthcare. But two-tier health care already exists. If a Vancouver Canuck player needs knee surgery, do you think he gets in a lineup that is about a year behind? Not on your tintype! The value of an injured Canuck to his team is such that the team has its own doctors to give the promptest of service—and there is no complaint from the Health Ministry. It is the same with the police and Worker's Compensation Board, though the latter organization has a truly fascinating double standard. If a worker's comp employee falls off a ladder while on the job and breaks a couple of bones, the government considers the loss of this person's contribution to the productivity of the province so important that he is sent to the head of the line and treated right away. If, however, this same worker falls off a ladder at home and has the same injuries, he suddenly loses his value to the province's productivity and has to join the lineup!

Now let's just suppose the brass at Station 600AM where I work looked over their staff and decided, "These people are so valuable that we'll hire private doctors so we can get them instant service." I needn't tell you what the government would do. And here's another anomaly of our present system: I have horrible knees (inside as well as outside), and there is nothing to stop me going to the US and paying privately to have them fixed. I am, after all, a free Canadian. But if I am truly a free citizen and if doctors are, too, why can't I make the same deal at home? And how is it possible that those with influence in our society, such as bigwigs in the health community or even Mr. Moneybags who knows someone who knows someone, often jump the queue?

There never was a magic bullet to cure our healthcare system. We tried cutting costs with miniscule results; we've tried rationing services by removing some procedures from coverage (unlawfully, it now appears), which in practice meant that only the poor, unable to pay for the uninsured procedures, suffered. But while it is true that no other health system in the world, however satisfactory it looks, is without problems, why are we so afraid to examine fully what these other jurisdictions do to see if there are lessons to be learned? The fact is that governments all over Europe and in Australia with similar cultures to ours operate systems that include a private factor, and I have said repeatedly (showing considerable prescience!) that Canada must do the same: Make peace with the private sector on our terms rather than dither until we have to do it on their terms. Now here we are, forced by the courts—which had to make the decision our governments didn't have the political will to do—to let private money come in, largely on their terms. And this is the most disturbing—and disgraceful—aspect to this court case: None of our governments were prepared for the outcome. It was scarcely a secret. The justices actually reserved for a full year before rendering their decision. I knew about it by simply talking to a couple of lawyers and doctors, and I warned over and over that there was a huge civil rights problem in Medicare. I interviewed health ministers on this point. Notwithstanding this, when the Supreme Court ruling came down on June 9, 2005, ministers across the country acted as if there was no reason in the world why they should have suspected this might happen! Instead of having fall-back positions, they were dumbfounded. It was a disgraceful example of political cowardice.

While it can be argued that what got us into this pickle were the rising costs and the expensive new procedures, there was plain political negligence as well. It started with the federal government back in the days when it agreed to pay half the cost of acute care hospitals. That was in the '60s and we certainly did need acute care beds—there's no question about that. What we didn't do at the time was look at the statistics and calculate when the baby boomers would stop needing maternity beds and start needing long-term care facilities. It wasn't until the '70s that BC Health

Minister Bob McLelland saw the horror story ahead and brought in a long-term care policy, but it was never properly implemented, due in part to the recession of the '80s. In my time we did bring in a better home-care program and, again in my time, decided to convert St. Mary's Hospital in New Westminster to extended care. This was a financially sound move as it was designed to take extended care patients out of acute care beds, which are much more expensive to maintain than extended or long-term care beds. There was, however, a huge campaign against my decision. Because St. Mary's is a Catholic hospital, the protesters even played the religious card, but when priests began sermonizing against the conversion of the hospital, I had to ask Archbishop Carney himself to call off the dogs. The decision, of course, had nothing to do with religion and everything to do with sound planning. The area in question—New Westminster, Surrey, the Coquitlams and Port Moody—had changed dramatically since St. Mary's was built. New Westminster was no longer a community of the young but quite the opposite; it was precisely where the aging population now lived. The young lived in Surrey, the Coquitlams and Port Moody and much had been done to cater to this new demographic, including the construction of Eagle Ridge Hospital.

However, the decision I had taken with such pain was annulled by political cowardice; shortly after I left the health ministry, my successor, Jim Nielsen, reversed it. Thus, for the next 25 years this partial solution to the shortage of acute care beds was not in place, and all because the government had buckled under pressure. (Now, as I write this in 2005, St. Mary's appears about to be closed again!) I tell this story because it underscores the fact that politics plays such a big role in determining health policy, and while the public must always be involved and informed, there comes a time when the brain must overrule the heart.

I would not want to be misunderstood. The pressure on government and especially the health minister is enormous and sometimes all but unbearable. The political heat from the Opposition can be considerable as well, although I'm bound to say that Dennis Cocke, the NDP critic when I held the portfolio, though tough as hell, always behaved responsibly. Now here we are in 2005 and a promise made four years ago of 5,000 additional long-term care beds in this province is not only unfulfilled but we have fallen further behind.

Another area where our medical system is only barely out of the Dickensian era is mental health. The first question that ought to come to everyone's mind is why do we set it aside from any other sort of health care? A person with schizophrenia is no less sick than someone with cancer, yet the mental health patient is treated much differently. Having been a mental health "consumer" for 15 years, this is one subject I know something about first hand, and I can recommend some things the government of BC must do to improve services to people with this kind of ailment:

1. BC now has a minister of state for mental health. It's a nice idea gone wrong. This semi-ministry should be abolished because, by its very existence, it marginalizes mental health. (Besides, this post is only used as a training school for ministers-on-the-make or people the premier doesn't quite know what to do with.)

2. The position of mental health advocate, a role so well performed by Nancy Hall, must be re-instated. One of the common characteristics of mentally ill people is that they are afraid to admit their malady because the stigma attached to mental illness is so very real. This is where the mental health advocate comes in; she searches out people who need help then puts in a request to the minister for financial assistance. This, of

course, makes her a nuisance to the minister who must, upon getting her advice, go to the minister of finance to ask for more money. Junior ministers don't like to do this because ministers of finance don't like hearing that sort of thing. The plain fact is that ministers of finance find it easier to balance their budgets when mentally ill people remain undiagnosed and untreated. If physically ill people were treated in the same manner by the system as mentally ill people are, the legislature would be stormed and there would be blood in the streets.

3. It must be a condition of practice that every general practitioner be able to diagnose mental illness. Imagine a woman with a lump on her breast going to her doctor and being told, "Sorry, I don't do lumps, but I can get you an appointment with a specialist in six months to a year." That wouldn't be tolerated for one second! Yet when mentally ill people, having fought through the terrible stigma of admitting to mental illness, finally go to a doctor, they are far too often sent home with a lecture on how to keep the chin up or at best a six-month-distant appointment with a psychiatrist. This is unacceptable in the extreme.

4. Family doctors should be properly paid for their time looking after mentally ill people. We mental health patients don't require x-rays, MRIs or any expensive diagnostic tools. What we do need is careful diagnosis, a process that often requires long and repetitive visits to the doctor. MDs simply are not properly compensated for this, and as human beings (their sometime claim to being super-human notwithstanding), they are, like all labourers, worthy of their hire.

I am currently involved in a wonderful exercise called "The Bottom Line," which grew out of an idea I presented a few years ago to Bev Gutray, executive director of the BC Branch of the Canadian Mental Health Association. We organize an annual two-day conference of health workers and professionals dealing with mental illness in the workplace in order to make new information available to them, though it has the added value of allowing people who seldom see each other over the year to compare notes. Thanks to people such as the president of the BC Federation of Labour, Jim Sinclair, and the well-known businessman Michael Francis, this conference has become a huge success and has lately added—at Michael's timely suggestion— a new wrinkle: At the end of each conference we set goals to be met before the next conference. I am very proud to have played a part in getting this going and am deeply honoured that the annual luncheon is called the Rafe Mair Luncheon.

We are making some progress in helping the mentally ill but it is slow. Very slow. Public attitudes are getting better and governments are responding, but again, very slowly. One day, hopefully, mental illness will be properly diagnosed and treated in timely fashion. Apart from helping those who need it, this will have the powerful monetary effect of getting sick people back into circulation both in the workplace and in society generally.

Sadly, we're still a long, long way from home.

Sex Offenders are Sick People

In this country and province there is a staggering number of abductions and attempted abductions of youngsters by molesters. We'll never know what the real numbers are because sometimes the would-be abductor is scared off at the last minute or the youngster is too frightened by the experience to tell a parent what has happened.

This is where a very useful group in Vancouver called Put Kids First comes in. Their goal is to minimize and, if possible of course, eliminate child abductions by teaching young people to recognize the danger signals and to act upon them. I can only applaud the group's efforts and encourage everyone to look at www.putkidsfirst.org and, having done that, offer to help. Prevention is always better than any cure because in abduction cases the child is often killed and, if he or she survives, is scarred for life.

At present we are dealing with the problem of sex offenders after the fact, and I think we have it all wrong. The Michael Jackson case should teach us something about this: sex criminals, including the despised child molesters, are sick. And we should think that through because if we do, there's a better way to do things.

What I am suggesting is radical and at first blush repulsive, but I urge you to think along with me because my idea will never pass the House of Commons until we the people make it clear to those in charge what we want done. In a nutshell what I suggest is that, subject to legal word polishing, the following be added to the Criminal Code of Canada: "In any case where an accused is convicted of sexual assault of a child, the judge shall make a finding as to whether or not the accused person is a pedophile and, if he so finds, a finding of Not Guilty shall be entered and the accused shall thereafter be detained at Her Majesty's pleasure." While the power to do this may well be inherent in the Criminal Code as it now stands, I believe that prosecutors and judges should be under no illusion about what is expected of them.

To get to this point the public must do some serious soul-searching. What happens under our present laws if a Robert Noyes is accused of molesting little children? He goes through a trial and if found guilty may—only may—go to prison. He will receive little if any treatment and he must be released under the same conditions as apply to all ordinary offenders. If he is paroled, the restrictions will be minimal and certainly will not deter him from offending again. In short, those who commit sex offences on the young are penalized for being caught and then sent back into the community, in most cases uncured.

But is the justice system the place for such people? To answer that, another question must be posed: is the sexual predator sick?

Of course he is. That's the first thing we say when a little girl or boy has been assaulted or assaulted and killed. We know the perpetrator is sick but we can't bring ourselves to treat him as sick and quarantine him until he's better. We are so horrified by the crime that all we can think of is punishment, forgetting that those punished by being imprisoned will sooner or later—usually sooner—be released. We still demand that all who do wrong should go into the justice system even though we know that the justice system will fail us, as it has over and over again. This isn't the fault of the police, crown attorneys, defence counsel, judges, parole boards or anyone else in the system. The fault is the system itself and, by not demanding change, we connive with that system. It makes as much sense to send someone with a severe stomach ache into the criminal justice system as it does to send child predators there.

How does detention "at Her Majesty's pleasure" work in the case of sexual predators?

At present the predator is detained for as long as it takes to demonstrate that he is no more likely to offend than any other citizen. In the best scenario, he receives treatment in the hope that he can return to life outside, but he is only released when government psychiatrists certify that it is safe to do so *and* the cabinet so approves. Even at that, stiff requirements as to medications and reporting are enforced. I spent five years on the cabinet committee that heard these matters as a final court of appeal, so to speak, and I can tell you that when this system is used, it works very well indeed. And where it didn't work, we were hardly worse off than we are now when, in most cases, release is inevitable.

But won't this be costly to use in the case of all child predators? My answer is compared to what? Is it the position of our society that we cannot afford measures that will keep the streets free from sexual predators and that the cost must be borne instead by emotionally scarred, physically abused, too often dead children and their families and friends? If we really believe that the present prison system adequately addresses sexual predation, then all we can do is educate kids and hope for the best. But I say the criminal justice system cannot possibly deal with this scourge and we must treat pedophilia as the illness it is, thus taking advantage of the availability of detention for as long as it takes for the predator to be cured, if he is.

The notion of hospitalizing sex offenders instead of jailing them is a hard sell mainly because we so revile the child molester that we don't give a damn how sick he may be. But we have to think this through. The present system generally incarcerates them and *always* lets them out in no better—and probably worse—shape than they went in. Hospitalization recognizes that which we hate to admit but know is the case—the offender is sick—and hospital incarceration does not mollycoddle. Rather it is jail that does that.

To do as I suggest will take a radical change in the public's attitude, but if we're going to save our kids, we must make this change and the sooner the better.

Part Seven

BEEFS

The Worst Law Money Can Buy

Since I first wrote my thoughts on lawyers and judges in 2002 (in my book *Still Ranting*), my views have if anything hardened against my old profession (the one that vies for the distinction of being the oldest with the one that represents the ladies of the night—the latter being the more honourable of the two, I'm sad to say.)

First, some background. In 1956 I graduated from the UBC School of Law and then practiced in Vancouver and Kamloops for nearly 16 years. While I was at it, I saw nothing especially wrong with the system, but that was because I never asked myself why I should make so much money out of other people's misfortunes. Things were pretty laid-back in our office. I did a lot of personal injury work on a 20 percent contingency fee plus the taxed costs, and though lawyers today would consider that almost doing it for free, my family and I lived well. On other non-contentious matters I charged an hourly rate, but the record keeping was lax to say the least and certainly not in my favour. But those were the days before IBM took over the law offices of the world with new time-recording systems that enable lawyers to charge when they are sitting on the pot if they happen to be thinking of a client at the time. When I practiced, every so often a salesman would appear on the scene with a foolproof way to keep record of time and thus greatly enhance our incomes, but after a brief flurry of interest amongst the partners, momentarily overcome with the zeal of a convert within the ranks, we all slipped back into former habits. Deep down I don't think that most of us believed our clients would pay the enhanced accounts, although future events showed they would when there was no alternative. I left law at the end of 1975 when I was elected to the BC legislature and went into cabinet. I never went back, although my old Kamloops firm, now huge by BC Interior standards, still bears my name.

Now it is not my intention to kick my old profession in the crotch—well, maybe it is, but not too hard—but the whole thing has got out of hand. There are many more lawyers in BC than in the whole of Japan. Indeed, most other western countries do their business with very little involvement by the legal profession. Here, lawyers have the kind of closed shop that any union leader would die to have. They have their own act of the legislature, the Legal Professions Act, which not only allows them to decide who will be lawyers and what behaviour will disqualify them but also what to do about other practitioners who might be poaching on their territory. This latter has been relaxed considerably in recent years to allow notaries public more latitude, but that had less to do with generosity on the part of lawyers than it did with their disdain for work that was no longer as profitable as the other stuff they were doing. The cost of dealing with lawyers today is prohibitive. Even the cost of entering their offices has gone out of sight since they got into the habit of pulling out a mike and declaring every breath they take for a client at a minimum of point one of an hour per. But let me explain that "point one" bit for you. Every time a lawyer takes a phone call on a client's behalf, he speaks into a recorder that is hitched up to a master billing system. He says, "To call for Mr. Smith, point one." Now that is minimum. Even if he only says to his opposite number, "Hi Charlie. Is the examination for discovery still on for this afternoon? Good, let's have a drink afterwards," and if this bird is charging his regular $300 per hour, he will be billing his client point one of that $300—or 30 bucks. Anything from ten seconds to sixty seconds costs $30! Only teenage girls stay on the phone for six minutes, but you will get bills for phone calls much longer than that. And remember, if the call takes six minutes and ten seconds, it's a charge of point two of an hour or 60 clams! Now here's the rub: It's only your word against his that he made any of these phone calls or how long he spoke or even if they were on your business or his pleasure.

And there are other difficult-to-refute charges. Conferences are one good way to pad the tab. It is also not hard to put a couple of conversations with a junior or a partner or the other side's lawyer on the slate. Some lawyers even charge for secretaries bringing them your file, and it is not unknown for a lawyer to charge for preparing the bill!

Any time a lawyer goes to court there's a charge. It may be a visit to chambers, the place where a judge or master sits to deal with interlocutory or interim matters. It may and often is just a matter of routine such as getting an order in a civil case for a jury trial. But sometimes these visits are not so routine and involve lengthy arguments with other counsel, and that's a grand way to run the bill up because here they aren't charging their hourly rate but their court appearance rate, which is, of course, much higher.

Examinations for discovery are a marvelous way to turn a tawdry little "tuppenny-ha'penny case," as the Brits call them, into a nifty little moneymaker. This process permits your lawyer to cross-examine the other guy and his lawyer to cross-examine you under oath, during which, it is hoped, vital information and exciting confessions will be extracted to be used at trial. Naturally these things aren't arranged overnight. Many phone calls and letters, all duly recorded in fractions of an hour, are needed to establish when these mini-hearings can be held and where. There are no rules here. You might be going through a hearing where your wife is demanding an increase in alimony. This will mean hour upon hour of oral examination with all your records gone through with a fine-toothed comb. Your accountant will provide your tax returns—at your expense, of course—and all your possessions will be examined as to worth. I went through such a case and it makes going to a dentist for a root canal without anesthetic seem pleasant by comparison.

One of the rules of the examination for discovery is that it ought neither to be a "fishing expedition" nor should the questions be repetitive. But suppose your lawyer thinks that the other guy is on a fishing trip and is being repetitive. Guess how that's resolved? You got it! Off to court to see the judge, and that's when all the foregoing examples of scheduling problems, availability of judges, kids with measles and the lot come into play. Another hearing is held and you get the bill. All these utterances are taken down by a court reporter and transcripts prepared for which the loser of the lawsuit will pay big time. And then let us assume, alas, that you lose the case. You not only must pay your own lawyer but a whacking chunk of the other guy's legal costs, too. At this point your lawyer tells you that the judge was clearly wrong and that you should take the matter to the court of appeal. Here the possibilities for running up the bill are a bit limited because there are likely to be fewer interlocutory matters and adjournments, though they do happen. What does run up the tab are appeal books, the entire transcript of the proceedings at trial. These can cost many thousands of dollars, and if you lose, you'll be paying for the other side's transcripts too. Far cheaper to buy all the bestsellers of the past couple of decades than to pay for the transcripts of all that crap heard in the court below, but without the transcript you can't get your case heard by the court of appeal. But for God's sake, don't even dream of going to the Supreme Court of Canada, which is about $3,500 business-class airfare away for your lawyer, plus another $3,500 for his junior.

But I have saved the best for last. Courts are crowded places and require the attendance of three people—your lawyer, the other guy's lawyer and a judge. Invariably, calendars clash and your lawyer must hie to the courthouse to get an adjournment of the matter. Now the last thing you wanted was an adjournment, but the other lawyer's kids have come down with pellagra so an adjournment he must have, and that costs you money. It doesn't cost either lawyer a penny; *au contraire*, they make money out of adjourning it. Sometimes it is the judge who is sick or—and this happens a lot—the judge says he's sorry but due to a scheduling problem he can't sit on your case today and he knows everyone will understand. The problem is that he is, as legal terminology puts it—"seized of the matter," that is, since the trial has already started, you must all go home and wait for him to be available again, which may mean months. Meanwhile, the lawyer adds another half day in court onto your bill. Adjournments happen frequently these days. Lawyers are evidently much busier than they were in my time and, like airlines, they overbook. As do judges. When those overbookings cause scheduling problems, everyone in the courtroom is kind and polite for they are all being paid by you whether as client or taxpayer.

Then there is the length of the trial and the payment of witnesses. Your lawyer and the other guy's lawyer will estimate how long the trial will last, and thus you know how many days you'll be paying to watch them at work. This is also supposed to help you estimate the cost, but the estimates are seldom accurate and never on the short side. Witnesses can't be found or get sick or their planes are late or they thought it was tomorrow they were to appear. The costs of these witnesses are, of course, paid by the litigants, and if you lose, mostly by you.

By this point, you may have got the hang of it. This isn't "piece work" your lawyer is doing. He's not like a berry picker who only gets paid when he delivers a bucket of berries. The incentive for the lawyer is to do as many money-producing things as he can in a case, and it matters not a whit that what he does has no value to you. He does it and you pay.

What all this means is that going to law is for the rich only.

No matter how just your cause, the courtroom is not for you unless yours is an injury case and your lawyer will take it on a contingency basis, that is to say, take a percentage of your winnings. Assuming that you win, of course. It demonstrates a huge failing in our system for, if only the rich can use it, it is not only useless to those who are not rich but allows those who are to "money whip" those who are not. It's a national disgrace—no, an international disgrace—that the court system is reserved for the well-to-do. (Though even the rich have their reservations about it. An English nobleman was once advised by his solicitor to sue. He replied, "No. I've already been ruined twice in my life—once when I lost a lawsuit, the other when I won.") Many chief justices have tried to streamline procedures, but alas they have most often simply aggravated the problem. For example, there is now a mandatory pre-trial conference where the judge explores the possibility of settlement and, if that proves unlikely, to get the lawyers to admit some facts in order to eliminate the need for them to be proved. This process may or may not help. I fear that many times it just adds one more procedure lawyers can charge their clients for. Moreover, the unintended consequence is that instead of settling earlier (the traditional time for this was after examinations for discovery and the exchange of medical reports), the inclination now is to go before the beak and perhaps get a preview of what he thinks of the case.

I raise one final matter with some reluctance. There is no training for judges. At present they are selected because they are eminent lawyers—which is helpful but scarcely definitive of the matter because being a judge isn't like being a lawyer. The new judge may have done little or no court work. And if he did court work, he may not have done much other than, say, divorces but no criminal law.

The entire situation cries out for reform. Some improvements have been made, especially in the area of voluntary arbitration. The trouble is that this has become most useful once again for the well-off. There isn't a good arbitration system for ordinary people. An exception to this statement must be made, however, for the small claims division of the provincial court. For cases involving $25,000 or less, citizens without the aid of a lawyer (in fact, they are rightly discouraged from using a lawyer) can have their day in court, and there is a compulsory settlement conference in front of the judge. It seems to me that the more the jurisdiction of this court can be practically expanded the better. There is no reason why the limit cannot be raised to $100,000 or even more, permitting reasonably serious personal injury cases to be tried. After all, the criminal division of this same court decides 90 percent of the criminal cases in the country. And the judges on the provincial court, of which the small claims division is part, have a hell of a lot more street smarts than the well-to-do Supreme Court judge whose entire contact with the people is at a ritzy club for a tax deductible lunch or a martini or two.

The "rule of law" has become a bad joke because the people have effectively been denied access to the courts of the country. It's little wonder that courts, judges and especially lawyers are held in such low esteem.

Piss-offs

Things that piss me off:

Women and dogs who, just as you've settled into your La-Z-Boy chair—properly tilted, with a drink on the table, book in hand—announce in their own way that since you don't appear to be doing anything, would you mind just et cetera, et cetera. Parking ticket meters where, if you can make the damned thing work at all, you ought to get a prize. Financial experts who moan when the dollar is down and set their hair on fire when it goes up, using whichever is handy to explain why your savings plan lost all that money last year. Being considered part of "the West" by central Canadian politicians and *Globe and Mail* writers. Christians who say that I am not a Christian because I don't agree with their version of Christianity. Speed traps and the cops that use them. Sheila Copps just for being Sheila Copps. Papers that refer to people like me, who do twice as much work as any of them, as "elderly." Rear view mirrors that say "objects are much closer than the appear," to which I ask, why? Toronto the attitude, not Toronto the city. Huge corporate welfare bums like Bombardier. Journalists making jokes about mental illness and the medicines mental health patients use. Being accused of anti-Semitism for criticizing Israel and its bully boy, Prime Minister Sharon. TransLink, which has no direct connection to the public and is afraid to put the RAV line to a plebiscite. The BC Liberals who intentionally bugger up the environment so as to split the Left votes. The federal Liberals, period. The Vancouver Airport that continued to collect money for improving the airport after it was done. Whistler-and-back sports utility vehicles travelling the Sea to Sky Highway at unbelievable speeds and all too often causing deaths and serious injury so they can get to their chalets and martinis three minutes faster. Places called "service stations" where there is no service. Growing old. Hell, being old! Electronic equipment that doesn't mark the buttons so you can read them without getting down on your hands and knees with a flashlight. TV "clickers" that give me anything other than the ability to change the channel and the volume, which is all I want. CDs that have the price labels right over the names of the songs and the part that says whether or not it has been re-mastered and, if so, to what degree. CDs that look great but don't tell you whether or not they are re-mastered. CD shops that pay only token attention to jazz and "easy listening" (you know you're old when you find Elvis Presley in the "easy listening" section). CD cases generally. People who don't like dogs, especially chocolate labs. Computers that lock. Spam. Telephones in general but especially ones that have a sales person or a pollster on the other end. The "help" command on the computer, which is the very last place to go if you need help. Toilet paper that won't roll freely and give you enough to get the job done without your fingers getting directly involved. The air in airplanes that exchanges your health for lower fuel consumption by the plane. Smoking outside restaurants, which means that on nice days only the smokers get to enjoy the sunshine. People reading over my shoulder. Classical music that has bits too low to hear and other bits too loud to hear. Big bookstores. People who, when traffic is merging from two lanes to one, always try and often succeed squeezing in before their turn, thus buggering up the rhythm. And those who won't let you merge when it's your turn. Servers in restaurants who interrupt right at the punch line of a joke you're telling. Lining up anywhere, anytime for anything. People who eat steak-and-kidney pie anywhere in my smell zone. Even within my sight. The same with fried liver. People who ask about or comment upon your weight. Dinners where all anyone talks about is the diseases and deaths that have recently occurred to those around you. Receptionists in medical and dental offices who call you by your first name. This is especially a piss-off when you are actually called by your second name. Policemen who do the same. Doctors and doctors' receptionists who forget who the paying customer is in the relationship. The *Globe and Mail* which, despite the fact it's a Toronto paper and not a very good one at that, calls itself "Canada's National Newspaper." Right wingers who think the poor like it that way. Drivers who ride your ass when you're obeying a construction area speed limit. Highway signs that say, "Watch for Falling Rock" or "Blasting Area, Proceed with Caution." What the hell are you supposed to do about that boulder rocketing down the hill or the sudden explosion that sends you to kingdom come? Signs on the backs of cars saying "Baby Onboard." Who cares if they've got a brat? I've had a few of them myself. Politicians (which is to say, all of them) who can't see past the next budget or at best past the next election date. The star candidate lured by the premier and parachuted into a safe riding with both premier and candidate vigorously denying that the star has been offered a cabinet post. Court of Appeal judges and presidents of the CBC who deny they don't have a cabinet post assured and pretending they just can't wait to get into the BC legislature and warm their bums on the backbench! The fact that wild animals you don't want to die off—such as whales, bears and tigers—do die off and imported animals—such as the Australian possum in New Zealand, rabbits in Australia, and rats in Hawaii—are indestructible. The fact that visionaries may accidentally get into government but never run them. And that those who would use the environment for profit don't have to prove they will do so without adverse impact and that this proof is left to ordinary citizens. Rapists of the environment who are never charged and, if they are charged and convicted—such as BC's fish farmers, get their money returned to them. Car horns that only students of Braille could find when it's time to blow the horn at that idiot who just cut you off. Christians and especially fellow Anglicans who get so worked up about homosexuality. What are they afraid of? People who double park and think that their "hazard lights" give them the right to do so. People who cheat and use handicapped parking when they aren't. Cocktail parties. People who come up to me in restaurants and want to know why I said what I did in an editorial. People who think that just because the water is still there that the fish are, too. Governments that don't police the environment or charge environmental miscreants and dump on them hard. Fish farms and fish farmers. Politicians who think that being elected confers wisdom, but especially politicians who become cabinet ministers and think that their new "honourable" means they know how to run, for example, BC Hydro. PR flacks, especially those who make a disaster seem like the person responsible for it has actually conferred a benefit on the public. Politicians' aides who act as if they themselves are important when it's doubtful that even their employers are. Pilots who interrupt your sleep with the breathtaking news that you're over Lake Athabaska. Flight attendants who keep running into you with the drinks trolley. Fellow passengers who want to talk when you want to read and vice versa. Announcers in airports and train stations (especially British ones) who are loud but utterly incomprehensible.

Part Eight

A SPORTING LIFE

The End of a Pastime

Not long ago, during an interview with an animal rights activist, I announced that I was no longer fishing. Before I tell you why I made this decision, let me tell you about my sports fishing history and why, if there is a cross-examination at the Pearly Gates, I will need a very good barrister indeed.

There are pictures of me around the age of four or five fishing for shiners off the wharf at Granthams Landing, just as my dad had done before me when he was young. There is another of me on Keats Island, where our little family used to picnic on those days when we went salmon fishing with our bamboo salmon rods, cotton lines and catgut leader. I'm holding, very proudly, two small grilse caught on my hand-line, which at that age was all I was permitted to use because rods and reels were only for grown-ups. During my teenage summer days at Woodlands I caught shiners and sea perch then used the shiners as live bait to catch rock cod. I filleted the cod, sold the meat locally, and used the cod heads in the crab net.

I remember catching my first steelhead in the Nanaimo River back in the '50s. I was so afraid that I would lose it I threw myself on it as I pulled it ashore. Trouble was, I was wearing my only suit and was on my way to Victoria on business. I remember the wonderful days in the Atnarko and Bella Coola rivers when the steelhead were so plentiful the fishing was rather boring.

Over the years, and especially after I moved to Kamloops in 1969, I went to flies only and started tying my own, the latter giving me enormous pleasure until fairly recently. In fact, I became not bad at it, although when I took lessons from the legendary, late Jack Shaw in Kamloops, he rightly pronounced me his worst ever student. At least my flies caught fish and I became the tyer for a number of friends.

I had some wonderful days—and some not so wonderful—on my favourite river in New Zealand, the Tauranga-Taupo, where the name I gave to an upriver pool, Cathedral Pool, stuck. I remember with pleasure and bitterness losing a 45-pound chinook after an hour chasing him in a jet boat. I was using a nine-foot number eight fly rod with eight-pound test leader because I'd been fishing for the much smaller sockeye. How did I lose him? The nail knot connecting the leader to the line came loose. It had been tied on by my young guide against my wish to tie it myself. I admit I was just a bit cross, having come so close to doing the utterly impossible and having my hopes dashed not by the fish but by my guide. I've spent many a happy hour on the lakes of BC, the lochs and lochans of Scotland and Ireland and the beaches of the Sunshine Coast fishing for sea-run cutthroat.

So what happened?

All sports fishermen, I daresay, ask themselves if what they are doing is right. They are not fishing for the table out of necessity and they are fishing with equipment that makes it impossible for them to quickly reel in and kill the fish. They want to "play the fish."

For me I suppose it was decades ago that I began hating the killing process. Every fish I killed was just a teeny bit harder than the last one. Then catch-and-release became the fashion and I was saved! No longer did I have to kill my prey so my conscience was clear, that is, until I read a book by the late and famous British fly fisherman, Hugh Falkus, who was sharply critical of the releasing of fish. His point was not one of conservation; he limited his own take to what he could put on his table. No, Falkus made the disturbing observation that if you don't kill the fish, you have simply played with him cruelly as a cat does with a mouse. I didn't agree with Mr. Falkus, not because I could demonstrate he was wrong, but because I didn't want to deal with his argument.

For years I subscribed to British fly-fishing magazines, and over time one by one they took the editorial position that to be consistent, we fishermen and women had to support hunting, both for game and with hounds for the fox. Again I rejected these arguments because I didn't want to deal with them. Fox hunting? Agggh! Wasn't it Oscar Wilde who called it "the unspeakable in full pursuit of the uneatable?" Besides, didn't some scientist or other say that fish don't feel pain? But I knew deep down that the editors were right.

Then I had something happen that I'd seen before, except this time it shook me. I was landing a fish in the Tauranga-Taupo, and two other fish swam alongside my prey, following it to my net. It just did something to me. That was five years ago and something else happened on the same trip. My wife Wendy and I went for dinner at a fish and game club near Whangoroa and saw these beautiful marlin strung by their tails, and we felt ill. How could anyone kill such magnificent beasts?

So I've decided not to fish anymore. Whatever pleasure it gives is more than offset by the realization that I was still tormenting one of God's creatures for personal pleasure. But let me make this clear: I'm not telling others what they should do. This is a personal thing. I still eat meat though I have dabbled with vegetarianism for health reasons. I still wear shoes made from leather. I can't see that I would ever stop eating shellfish, though I never thought I would quit fishing either. I'm not going to throw stones into pools where others are fishing nor am I going to clang horns to scare the deer away. I have no sermons to preach and no demonstrations in mind. It's just that somehow the thrill of tossing a dry fly of my own invention and manufacture at a rising fish and hooking it now gives me more pain than pleasure.

And when that happens, it's checkout time.

The Forgotten Hero

Every year we remember Terry Fox and his gallant attempt to run across Canada to raise money for cancer research. Terry, as we know, couldn't finish his trip because of a recurrence of cancer that on June 26, 1981, took his young, courageous life. The annual Terry Fox Run and other endeavours of the Terry Fox Foundation have raised several hundreds of millions of dollars for cancer research over the years. Terry was awarded the Order of Canada and was declared the most famous Canadian of the 20th Century by Macleans Magazine in 1999 and second greatest Canadian (#1 went to Tommy Douglas) by the CBC in 2004. He rightly remains an ongoing inspiration to all who suffer, especially cancer patients.

But there was a sidebar tragedy, a companion story to Terry's run, which occurred in 1984 and now seems utterly forgotten. That year I was doing a midnight to 2 a.m. talk show and we got wind of a young man named Steve Fonyo who was trying to complete Terry's ambition of crossing Canada on one leg and an artificial limb. Steve, you see, was in the same physical situation Terry was in. He, too, had lost a leg to cancer at 13. A Vernon kid, he was a rough diamond but plucky as hell. On March 31, 1984, he went to St. Johns, Newfoundland, dipped his artificial limb in the water and started his run across Canada. During the run we kept in touch and did some clips with him from time to time, and when he took time off, he came into the studio for longer interviews.

It was strange following Steve's progress. It was almost as if he was resented for trying to do what Terry Fox had been prevented from doing. The media coverage until he reached Thunder Bay was almost nil, and the only Vancouver media that stayed with him and interviewed him along the way was my show. When on May 29, 1985, Steve dipped his artificial leg into the Pacific at Victoria, he had completed that which Terry certainly would have done if he had lived. The press coverage was there but tentative, almost as if the media was too embarrassed to do too much for fear they would be seen as disrespectful of Terry's memory. There was no denying, however, that Steve Fonyo had not only done what Terry couldn't do but raised $13 million for cancer research while he was at it.

Steve Fonyo did receive an Order of Canada but it seemed he was being hit from both sides—he had trouble handling the attention he got while at the same time he believed he wasn't getting his due. The real problem was that he wasn't Terry Fox, who had, in addition to enormous courage, good looks and charisma. You couldn't help but be drawn to him. Steve, on the other hand, while by no means ugly, didn't have that tousled hair, that bearing and the movie-star looks.

Not long after he got home, Steve began to drink and he was nailed for impaired driving.

During that time I tried to counsel Steve without success and he wound up in court on sixteen charges, including assault with a weapon, fraud, theft and firearms offences. Fonyo simply stated, "I am very sorry for the crimes I have done." The Judge took into account the problems Steve had been thorugh and obviously understood the stress and strain and he was given an 18-month, conditional sentence, meaning that he would stay out of jail unless he breached any of a lengthy list of court-ordered conditions. Fonyo has, by all accounts, overcome his substance abuse problems and seems to have overcome his quick rise to fame and the repercussions it caused a young man. He has studied aircraft engine maintenance and earned his helicopter pilot license. He now works and lives near Cultus Lake.

Clearly, Steve suffered from depression and how much of it was caused by his run and the public reaction is hard to say. I wouldn't want to leave the impression that the media and public shunned Steve, because they didn't. I think the problem with Steve was that he thought if he surpassed Terry's accomplishment people would love and respect him and that he would be a hero forever. It didn't work out that way, and I know from my interviews with him so many years ago that he felt a certain resentment. I have no doubt that he was self-medicating with booze and drugs. As mentioned, Steve has completely rehabilitated himself from his days of substance abuse and trouble with the law. Yes, he had his problems and he did not suit the role of hero as well as Terry Fox did, but I think Steve should be recognized for the hero he was and the courageous man he became thereafter. Not for one second would I diminish Terry Fox's achievement. I just think that Steve Fonyo was also a hero, first class, and ought to be remembered and recognized as such.

Baseball

Baseball is the greatest team sport of them all. No argument. It's the best by a country kilometre.

But, say you, you're a Canadian, Rafe! How can you possibly put baseball ahead of ice hockey? Or soccer, for that matter. Isn't soccer the most popular team game in the world?

Of course, it is. And there will be those who see college football on a cold crisp autumn as the *ne plus ultra* of athletic experiences, and some will plump for rugby. But I have to say, sorry, you're all out to lunch. It's baseball and ol' Uncle Rafe will tell you why.

To begin with, the basic design of baseball is so symmetrical. The diamond, laid out by Alexander Cartwright (I once dated his granddaughter, to which you may attribute my crass prejudice, I suppose) is no less than perfect, and where it is a bit flawed, it doesn't matter. The distance between home plate and first base is just right so that a sharply hit ball to the infield means an easy out, a not so sharply one may be safely run out, and a bunt or ball hit in an awkward place will bring intense excitement or pain, depending on who you're pulling for. If there is a man on first, the distances are such that a sharply hit ground ball in the infield, depending on where it's hit and the skills of the infielders, brings or doesn't bring a double play. Can there be a more exciting moment than the three seconds or so it takes to see if the rally is snuffed out or just beginning? Isn't, surely, the infield double play the loveliest sight in sports?

The 90 feet between bases is perfect when a man is on base and is contemplating stealing a base. A fast runner, a slow pitch, an errant throw and the man on first is suddenly on second. The good base stealer on first with a left-handed pitcher brings on a drama all of its own as the pitcher snarls and stares at the runner, daring him to go, while the runner takes more and more liberties, a half-step further, then another half step, then a face-first dive back into first as the pitcher tries to catch him out. But there's more than just the pitcher and the runner. How good is the catcher at taking a curve ball off the plate and then, from a crouched, off-balance position, at firing the ball to second in time for the out? And what about the shortstop or second baseman? Can they move quickly enough and be stoically unafraid of being spiked as the base runner tries to break up the double play? The steal of a base in itself provides drama and skill enough to be a whole game!

There is, of course, the more standard contest between pitcher and batsman. While this waxes and wanes in excitement depending on the state of the contest, it's always interesting to see the pitcher concentrating on the sign from the catcher, sometimes shaking his head, sometimes nodding, with the batter concentrating as if his life depended upon what he did. When this contest comes in a critical situation, a lack of action, the pumping of the pitcher, the bat waggling by the batter can become almost unbearably exciting. And that is one of the great things about baseball—it's an anticipation sport. Some of the most dramatic moments come when absolutely no action is happening.

Because success one-third of the time would make any hitter rich beyond all possible dreams, the base hit itself is an accomplishment. Sometimes, indeed often, the base hit is much more than that; it is a sublime revenge or an unbearable loss. The hit that starts a rally or keeps it going or, most exciting of all, wins the big game thus is precious and never to be forgotten. There was a time, indeed a long time, when the homerun was the only hit one got excited about. But it wasn't always that way because before Babe Ruth, who began his illustrious career as a very good pitcher with the Boston Red Sox during World

War I, the hitting of Cap Anson, Tris Speaker, "Shoeless" Joe Jackson and, of course, the Georgia Peach himself, Ty Cobb, thrilled crowds. With and following Ruth, the slugger became the hero, but even then the smooth double by Joe DiMaggio or the last-minute swing by Hank Aaron, pushing a single to his off-field, brought the crowd to its collective feet. They used to say of Aaron "getting a pitch by Hank Aaron was like sneaking a sunrise past a rooster." And, of course, there was the "Splendid Splinter," "Teddy Ballgame" himself, Ted Williams, perhaps the best hitter of them all. One can only imagine what records would have fallen if Williams had not spent three and a half years in the service in two wars. Now, of course, the "single" has become a thrill again as Ichiro Suzuki has happened upon the Seattle scene.

Everyone has a special memory of batsmanship that sticks in the front lobe of the brain. Mine is 1988. It's game one of the World Series between my beloved Dodgers and the hated As of Oakland, clearly the better of the two teams on paper and on the odds board. In the second-inning Oakland has loaded the bases and Jose Canseco, their feared slugger, is next up to bat. I curse aloud as I hear the announcer say, "There hasn't been a grand slam…" for however long. "Shut up you, bloody idiot!" I cry as the pitch comes in and Canseco knocks it out of the park for that grand slammer. Four zip for the hated A's. But it's the bottom of the ninth and the Dodgers, trailing by one, have one on base with two out and pinch hitter Kirk Gibson at the plate. Now you must know that Gibson is hurting so much that despite his prowess at the plate and on the field, this is the only appearance he will make in the series. It's three and two and the superb reliever Dennis Eckersley throws the perfect pitch for the situation, a curve down and away. Gibson, in obvious pain, reaches out and literally scoops the pitch from the catcher's grasp and poles it over the right field fence for a home run! The Dodgers win game one and go on to beat the hugely favoured As in five. The following year my son got hold of a video of the sports highlights of 1988 and I watched that homer time after time, each time not believing that the wounded Gibson could even reach that pitch much less turn it into so much drama!

In 1951 I was at university and one of my pals, a devoted New York Giants fan, and I, who bled from every pore for the Brooklyn Dodgers, were listening to the third and final game of the playoff that would decide the pennant. We were in the front seat of my car listening to the radio as live TV hadn't reached Vancouver yet. The Dodgers, at one time leading New York by thirteen and a half games, needed some heroics from Jackie Robinson in the last game of the season to hold the Giants to a tie. The Giants had won the first game and the Dodgers had blown them away in game two. Now it was the bottom of the ninth, two out, two on for New York, the hitherto rather undistinguished Scots-born Bobby Thompson at the plate and Dodger ace Ralph Branca on the mound.

Strike one! I heard. Then after a silence, everything went nuts. I heard Red Barber saying, "It's a long fly ball to deep left field...The Giants win the pennant! The Giants win the pennant! The Giants win the pennant!" And so on, ad nauseum. Needless to say, the moment wasn't helped by the screaming of my pal beside me. It was horrible. But it was baseball at its best.

Baseball has been a social issue up close. Until April 1947 no Black in modern times had played in the major leagues. The previous year an outstanding young black man had played for the Montreal Royals in the Triple A International League. He was the batting champion, the best base stealer in the league and was named the league's most valuable player. His name? Jack Roosevelt Robinson. (His brother, in case you like trivia, was runner-up to Jesse Owens in the 200-metre dash at the 1936 Olympics in Berlin.) It's been said that Branch Rickey, the general manager of the Brooklyn Dodgers, was a social reformer. Maybe. But I think he signed Robinson to play for the Dodgers because he saw one hell of a ball player and knew that there were lots more like him in the Negro Leagues.

On opening day of the 1947 season, Jackie Robinson—the first and only black man in the league—kissed his wife Rachel goodbye as he left the apartment for Brooklyn's Ebbets Field and said, "Honey, look for me out there on the field. I'll be wearing number 42!" Under enormous pressure, as no athlete has felt before or since, Jackie Robinson hit .296 and became Rookie of the Year. In 1949 he won the batting title with .349 and was the National League's MVP.

Baseball reflected society in general in those days, and when Jackie Robinson joined the Dodgers, he started a revolution that would see Rosa Parks refuse to go to the back of a bus, and we all know what happened then. When I think of the players we would have missed if the white players who had tried to prevent Robinson from playing had been allowed to have their way, it truly does boggle the mind. Not only no Jackie Robinson but no Willie Mays. Or Joe Morgan? Or Roberto Clemente? Or Ozzie Smith? The list goes on and on of players who made such an impact that you really have to wonder just how good major league ball was when Babe Ruth didn't have to bat against Leroy "Satchel" Paige. When Paige was an old man—likely in his 60s—he was still playing for Portland in the old Pacific Coast League, which was AAA ball. I took my then six-year-old son Ken out to watch him pitch against the Vancouver Mounties so he could say later on that he had seen the best pitcher baseball had ever produced. Paige pitched seven innings, giving up but one earned run before being lifted for a pinch hitter. Quite a show!

Finally, I have two clinching arguments for why baseball is the greatest team sport. First, like no other sport with the exception of fly-fishing, baseball has a terrific literature built up around it. Yes, Grantland Rice did write that line "Outlined against the grey November sky, the four horsemen rode again…" which elevated the Notre Dame backfield of the '20s to a degree of immortality, and there has been good stuff written about boxing. But no one could possibly deny that the best sports literature—literature, not boosterism—arose and continues to rise from baseball. Read some Red Berber, Shirley Povich (a guy, incidentally), Ring Lardner, Roger Kahn, Roger Angell and others and you'll see what I mean.

Read E.L. Thayer's classic "Casey at the Bat." The entire town of Mudville is in the stands. It's the bottom of the ninth, and the mighty Casey, the hero, the man most feared by all pitchers in the game, is at the plate. All will surely come out well. The suspense builds. You can see the scowl on Casey's face as he sneers at the pitcher who is promptly roundly booed by loyal Mudvillers. Then, suddenly, the suspense vanishes like the air from a punctured balloon. "There is no joy in Mudville, Mighty Casey has struck out!"

My second clincher is that baseball is a game everyone can and does play. Look at any company picnic and what do you see? Men, women and kids playing softball. It's everyone's game because it's the best there is.

Oh, yes, I completely forgot the allegations that it takes too long and it's dull. A hockey game, with its endless time-outs for TV ads, takes three hours. A football game, with endless time-outs for ads and stuff, takes three hours. The 2004 Super Bowl took three and three-quarter hours. Baseball takes about three hours.

But there is more. Hockey, football and soccer crowds are mean and ugly. There is something about those games that makes people feel that they have been personally reviled if their team loses. I went to my last football game 20 years ago when, while getting my grandson and I hotdogs, we were met by four drunken hoods who wouldn't let us pass. They had great fun frightening a six-year-old kid and his grandpa half to death. But it isn't just isolated incidents for, even though most crowds are civil, there is an air of antagonism in a football stadium or hockey arena. The language—and God knows I'm no prude—is vile by any standards with no attention paid to the sex or youth of bystanders. Sure, baseball fans want the home team to win, but for the most part there's an air of resignation when defeat comes, as it must often do. There's something about a beer and a hot dog in the bleachers with young kids that always reminds you that it really is only a game and better called a pastime. And I think there is another factor: Even though the score might be lopsided against you, you know that the game is never over until the last pitch. No lead is ever insurmountable, however unlikely a comeback might seem.

I guess the really interesting part of baseball is that whether you are an occasional attender or an aficionado who marks his own scorecard, the time spent is well spent. Without knowing anything about the game, a spectator can marvel at the grace and speed of the game and go home well satisfied. The true fan, on the other hand, can do a complete box score on his own and second guess, with some reason and expertise, every move the manager makes and give him hell if it turns out he was wrong.

There is no game in the world that can catch the attention of everyone like the American League Championship Series between the Red Sox and the Yankees did in 2004. There could scarcely have been a soul in North America, much of the Caribbean and Japan who didn't pull those Sox back from a 3-0 deficit to victory in the seventh game over the mighty Yankees.

Baseball is, simply put, the best.

Profiles from the Locker Room

Tommy Lasorda

I have been a Dodgers fan since I was a child and that covers a lot of ground.

Back in the late '70s the Boys and Girls Club of Kamloops invited Tommy Lasorda to be the guest speaker at their annual banquet. I represented Kamloops in the BC legislature at the time so I was at the head table. The time had come and gone for Tommy's arrival when someone came to the chairman to say that Mr. Lasorda was on the line.

He had started the day in Chicago, but when the plane that was to take him to Seattle—thence Vancouver, thence Kamloops—could not land in Chicago due to a blizzard, he had found a plane already on the ground that could take him to Dallas. From Dallas he flew to San Francisco, then Seattle, then Vancouver, finally Kamloops. He came into the banquet apologizing profusely for being an hour late. No one would have blamed him for a second had he canceled the engagement. I've seen a lot of standing ovations in my life but nothing could match that one. He went on to give a wonderful talk, mostly to the kids, and had them rolling in the aisles then listening very carefully as he gave them advice on living through their youth to adulthood.

We tend to think of jocks as greedy, inarticulate boors—which some of them are. But Tommy Lasorda, by any yardstick, is a class act and a gentleman, and so say all of those at that Boys and Girls Club annual dinner.

Don Larsen

In October 1956 the Yankees beat my beloved Dodgers 2-0. That wasn't a big deal but not only did Yankee pitcher Don Larsen throw a no-hitter but not a single Bum reached first base. A perfect game. Now there I was in October 1983 interviewing the great man himself. He was the soul of grace and friendliness. He took me through the game and its emotions pitch by pitch to the point where the Yankee catcher Yogi Berra jumped on him with a bear hug that would have killed most men.

As the interview ended, I—who had endured with a mix of hatred and envy every pitch he threw in that famous game— said, "Don, like many others I thought that third pitch to the last batter, Dale Mitchell, should have been called a ball." Larson snarled, "It was a goddam strike, goddam it, and I don't give a good goddam what sportswriters and Dodger fans think!"

I got the impression he'd heard the line before and it wasn't one of his all-time favourites!

Enos Slaughter

The same day I interviewed Don Larsen I also had Enos Slaughter on the show. He was a great player who had finished up with the Yankees after a long and illustrious career with the St. Louis Cardinals. His greatest claim to fame came in the 1946 World Series between the Cards and the Boston Red Sox. In the top of the ninth Slaughter scored from first base on a double by Harry "The Hat" Walker, mainly because Boston's shortstop, Johnny Pesky, delayed with the relay home. The run held up in the bottom of the ninth and the Cards won the Series.

But Slaughter was known for other things. In 1947 Jackie Robinson became the first black playor in the majors. At their first meeting, the Card players, led by Slaughter and Harry Walker, threatened to strike if Robinson was to take the field against them. The league commissioner, Albert "Happy" Chandler, was a southerner and had scarcely distinguished himself as commissioner. Now here he was with the Dodgers general manager, Branch Rickey, on one side and the Cards general manager, Sam Breadon, breathing down his neck on the other. What the hell was he to do? But events sometimes make the man, and Chandler told the Cardinals to take the field or it would be the last game of major league ball they would ever play. The Cards took the field. Meanwhile, in Brooklyn, Harry Walker's brother, outfielder Dixie Walker (called the "People's Cherce" because he was so popular) announced that he and pitcher Kirby Higbe didn't want Robinson as a teammate. "Right," said Branch Rickey. "Don't give it another thought," and he shipped them both unceremoniously to the lowly Pittsburgh Pirates.

After I'd let Slaughter tell my listeners all about his illustrious career, I asked him about the double Jackie Robinson had hit over his shoulder to win a game in the 1956 series. Slaughter growled that he had lost it in the lights. I then sweetly asked if the reason he wasn't in the Hall of Fame was because of the time he had slid into first (!) and deliberately spiked the first baseman who happened to be Jack Roosevelt Robinson. Slaughter growled, "I didn't deliberately spike that Nigra!"

A great ballplayer, a certified bigot and a man who had to wait until he was old before the veterans' committee finally let him into the Baseball Hall of Fame at Cooperstown, which would no doubt have welcomed him earlier had he behaved better.

An unpleasant bugger, if you ask me.

Tommy Bolt

Tommy "Thunder" Bolt, winner of the 1958 US Open and one of the finest ever golf swingers, was once asked who was the better golfer, Jack Nicklaus or Ben Hogan. After a pause, he said, "I've seen Jack Nicklaus out on the practice tee watching Ben Hogan but I've never seen Ben Hogan on the practice tee watching Jack Nicklaus." Tommy Bolt idolized his good friend Hogan.

It can only be speculated how many majors Tommy Bolt would have won if he'd been able to keep his temper under control, a temper I saw up close at a pro-am golf tournament at the Royal Victoria Golf Club in Oak Bay. The other pro with us was Bob Rosburg, a former winner of the PGA and long-time golf commentator on TV. We were watching when, on a short par three on the back nine, Tommy (who had not had a good day) missed the green and stomped off toward the clubhouse.

For all that, he was fun to watch, and Bob Rosburg's hilarious stories of the golf tour made the day for me.

Rick Hansen

I met Rick Hansen in my tenth-floor studio at the old Holiday Inn on Hastings Street. I was doing the midnight to 2 a.m. and it was 1 a.m. when he came in. No one else in the talk show business was interested in the story of this "Man in Motion" who was going to go around the world in his wheelchair. But I was interested, and Rick told my tiny audience of his plans. Fast forward to a sunny day when Rick Hansen, having successfully completed his amazing journey was being courted by all the talk show hosts. No, said Rick. First it's Rafe because he alone showed interest when no one else did.

A class act.

Maurice "Rocket" Richard

The "Rocket," Maurice Richard, was a hero of mine, big time. I hated the Toronto Maple Leafs with a passion and he embodied that hatred. As a sports fan, my finest moment came in game four of the 1960 Stanley Cup in which the Habs beat the Leafs four straight (winning the Stanley in eight straight) when the Rocket scored the fourth and final goal in a 4-0 game.

To say that Richard had a tempestuous career would be to put it mildly. A high point was the riot in Montreal on March 17, 1955, triggered by his suspension for slugging a linesman. In the late '60s I watched him in an old-timers game at the Vancouver Coliseum and will never forget seeing him, sent in the clear, miss beating Terry Sawchuk, then smashing his stick on the ice in anger. Just an old-timers exhibition game but the competitiveness was still there. None who watched will forget the 12-minute standing ovation he got in the ceremony marking the end of the old Forum in Montreal.

I interviewed the Rocket in the nineties when he was touring on behalf of the prostate cancer people. It was a tough interview because he was very shy. I don't remember much of our conversation but I did become aware that here was a very charismatic person, and I understood why the people of Quebec saw him as a leader. It was also why a few years later he was given what amounted to a state funeral.

He may not have been as good as Gordie Howe, but for my money, in a tight spot like an overtime Stanley Cup game, the Rocket would be my number one choice on the ice, and that contest isn't even close.

Bobby Orr

I interviewed Bobby Orr twice and he was, like Jean Beliveau and Tiger Woods, one of those rare athletes who could actually think something out and present it in good English.

On air I took Bobby back to the 1971 Stanley Cup between his invincible Boston Bruins and the no longer invincible Montreal Canadiens. It was, I recollect, game four in Boston and the Bruins went into the last period up 5-1. Then summoning up the ghosts of the past, I suppose, Montreal scored six unanswered goals to win 7-5. The next game was in Montreal and that was the game I wanted to talk about. "You were the team of the century," I reminded Bobby, "but the Habs blew you out 8-3. What the hell happened?"

Orr gave that boyish grin of his. "We never had a chance. When the Canadiens came on the ice, it was like an electrical storm inside that Forum. You could cut the atmosphere with a knife. Even in the warm-up the Habs were skating like the game was on. I went over to Yvan Cornoyer and asked him why he was skating so hard, and he replied, 'Bobbee, zee wind is at zee back tonight!'" Incidentally, the Canadiens won the sixth and final game 4-2 in Boston and went on the beat Chicago in seven games to win the Cup.

Bobby Orr? Not only the greatest player ever but a gentleman prepared to revisit the bad as well as the good. Super guy.

Ken Dryden

Back about 1977 I attended a constitutional conference at McGill University in Montreal as BC's minister responsible for the Constitution. Sitting next to me was Ken Dryden and I got to know him in a chatty sort of way. I could tell very quickly that, although this man was a great athlete, he also had quite a mind.

After Ken left hockey, I interviewed him on my show several times when he was on tour promoting one of his books, the most well-known being *The Game*. I remember asking him if he sometimes viewed the game he was in with a certain detachment. I reminded him of the pictures of him standing, gloves on top of his stick, as he watched the action at the other end of the arena. He said he did. He mused about the meaning of hockey, the meaning of life and social things of that sort. I was surprised not only that he thought so deeply about social issues but also that he was able to articulate them so well. But I was not surprised to see him take on senior posts nor to see him promoted to the federal cabinet when he was just a rookie MP.

When he eventually retires, it's my bet that his bio will tell more about his public life than his hockey career.

Part Nine

THE LIGHTER SIDE

Benny Goodman

One should be very careful when questioning someone else's taste. My father was once asked by his then best friend (who was also one of my godfathers) what he thought of the girl he loved and was about to marry. My dad told him. They never spoke again.

Music is a lot like girlfriends—or boyfriends, for that matter—it's a matter of individual taste or (he says nastily) the lack of it. My ever-growing love of what is sometimes called classical music (some arrogantly call it "serious" music, as if Duke Ellington wasn't serious!) came late in life, so I am only beginning to work my way through what is a concerto, what it a symphony and why so many violins.

I have written about my love of music in the past and I see that I change my mind with some frequency. This is not as air-headed as it may appear (though, for that matter, it could be), but I think reflects the greater availability of past excellence on digitally re-mastered CDs. My recent acquisitions have put Benny Goodman in a new light and I have discovered how much of my "music memory" was owed to him. The latest catalyst to this re-writing of my musical history came by accident two years ago when Wendy and I were in our favourite classical music shop right at the South Kensington Underground station. (Unhappily the shop recently went under, though certainly not for lack of business from us!) This shop had some neat jazz stuff, often under the Naxos label. On this occasion Wendy, a better snooper by far than I, asked me if I'd ever seen this? "Seen what, woman?" I said with some impatience, then saw she had in her hand a boxed set of 20—yes, 20!—Benny Goodman CDs from all eras and all aggregations. I went to the young man at the desk like a flash, afraid someone would snatch it from my hand crying "Eureka!" and I asked him about the quality of the disks. "Are they digitally re-mastered?"

"Damned if I know," was the reply.

"May I break the seal and listen to one?" I begged.

"Afraid not. I just work here and the guv'nor wouldn't like it."

Believe it or not, the whole boxed set was less than 20 quid, so I said to my bride. "Bride, what the Hell, let's take a chance. Columbus did!"

Our hotel, Jurys, has a CD player, making my purchase of a portable the year before a big waste of money, so I tried them. Magnificent! Great sound! Benny moved up the line of my all-time favourites faster than Tiger can catch an opponent.

So-called "popular music" is a term as difficult or perhaps more difficult to define than "classical music." For these purposes, I will define it as the noise you heard during your hopping hormones years, a noise that—now that your hormones are crawling if they're moving at all—provides you with "music memories." I'll refine that further by saying I mean the real music memories, not the stuff you sang around the beach bonfire or the novelty tunes you remember during those spontaneous musical trivia games that are so much fun for those of a certain age when the spirit and spirits move you to think back to a time that in retrospect seems to have been so carefree.

My music memories are from the "swing era," but that also is as hard an expression to define as "classical music." I say that because strictly speaking "swing" cannot be defined "strictly speaking." The man known as the "King of Swing," Benny Goodman, was actually a jazz virtuoso, and to include him with, say, Sammy Kaye, Guy Lombardo or Wayne King is ludicrous. But if Benny Goodman was a jazz artist, not a swing bandleader, where does that put Glenn Miller? And Tommy Dorsey? And what about Count Basie, Woody Herman and the great Duke Ellington? Without too much exaggeration, given a few lessons I could play the trombone as well as Glenn Miller or, for that matter, the clarinet as well as Woody Herman, but Miller was no Guy Lombardo. His music was different. And where do you slot Tommy Dorsey or his brother Jimmy who played Miller-like swing but some pretty jazzy stuff, too? Probably the best example of a man who was a jazz perfectionist yet a commercial turncoat was Nat "King" Cole, who went from being one of the greatest jazz pianists of all time and the inspiration for the great Canadian pianist Oscar Peterson to a flogger of love songs and even a few novelty hits. I think, as I ramble, I am saying that one should shy away from labels and simply talk about what one remembers with great fondness. One of my favorite male vocalists, a man I got to know a bit personally, was Frankie Laine, who did some great jazz stuff in his earlier years, as possessors of his classic jazz recording with Buck Clayton will know. Unfortunately, after his lifelong pal and pianist, Carl Fischer, died, people like Mitch Miller came along to produce awful crap like "Mule Train" and even western stuff, and it took more than a bit of imagination for the kid from east Chicago to put his heart into it.

My teen years—when every love was true love to last all time—came in the interregnum between the swing era and rock and roll. "King" Cole was still doing jazz but he was experimenting with in-between stuff like "It's only a Paper Moon," "Route 66" and "Straighten Up and Fly Right" and the strange but hugely popular "Nature Boy." He did a marvelous duet with June Christy called "Nat Meets June" which in many ways epitomized the lull that was taking place as big bands and big expenses were being replaced by the band singer gone single, Frank Sinatra and Ella Fitzgerald being two pretty good examples.

There was some really neat stuff in those years from roughly from 1946 to 1950. Johnny Mercer became a bit of a singer in addition to being, perhaps, the best lyricist of his time. Stan Kenton and Duke Ellington (whose singer, Maria Ellington— no relation—was to become Nat "King" Cole's second wife and the mother of the magnificent Natalie) tried to keep the big band going with new methods, but they played to an enthusiastic but aging and diminishing crowd. One of my favourites during that era was a little lady from Seattle named Ella Mae Morse who, with Freddy Slack and his orchestra made the best boogie woogie of them all, the 1947 "House of Blue Lights." (Slack, with Will Bradley, did the second best boogie woogie called "Down the Road Apiece," later reprised by Ella Mae and Freddy Slack's orchestra as "A Little Further Down the Road Apiece.") I should be careful here because people will remember Albert Ammons and Pete Johnson, Meade Lux Lewis and Jack Fina's blockbuster 1945 version of "Bumble Boogie," a wonderful production which boogies up Rimsky-Korsakov's "Flight of the Bumble Bee." Incidentally, if you want a haunting wartime "torch" ballad, try Ella Mae and "Hey, Mr. Postman."

There were many, many wonderful artists of the swing era and they all have, justifiably, fans who say they were the greatest without question. Having conceded that, allow me to nominate my "greatest." Bear in mind that I think the greatest single performer of my era was Nat "King" Cole; even his crap, of which there is an abundance, makes good listening. But the greatest—a little fanfare please!—was Benny Goodman. Perhaps he wasn't as good a clarinetist as Artie Shaw but he was a good enough clarinetist to play by invitation with some of the best symphony orchestras of his day. And I don't say his bands were any better than lots of others. But I contend that the Benny Goodman Quartet when it consisted of the great man on clarinet, Teddy Wilson on piano, Gene Krupa on drums and the incomparable Lionel Hampton on vibes was as good as it ever got. Goodman, though not the first to combine blacks and whites, was a pioneer in colour-blind music with Wilson and Hampton, blacks, combining with the Polish Krupa and the Jewish Goodman. I have no idea how many songs they recorded, but I have more than a hundred and I'm still finding more. I suppose that Benny Goodman's musical epitaph will be the great Carnegie Hall Concert of 1938, the "masters" of which came serendipitously into daylight in the late 1950s and featured the members of his quartet and such other luminaries as Harry James. But for me it's the quartet.

What is my best live "music memory?" That's hard to say because I saw so many of them, ranging from the wonderful-to-listen-to Mills Brothers to Ella, Sarah, Louis and Nat "King" Cole. But there is one night in about 1953 that sticks in the memory. It was in the old Denman Auditorium, now long gone, and it was a triple-header—George Shearing, the marvelous, blind English pianist, followed by Count Basie and his Orchestra and finished off with Billy Eckstine. A fantastic night. A close second, which I have related elsewhere, would be the Saturday matinee by Ella to which only a handful of kids showed up, and Ella asked us all to sit on stage with her while for two whole hours she sang whatever we asked for.

The main difference between then and now, I think, is that back then most, though not all, of the performances were in night clubs, while it is all concerts now and they lack the intimacy the smoke-filled night clubs provided. However, as I digest my music memories, I find that the good ones are always with me.

Scots Wha' Hae

Everyone wishes he were a Scot…c'mon, admit it now! The Scots are the people who built the empire. They were the most feared fighters in the world, with the possible exception of the Gurkhas. They had a culture that vastly exceeded the English except in one respect—the English wrote all the histories and saved the good bits for themselves.

While I'm of Scots descent on both sides, I am English, too. Through my maternal grandmother I'm descended from the Leigh family of southern England, especially the Isle of Wight. One of my direct ancestors was an editor of *Punch Magazine* and has his name carved on the famous Punch desk that used to be in the Punch Tavern on Fleet Street and may still be, for all I know. Through the Leighs I'm related to the Spencers and the Churchills and descended from the Drakes of Devon (Francis had no children so no one is directly descended from him). But actual descent isn't as important as what you feel you are, and I am a Scot descended from the Mairs of Banffshire and the Macdonalds of Skye. The hair on the back of my neck rises when I hear the bagpipes, especially "Scotland the Brave." That sound immediately has me ready to go to war—anyone will do. As a little boy during the war when I went to the parades, I always waited, often holding hands with my Gram, Jane (Macdonald) Leigh, for the Scotties to come by. When they did, I gave a great shout that was probably the shout of the highlanders at the Battle of Culloden. There was a picture in the papers one day of a parade and there I was, leaning out to look for the Scots and their bagpipes. And whether it's for the foregoing reasons or not, I've spent a lot of time in Scotland and especially in the Highlands, and when I pass through the

Glen of Coe, I feel the pain of my Macdonald ancestors slain in their sleep in 1692 by the hated Campbells.

Once, towards the end of August, Wendy and I were lying on a lovely grassy hill, cheese sandwich and beer in hand, looking out over the lovely turquoise blue water below. It was sunny, about 25 Celsius, with no wind. It could have been a lovely spring day in the North Island of New Zealand or on the Oregon coast but it wasn't. It was the Inner Hebrides Isle of Mull and it was magic. Next to Mull, incidentally, after a short ferry hop is the famous Isle of Staffa with its Fingal's Cave, the inspiration for Mendelssohn's famous music of the same name. This is, actually, the eastern end of the Giant's Causeway that starts in Northern Ireland.

When Wendy and I tell of our love affair with the northwest corner of Scotland and the Isles, friends think we've gone mad. Doesn't it rain or sleet all the time? Doesn't the wind always blow and isn't that why they call it Cape Wrath? The answer is no, but I really shouldn't tell you this because you'll go there, then tell all your friends and the place will be ruined. The goddamned government has already ruined Skye by putting a bridge across Lochalsh against the wishes of the residents. So you had better go to the uninhabited and little explored northwest of Scotland while there's still time.

My love affair with the Highlands started in about 1972 when my first wife, Eve, and I took a whirlwind tour. I made the big mistake we all do—I wanted to see everything in two weeks—so we went at full gallop. Our first stop in the Highlands, just past Tyndrum was at the Bridge of Orchy where I was introduced for the first time to single malt whisky. It happened this way. There is a wonderful old hotel there, run at the time by the delightful Angus Macdonald to whom I had a letter of introduction from an old friend, the late lawyer, Dave McDonald (bad spelling, that!). I left Eve in the car as I went in to see about a room, whereupon Angus, seeing the letter and commenting that I must work on Dave to get the spelling right, invited me into his office. It was just before noon and Angus drew a bottle of Glenmorangie single malt from the desk drawer and offered me a small shot. Well, the previous night Eve and I had been in a small hotel pub in Penrith in the Penines, and I was feeling a bit fragile so, for medicinal reasons, I took it. One led to three and it was an hour later when I went back to the car, half (at least) pissed to find a somewhat irritated, to say the least, wife.

Angus had no room for us but he had found us a lovely bed and breakfast owned by the Fletcher family just up the road. This was a historic spot for it was in their stable, which was still standing, that the Campbells had spent that February in 1692 before taking off for Glencoe and doing their dastardly deeds to my ancestors. That afternoon at Angus's suggestion we drove down to Inverary Castle, the ancestral home of the Black Campbells, and though it was beautiful I was sure I could hear Gram whispering "traitor!" in my ear. The next day we drove to the Kyle of Lochalsh and took the ferry over the sea to Skye, about a 15-minute journey. We drove alongside the Sleat of Raasay, with the Isle of Raasay easily visible, to the "capital" of Skye, Portree, and the Portree Hotel.

The next day, Sunday, we drove around the island out to the statue of my kinswoman, Florence Macdonald, alongside the beautiful Black Coulins and then back to Portree. (In case you're a sassenach and don't know better, the "coulins" are mountains, as Sir Harry Lauder sang in the "Road to the Isles," "there's a far coulin is putting love on me, as tak I wi' my cromach to the Isles….") It was a very good time for a beer, I thought, and it was then we learned something about Skye: The Macdonalds were Protestants and wouldn't touch the stuff on the Sabbath but, fortunately, the Macleods were Catholics so there was one tiny pub around the corner if we truly wanted to break the holy day. We did. That night at dinner a pretty lass of about 18 served us and I asked for the wine list. She recoiled in horror, threw up her arms, waved them about and hollered, "On the Sabbath, Sirrr?" Clearly a Macdonald, she ran from the table never to be seen again. A few moments later the guv'nor arrived with the wine list and advised us that Flora (I just made the name up) was an excitable lass, but he would be glad to serve us the wine of our choice.

In the years to come, I went to the Cape Wrath area on the northwest tip of the Scottish mainland to hike in the hills and fish the wee lochs and lochans that abound. For the most part it's all public water and I must say I was more hooked on the scenery and the hiking than were the fish I was attempting to catch. This trip became an annual event and sometimes I even went back, time and money permitting, twice a year.

Wendy and I got married on July 29, 1994, and took our honeymoon to the Highlands, first spending several days on the Isle of Raasay in a bed and breakfast owned by a delightful lady named Rebecca Mackay. All through the house were religious pictures and icons, some with pithy little quotes such as "Lips that touch liquor will never touch mine." When we went out for dinner, we would come back with a few beer hidden in our coats, hoping they would not be noticed, but as we opened them in our room, we feared that the hissing of the process would alert Rebecca in the living room down the hall to our sins. We could only ponder what our fate would be if what we were doing ever came to the attention of the master or mistress of the house.

As we came in the door on our last night, Rebecca asked if we would care to join her in her den before we retired. I thought of the long hour plus listening while dry to two women gossip, so made my excuses and adjourned to our room for a beer. An hour passed, and I (by now on my third) could hear great merriment down the hall. At about the second hour mark (I will not confess what beer I was on by then) down came Wendy at least half pissed! What had happened? Well, it seems that Rebecca's sourpuss husband, whom we had met and instantly and intensely disliked (demonstrating immaculate perception on our part), was the Presbyterian and non-drinker in the house, and he was responsible for all the religious and temperance messages about the place. Rebecca, on the other hand, just loved to snort a few vodkas from time to time. All was now clear.

After we left Raasay, we went north to a place called Scourie where I had stayed a couple of times before. This was the quintessential Scots Highland fishing hotel with one of the guests appointed master of the fishery, in charge of selecting the lochs where everyone would fish the following day. Even though we pleaded that we were on our honeymoon, as newcomers we got last dibs, so we were assigned, given oarlocks (to prevent the boats being stolen, the oarlocks were always removed after use), an ordnance map and good wishes to find our assigned loch. The day was magic. We hiked up lovely heather-covered hills where the heather was just coming into bloom, and below us we could see the sun glinting off the ocean. I'm not sure what lochs we actually found but they were plentiful, and though the brownies we caught were small—as the Scots would say "two to the pound"—it didn't matter. That night when we met the "master," he surprised us with the good news that one of the guests had to leave early so that on the day after tomorrow we would get one of the salmon beats. But as we had just two more days to spend there, and Wendy and I had fallen love with the lochs, we declined his beneficence and opted for two more days hiking. I pause here to say that the hiking to some of these places can be strenuous but to many they are just pleasant walks. We had a bit of both.

The following year I was pursuing my second favourite hobby—the first being traveling, the second being the planning—when, pawing through a British fly-fishing mag, I chanced upon an advertisement for a place called Rhiconich, north of Scourie and near Cape Wrath itself. What really caught my eye was that the owner's name was Helen Fish, and this I regarded as a very good omen indeed. A few minutes later I had a fax (this was before emails became the rage) saying that she would be pleased to take us for a week.

Experienced travelers know that the picture in the brochure never looks anything like the near dump that is the reality. That said, the brochure scarcely did or could do the place justice. The Rhiconich Hotel and the sea loch, Loch Bervie, are magic. (Incidentally, the long ocean bays are called sea lochs in Scotland.) We had a lovely suite overlooking the loch and the hills behind, and it was as if we had died and gone to heaven. The hiking was of the more strenuous sort but Wendy and I, both being pretty fit, had no trouble negotiating the heather-covered hills with their little babbling streams. I couldn't begin to count the lochs and lochans. They were everywhere you looked. Again the "troot" were two, maybe three to the pound but, since by this time I was using my own ties copied from fly-fishing books, even the small fish gave great satisfaction. And the nightly entertainment in the hotel's small but very cozy bar was listening to old Mac Smith regale us in his wonderful Scottish brogue with stories of the fishing of yesteryear.

But there is more, much more than the fishing at Rhiconich. If you drive down Loch Bervie to Kinlochbervie ("kin" means "head of") and turn right, you will come across one of the loveliest beaches you'll ever see in the world! Unused, except by locals walking their gull-chasing dogs (never has a gull ever been caught, I'm told), it's like paradise on top of the world.

If you drive north of Rhiconich only a few miles, you come to the pleasant seaside town of Durness, and here you have a treat in store for just a mile or so away is an artists' colony with some really super crafts for sale. Now, you might say "seen one artists' colony, seen 'em all," but after you visit the studio of

Lotte Globb, a Danish lady of great international fame in her craft, you won't sing that song. After you look at what she has to offer, you'll be blown away that this kind of art is available so far off the beaten track. She collects rocks from the surrounding hills and then, in furnaces at unbelievable heat, fires and molds these rocks into the most wonderful designs and colours. Some of the things she makes are practical, such as cups, saucers, bowls and the like, and to possess them is to possess a lifelong object of pleasure. Some are simply artistic pieces for display on a table, but it is a wonderful experience just to visit her studio.

While I don't want to move us away from the Cape Wrath area in Caithness and North Sutherland, I must tell you that, if you turn right out of Durness and take the coast road to Tongue, you will see one of the most spectacular sights in the world. The water here is Caribbean turquoise in colour, and the mountains are the ones just back of the lochs we fished, and they make a spectacular backdrop. The drive is breathtaking. So if you're going to head for the east coast of Scotland this is the way to do it. Furthermore, if your meandering takes you to Orkney, the ferry from Scrabster—just a short hop from the northern tip of mainland Scotland at Dunnet Head—is only about an hour from Tongue. (Many, including the people in the tourist shops there think the top is at John O'Groats but it isn't.)

The beautiful seaside town of Lochinver lies to the south of Rhiconich, but though the scenery is spectacular, be advised that much of the drive is on one-way roads with lay-bys. This sort of road is common in the north of Scotland and isn't too bad except on winding roads as the road to Lochinver most certainly is. One the way home you can, however, go back to the main highway.

The northwest of Scotland—give it a try. You'll be glad you did. Just don't tell too many people about it!

How Lucky I Am to Have Been Born to English-speaking Parents

A few years ago I was the dinner guest of my old friend, the Impressionist artist extraordinaire, Daniel Izzard, and my partner at the table was a fascinating lady named Judith. This lady was eastern European in origin and she was fluent in countless languages including English, which she spoke with just that trace of an English accent that identifies people whose mother tongue isn't English but who mastered the language in England not America.

As we chatted, Judith asked if I spoke French. I confessed that I did not despite a dozen years of French courses in school and university. I told her that I had tried to learn by watching the Montreal Canadiens on the French channel, but I couldn't pick up what the commentator was saying even though I knew what he was describing. I opined that I just didn't have the ear necessary to pick up foreign tongues. Her short and caustic reply was, "How fortunate you are to have been born to parents who speak English." Touché.

Or was it? Will my descendants and I have the last laugh as English continues to be the world's lingua franca? I confess I did feel uneasy at Judith's bit of sarcasm because I was aware that a knowledge of languages is an extension of one's knowledge of the world. I was easily persuaded that reading Goethe in German or Victor Hugo in French was different—and much better—than reading the English translations, just as German friends have told me that Shakespeare, though tolerable in German, loses a hell of a lot in the translation. I was reminded of Churchill who wrote that when he was in school all the clever boys learned

Latin and Greek while he was forced to master English—and master it he did!

Over the years I have thought about what Judith said, and while I must confess an envy of those who can speak other languages, I am forced—perhaps because of my own linguistic inadequacy—to come to the defence of us unilingual Anglophones. Not understanding other languages, I must have the boldness of the American chauvinist—so well-known as the Ugly American when he travels—and allege without a shred of evidence except my own prejudice that English is far and away the most wonderful tongue on the planet. Paint me in Bermuda shorts, huge camera around my neck, gigantic stogie in my mouth as I wander down the Champs Elysees, complaining loudly that I can't make myself understood. That's me—sans cigar, of course! When it comes to the English language, since I have no evidence, I must do as all good lawyers do in such circumstances, pound the table and shout. I suppose I am of the Mark Twain school; upon visiting Paris for the first time he remarked, "I couldn't make the damned fools understand me even though I spoke to them in their own language."

English has two great advantages over most tongues. First, although all languages—way back, I'm told—bear relationships to other tongues, English is the one language that has not just accepted but greedily snatched words from foreign tongues for its own. It's not just the Norse, Celtic and French words that came with conquests of Britain—that part was easy—but we have taken words from places Britain conquered and absorbed them just as though we'd thought of them ourselves. For example, we got pajamas, bungalow and khaki from India. The French Academy has taken quite the opposite tack. Petrified at the possibility of language pollution, it outlaws words on a regular basis. It can't enforce its rulings, of course, but it is deadly serious about keeping the French language as pure as possible.

It's interesting to contrast English and French in other ways as well. French is a tidy language except for its insistence that each noun have a gender. Why? What does gender add to a language except an annoying linguistic excess? At the same time French is a longer language, as I'm sure you've noticed when you see instructions in English followed by the French version. Treaties were once written in French because their words were believed to be more precise, although, in fact, they weren't and that caused all sorts of trouble. Because French hasn't permitted new words to creep into the language, there is more likelihood of a single French word having to do the work of a half dozen English ones and more possibility of an error in translation. English, because it readily absorbs foreign words as its own, is a language of synonyms and thus a language of shades of meaning. No matter what your discourse, you can alter the meaning ever so slightly by using your thesaurus. This is no doubt why, even though it's a hard language to learn, it has become the worldwide language of commerce and international affairs.

Choosing Books for the Long Haul

Lists are very fashionable these days—a list of the best and worst of this, that or the other thing. After browsing through a book of lists recently, I thought I might compile a list of books that have affected my life but dissuaded myself quickly because I realized that, to be absolutely faithful to the test, I would have to list such classics as *Jerry and Jane, Mr. Popper's Penguins, Latin For Today,* all of Thornton W. Burgess' books, *The Coral Island: A Tale of the Pacific Ocean* by R. M. Ballantyne and my English 202 textbook. One doesn't hear of most of these books now, I suppose, but for me *The Coral Island* was a riveting experience, my first can't-put-it-down book. I would also have to include books I knew about in school but didn't really understand until I got to university, Jonathan Swift's *Gulliver's Travels* for one. Then there would be books I was supposed to have read—and perhaps did read (the Bible being the first that comes to mind)—the listing of which would be the height of pretentiousness.

Then I had a brain wave. We all have loaned books (and I hate to say borrowed a few) that have never been returned. If I were forced to loan out with the expectation of never having them returned all but, say, 25 of the books I possess, which would I save? I must warn you that they are mostly non-fiction and this I regret, but I must play fair with you. I regret also that I didn't have room to include *Jane Eyre*, which I enjoyed immensely while on a 23-hour flight back in 1990.

My selections were not made with particular care because I knew I could do ten times 25 and still have had plenty of books to choose from out of a library of about 3,000 books.

I am as you know or have deduced, a bookaholic badly in need of a 12-step program. I look up from my computer now and see more than 50 fairly current books that I have not begun. To Wendy I excuse myself by pointing out that there are more expensive hobbies, though I must admit my case is better made by observing that she's damn near as bad as I am.

So here are my 25 with absolutely no attempt to grade them.

1. *The New English Bible*, not for spiritual guidance—at least by no means exclusively for that reason—but more to continue my ongoing test of Christian dogma. How could I argue with my fundamentalist Christian friends in the Fraser Valley or debate points of faith with Catholics without this basic tool?

2. Volume V of Sir Martin Gilbert's eight-volume truly magisterial biography of Winston Churchill. This volume is entitled *Finest Hour* and tells, essentially, how in 1940–41 Britain stood alone. My fascination with it is this: Though you know how the story turns out, as you move through the book, you can't begin to believe the ending. I keep saying but they can't possibly make it! Inside this volume I would paste that wonderful cartoon by David Low that shows a British Tommy standing on the Cliffs of Dover, shaking his fist at incoming bombers. The caption, which says it all, reads, "Very well. Alone!"

3. A.J.P. Taylor's biography of Beaverbrook, aka Max Aitken, the Canadian who went to London to make his pile and wield influence. He did both in spades. He was a towering presence on Fleet Street, becoming one of the great newspaper moguls, a clan which—though the members have changed, of course—remains to this day. Though he often opposed his great friend Churchill, for example over Munich, Churchill made him minister of aircraft production in 1940, and it is to Beaverbrook

that Britain and, in a larger sense, the world owe a huge debt of gratitude for the superlative results.

4. *The Proud Tower* by that wonderful popular historian, Barbara Tuchman. This brilliant book encapsulates pre-1914 European society and takes the reader step by step to August 6, 1914, when World War I broke out. It is amazing to be able to look back from this distance at how the great powers slowly but surely, and without some of them knowing it was happening, marched down a path that almost, in retrospect, seems pre-ordained. Churchill, though best remembered for his World War II heroics, also played an important role in the pre-war countdown. In 1911, while First Lord of the Admiralty, he switched the Royal Navy's ships from coal to oil power, thus very much increasing the range of the fleet and making supplying it infinitely easier. On August 1, 1914, while most in Britain including his colleagues saw war as unlikely, Churchill sent the fleet to sea in full battle array, thus saving it from attack in the harbours and permitting it to start blockading the continent.

5. *Pride and Prejudice* by Jane Austen, perhaps the most enjoyable work of fiction ever written, is a wonderful love story and at the same time a marvelous critique of the English upper middle class in the nineteenth century. Like all Austen's works, this book can be left for a bit then picked up as if you were never away.

6. *Sarum* by Edward Rutherfurd is the carefully and brilliantly told tale of the building of Salisbury Cathedral over several centuries. I have interviewed Rutherfurd in person for his books, *London*, *The Forest*, *Russka* and *Princes of Ireland*, all of which use the unique literary stratagem of tracing families from their beginnings until modern times, a bit of author's glue that adds very significantly to the tale being told. He is a wonderful storyteller.

7. *Five Days in London* by John Lukacs. It was May 1940. France was doomed. The British Expeditionary Force was trapped in Dunkirk, France. Britain was most assuredly going to be Hitler's next victim. If Britain could get favourable terms, why not negotiate for peace? At this point Winston Churchill had only been prime minister for a fortnight and, for all his personal strength, was far from secure in the job. He was not the leader of the Conservative Party, which included a large number who, to put it mildly, disliked him for the stand he had taken against the government during the '30s. Would he last or would he be replaced by someone who could make peace with Hitler? We know that he survived, and what this marvelous, fairly small book reveals is how that was due to support from the man he replaced, Neville Chamberlain. It's a compelling story that can't be told enough times to suit me.

An interesting sidelight was that Churchill, while having no intention of making peace with Hitler because he knew Hitler could not be trusted, did not discourage the "peace party" from talking with Hitler through private channels. This was a deliberate delaying tactic because Churchill knew that, if an invasion could be held off until September, it could not come until the following spring. And who could know what might happen by then? What did happen was Hitler turned his attention to the Soviet Union.

8. *From Beirut to Jerusalem* by Thomas Friedman. Though written in the 1980s this remains the most readable of his three books, and it is, I think, a most fair summation of the bottle that holds the two scorpions called Palestine and Israel.

9. *The Lexus and the Olive Tree* by Thomas L. Friedman. In the simple but thorough way that is the hallmark of this *New York Times* veteran, this extraordinary book explains globalization in all its manifestations.

10. *The World is Flat*, also by Friedman. Ever wonder why your Amex bill comes from India? This wonderful effort tells us what globalization has brought about and how to deal with it. It's scarcely all happiness and wealth, but Friedman shows us all sides and a common sense set of solutions.

11. *Wouldn't Have Missed It* by Ogden Nash. As a child I became hooked on the late American poet laureate of humorous verse. My mother would deliberately leave her *New Yorker* around where I might read it and I did. I think I've collected most of his stuff, this book being a compilation of some of his best. One doesn't hear much of Ogden Nash these days, but in the '30s and '40s he was a part of the Algonquin Round Table at the New York hotel of the same name and traded quips with the likes of Robert Benchley, Alexander Woollcott, Dorothy Parker and that ilk. He does live on with some short quips such as his "Reflections on Ice-breaking" which simply stated, "Candy is dandy but Liquor is quicker."

12. *The Complete Cartoons of The New Yorker,* numbering, as of the 2004 publishing date, 68,647! The majority are on CD ROMs but the book itself, which weighs in at 15 pounds, is the coffee table book to end all coffee table books.

13. *Franklin Delano Roosevelt* by Conrad Black. Lord Black is in some trouble as this is written and even when he isn't, he's as hard to like as his wife, the snooty Barbara Amiel. But I would keep this book for two reasons: It is well written and it looks at Roosevelt, the socialist, through the eyes of a man who is definitely of the Right. It may surprise you to learn that Black became a fan and it shows. Mind you, this is not a hagiography and it shows the warts, but you come away from this read feeling you know one of the greatest men of the 20th century much better.

14. *Churchill* by Roy Jenkins. God only knows how many biographies of the Right Honourable Sir Winston Churchill have been written, but I think I've read them all, and for me this one is the best in a single volume. (I say that because Martin Gilbert's eight-volume official biography is the one every Churchillian worthy of the name must read.) What makes the late Lord Jenkins' book so special is that he also wrote a biography of Gladstone (which would easily get into my second list) and after doing so, concluded that Gladstone had been 10 Downing Street's best. However, at the conclusion of *Churchill*, he gave him the nod instead. This one is the perfect present for someone who has admitted that he wished he knew Churchill a bit better.

15. *The Compleat Angler* by Izaak Walton. This should be required reading for all who would angle. Scarcely a purist, Walton fished for whatever was in the river with whatever bait would get the job done. There is a chapter by Charles Cotton on fly-fishing and devotees of that sport will marvel how so much of what Cotton writes resonates today. This book either carries you away into dreams of hours by the river or you weren't meant to be a true fisherman.

16. *The West Beyond the West* by Jean Barman. As a British Columbian I have long chafed at the lack of interest in BC's wonderful history. There has always been this official impression that BC came about as a result of migration of hardy Ontarians over the prairies and through the bitterly cold mountains and it is to them we owe everything we have. Nothing could be further from the truth, of course, and Jean Barman tells it like it truly was. A heck of a read, unless you're from central Canada and don't like your cherished myths shattered.

17. *Collapse* by Jared Diamond. This book, by the author of *Guns, Germs and Steel*, is surely a masterpiece as Diamond traces the environmental disasters that have shattered one civilization after another and concludes that we may well be on the path to a world environmental catastrophe. This is compelling reading, even for those who think that there is always another valley to cut, another river to deplete.

18. *Hitler* by Ian Kershaw. I cheat a bit here because this biography is in two volumes. It is, simply put, a masterpiece.

19. *Will in the World: How Shakespeare Became Shakespeare* by Stephen Greenblatt. This is the best and easiest to read of all the bios of the Bard and makes one feel part of late 16th and early 17th century England.

20. *Truman* by David McCulloch, more recently the biographer of John Adams and the chronicler of the American War of Independence. Harry S. Truman was one of those great surprises in the world of international politics. When he became Franklin Roosevelt's vice-president in 1945, few Americans knew much about him, and those who did likely saw him as a failed haberdasher from Missouri and part of the Kansas City Prendergast machine. When he became president on Roosevelt's death on April 12, 1945, those who know about these things thought they had a lightweight on their hands. To say that Truman fooled 'em would be a masterpiece of understatement. He became a much admired world statesman. On the domestic front he battled the highly favoured New York Governor Thomas Dewey for the presidency in 1948 and despite the fact that there were two splinter groups on the left, Henry Wallace's Progressive Party and Strom Thurmond's Dixiecrats, Truman won. McCulloch's biography is simply excellent.

21. *Nelson* by Carolla Oman. Admiral Nelson has been lucky in his biographers, of whom there have been several, and I pick Oman's book for no better reason than I liked it best. Nelson's life is, of course, one of great adventure, of magnificent and important victories at sea, and a love affair with Emma, the wife of his friend, Sir William Hamilton, who evidently considered it an honour to make this marital donation. It was probably Nelson's great victory at Trafalgar in 1805 more than the Battle of Waterloo ten years on that doomed Napoleon. After Nelson's great victory Britain was safe from invasion and able to help out on the mainland first in Iberia (Spain and Portugal) and later in Belgium at Waterloo. (Recently I was amused to see Nelson's name included on a list of prominent left-handers. He was left-handed all right but only because his right arm was blown off in battle.) This book is really a marvelous biography of the man who left the Royal Navy with the "Nelson touch."

22. *Tom Paine* by Sir John Keane or *Thomas Paine* by Jack Fruchtman Jr. These are both very good biographies of the dirt poor, uneducated Englishman whose pamphleteering inspired first the American then the French revolutions. *Common Sense*, the philosophical underpinning of the War of Independence ("These are the times that try men's souls…") was a runaway bestseller. I've elected to break the rules and keep both volumes because, next to Churchill, Paine is my hero, and both books, which came out at the same time, are superb.

23. *Oscar Wilde* by Richard Ellmann. It's hard to believe in today's world that a man could be brought down from the highest rung of society and the arts, sent to jail, abandoned and condemned to die of a broken heart because he was a homosexual. In fact, Wilde was what some would now call a

switch-hitter as he had a long-suffering and faithful wife and two sons (who eventually changed their surnames to Holland). Oscar Wilde's brilliant plays have not only stood the test of time but rarely has a season passed without one of them running on the London stage. This is an excellent book that tells of Wilde's roller-coaster life with understanding and accuracy.

24. *Mandela* by Anthony Sampson. What can be said about Nelson Mandela that hasn't been said? Nothing, I suppose, but if you read this marvelous biography you are left with a feeling of disbelief that this man could be imprisoned for 26 years, with much of those years being hard time, and not emerge mentally incapable of functioning. At the very best one would have thought that he would be a permanently embittered man. We know the story, of course, of how he became the first black president of hitherto segregated and discriminatory South Africa but, even knowing the outcome, the reader is still tantalized to have all the details behind this amazing tale.

25. *In Command of History* by David Reynolds. Finally there appears an examination of Churchill's place in history that is not hagiographic or fawning. David Reynolds dissects the war years and the decisions Churchill took in a painstaking but eminently readable fashion. Churchill once said that history would be kind to him because he intended to write it—which, of course, he did. But over the years, especially in the '80s and '90s, the revisionists went to work on Churchill's reputation with at least two, David Irving and Clive Ponting, all but concluding that he was little short of evil or at best hopelessly incompetent. But Reynolds concludes this excellent book thus: "Churchill had dominated the field for a quarter century—through speeches and deeds in wartime and, even more, by what he wrote afterwards. And he surely must have known, as he finally slipped away, that he had won the immortality he

craved. In death, as in life, Winston Churchill continues to glow. He remains in command of history."

And if I was to have, so to speak, one more book for the road? One that I should have included had it not been virtually a 25-way tie for the list? Indeed. And it is a delight because it is the writings of the most thoughtful man of the left in modern times (at least in my view): *Essays* by George Orwell.

So there they are—one man's list. No more than that.

Headliners

Dal Richards

Dal Richards was born, I think, just as Wellington was celebrating his win at Waterloo. He's been around so long that no one can remember when he wasn't part of Vancouver's entertainment scene. The entire west side of the city grew up knowing that a formal gown or tuxedo and an evening at the Panorama Roof at the Vancouver Hotel meant that they were grown up enough to smoke in front of their parents and that youth was passing.

When congratulating Dal on 60 years of entertaining at the Pacific National Exhibition (yes, 60!), I told the crowd that statistics showed conclusively that about 25 percent of Vancouver's births occurred nine months after a boozy evening at the "Roof," listening to the wonderful swing of Dal and his band, then to the strains of "The Hour of Parting," heading off to the back seat of the car.

As I write this, Dal is still working more than 20 gigs a month and doing his weekly radio show, "Dal's Place," on 600AM as well as making his never-ending efforts on behalf of the Variety Club. I'm fortunate to do the occasional guest bit with Dal on his radio show, and no broadcasting I've done or will ever do can match this time with him, remembering music and events of the past amidst the laughter he always inspires. A wonderful guy who truly is Mr. Vancouver.

Jack Webster

There has never been anyone quite like Jack Webster and there never will be. A gruff Scot from Glasgow with a heart of pure gold, Jack established talk radio in Vancouver and kept it going when it went out of fashion elsewhere. He wasn't the first—that honour goes to a minister who had a show (on CKWX, I believe) called "The Pastor's Study." And there were others who had very popular shows in the '60s and '70s—Pat Burns, Dave Abbott, Ed Murphy, Gary Bannerman and Barrie Clark come to mind.

Jack got his start in radio when he was working the police beat as a reporter for the *Vancouver Sun* and was assigned to cover a commission, chaired by Reginald Tupper, QC, that was looking into alleged wrongdoing by an ex-police chief named Walter Mulligan. Mr. Tupper would not allow tape recorders to be used in his court, but Jack knew shorthand, and during breaks he would go to a pay phone and give listeners at CJOR600 the word-by-word coverage. His radio career thereafter was spectacular, and he became the first talk show host in Vancouver to have bidding wars for his services and, later in his career, the first to be paid to stay in TV and out of radio.

I remember Jack as a fighter for causes, especially those of the less well-off. I first met him in the early '60s when he went to bat for a client of mine whose car had been seized by the crown and forfeited because the man's son had been pulled over on a Saturday night and the police had found a mickey of vodka in the possession of the boy's passenger. Under the law as it then existed, if any offence against the Liquor Act was deemed to have been committed in a car or other conveyance including a boat, said conveyance could be seized by the police and forfeited to Her Majesty upon conviction of the wrongdoer. When Webster learned about the case, he raised proper Hell, but it didn't dissuade the attorney general. (In the end to get his car back my client had to apologize for "his crime," but the car came back with a cracked block because it had been left out all winter without anti-freeze. It seems the car belonged to the Queen when the block cracked and she was not obliged to put anti-freeze in her own car!)

Jack went into morning TV in the '70s, and although his stature made certain he got all the high-profile guests, the show wasn't nearly as highly rated as was assumed, morning being a tough time to attract an audience to TV. But when his show was moved to the afternoon, he did very well.

Jack was rough, gruff, and a drinker of the old school. He was also charming when he wanted to be, kind to a fault and always on the side of the "little" guy or gal. I have told the story elsewhere of how he got me into the radio business, something for which I will forever be grateful, and it is fitting that the highlight of my radio career was when I won the Bruce Hutchison Award for Lifetime Achievement at the Jack Webster Awards in October 2004. And I'm sure I heard a gruff Scots brogue saying, "Not bad, Mairrrr, not bad at all fer a bluddy lawyer and politician."

Pat Burns

Pat Burns, the bigoted, lovable and loved Talk Show Host from the '60s until his death in the late '80s, had an audience like no other. When at one point he left Vancouver for Montreal so he could torment Quebec separatists and French-speaking Quebeckers generally, the send-off arranged for the Queen Elizabeth Theatre caused a traffic jam that lasted for hours. He was a true legend in the broadcasting field.

Early in 1981, while listening to his own station's 10 AM news, Pat learned that he was leaving the morning show at

CJOR600 and moving to the afternoon, with his morning spot being taken by a man without any radio experience and until a few moments before the BC health minister—yes, that's me, folks. You might have thought he would be bitter at this shabby treatment, but if he was it didn't show. Just before my first moment on air the receptionist came and said, "Rafe, a phone call. I think you should take it." It was Pat. "Break a leg, kid," said the gruff voice, the show biz equivalent of "Get out there and wow 'em!"

Pat listened to my show and, if the subject was baseball, never hesitated to call me on air. One day I said, "In 1946 Harry "The Cat" Brecheen was the first pitcher to win three games in a World Series." Moments later I heard the famous Burns growl. "I think you missed Christy Mathewson in 1905 pitching for the Giants." He was right. We used to see each other at the racetrack a lot and he had an encyclopedic knowledge of that sport, too.

Pat didn't care all that much about interviewing guests and much preferred open line where he would infuriate "Wimslibbers" by calling female callers "doll," and though he tended to be a tad on the racist side, he was always gentlemanly about it—if one can be a racist in a gentlemanly way. One of the greatest in his profession, loved by his fans, hated by the Establishment.

Vicki Gabereau

Vicki Gabereau is easily the most versatile broadcaster I ever saw or heard. Back in the early '80s when I was really a wet-behind-the-ears rookie broadcaster, I was asked by Peter Wilson of the *Vancouver Sun* to review a book she had written. I hope it wasn't professional jealousy on my part, but I didn't like the book and said so in no uncertain terms. Later I had second thoughts and tried to get Peter to let me change it, but he wanted to run it as it was. I must admit it was an unfair review, and in the years that followed I would see Vicki from time to time and was always sure she was going to level me, which she had every right to do. Not a bit of it. Every time we met she was super nice.

In the mid-'90s Vicki left her long-running radio show on CBC to go into TV, and she was a guest on my program, starting at 8:40 and running to 8:58 when, because of network commitments, I had to break right on the second for the news. I kept waiting for Vicki to say something about that review but she was just as nice as pie. Then at about 8:57, as I was working toward the break, Vicki, her eye on the clock, said, "Wait a minute, Buster. There's something I've been wanting to say to you for ten years!" And she let me have it with both barrels. She knew my time problems and ended her justified tirade right at 8:58 on the dot. I could only sit back and exclaim in admiration, "Vicki, that was one of the greatest 'gotchas' I have ever seen." I couldn't stop laughing and neither could she. What goes around comes around. I was and remain a great admirer and, I hope, a friend. She is the greatest.

Robert "Red" Robinson

Red has just completed 50 years in radio in Vancouver, an outstanding record by an outstanding person. As a disc jockey back in the '50s he interviewed and was master of ceremonies for all the great rock stars, including Elvis Presley and the Beatles when they came to town, and he has authored a number of books on the entertainment business. He is a member of every "Hall of Fame" associated with show business.

But Red has another feather in his cap. In an era where there was a considerable lowering of standards, professional and personal, Red has remained utterly incorruptible, has never been associated with drugs and has been happily married for well over 40 years to the lovely Carole.

When I was "between engagements" in June 2003, it was Red I turned to for help, and he gave it to me big time. Leo Durocher was wrong: sometimes good guys finish first.

Winston Churchill

Back in the '80s I interviewed Winston Churchill—not the original but his grandson, who was at that time a member of the British parliament—in the House of Commons about a book he had written. However, a far more memorable moment with him came during the VE Day celebrations on May 8, 1995. My friend Stan Winfield, who had been in London on that day in 1945 as a member of the Royal Canadian Air Force, was with Wendy and me as we went to Buckingham Palace for the re-enactment of the balcony appearance of King George VI, Queen Elizabeth, the two princesses, Elizabeth and Margaret Rose, and Winston Churchill. Of course, the King and Churchill were long dead but the others appeared. Vera Lynn and Harry Secombe sang, a squadron of Spitfires flew over and there were bands playing stirring marches. After the ceremony Stan, Wendy and I walked down Buckingham Palace Road amid the swirling mob in search of a pub. I was having a bad time with my knee so we stopped to rest. I had just said to Stan and Wendy, "Wouldn't it have been wonderful if, just for a split second, Churchill could have appeared on the balcony?" when out of the crowd came a middle-aged man with two younger men. "I see," he said to Stan, "by the medals you are wearing that you're a Canadian. I'm Winston Churchill and these are my sons Randolph and Jack." It was eerie. Mr. Churchill then alleged that he remembered our interview and we all had a lovely chat.

His son Jack is, of course, named after Winston's brother and Randolph after the wartime leader's father, a very prominent politician of the late 19th century.

Lady Mary Soames

I have interviewed Churchill's youngest daughter three times, twice by phone and once in person in the Hotel Vancouver. This last interview was about her biography of her mother, the remarkable Clemmie. We spoke of her father, of course, and I was astonished at the obvious love this lady had for her parents and the matter-of-fact way she described growing up in this remarkable family. A beautiful, gracious lady whose son, Nicholas Soames, and nephew, Winston Churchill, were both then serving in the Margaret Thatcher government, she obviously took great pleasure describing her father's life at centre stage. I was, quite frankly, star-struck. My hero's daughter!

Lady Soames has, happily, her mother's looks, though to listen to her, she was Daddy's girl, too, and as a child "helped" him build his famous brick wall and watched him paint. During the war she operated an anti-aircraft gun in Hyde Park, a job scarcely without its dangers.

The Churchills had five children. One, Marigold, died as a young child. Randolph, who inherited his father's writing ability, had a good war record but a serious alcohol problem. After he had a non-cancerous lump on his lung removed, his friend Evelyn Waugh commented, "How like modern surgery to remove the only part of Randolph Churchill that isn't malignant!" The Churchills' oldest daughter, Sarah, was a very talented actress and dancer who also had a serious booze problem and committed suicide late in Churchill's life, a fact that was kept from him. Mary, it is often said, was the only Churchill child who turned out well, which is pretty unfair given the accomplishments of the others despite their problems. But Mary Churchill, now Lady Soames OBE, is quite a lady and did manage the enormous task of growing up the daughter of, by almost universal agreement, the Man of the 20th Century.

Sir William Deakin

Bill Deakin was one of Churchill's history researchers and a don at Oxford. It was a thrill to meet him because here was a man who had been truly close to the great man. Although Churchill had wanted to win the Nobel Prize for Peace, after World War II he was given the prize for literature for his history of World War II. However, throughout the 1930s and spasmodically during the war, he had worked on his *History of the English Speaking Peoples,* which was intended to be, and is, a popular history, a genre which in Churchill's mind was a factual history but with his particular take on events. Bill Deakin did much of the research for this book.

He tells a wonderful story of phoning Churchill one Friday to tell him that he wouldn't be able to make it to Chartwell, Churchill's home in Kent, that weekend to work.

"Fine, Bill," said Churchill, "so we'll pick you up at Westerham [the nearest station to Chartwell] at 11 a.m., shall we?"

"But Mr. Churchill, I can't make it!" replied Deakin.

"Right then, Bill, there it is—11 a.m. on Saturday at Westerham," and he hung up.

Bill was there at 11 a.m. on Saturday.

Sir William Deakin became a world-renowned historian and a frequent contributor to dinners and the like in Sir Winston Churchill's memory and honour. He was a wonderful interview. He died in February 2005 at 92, full of honours and assured a place in history.

Grace Hamblin

Grace Hamblin was Churchill's principal secretary for many years and tells wonderful stories about him. He worked from a stand-up desk of his own invention, which still remains in his study at Chartwell. His secretaries were expected to be there whenever he wanted them, and because he did his best work after midnight, he often called on them to take dictation until three or four in the morning. As he moved around his den like a caged lion—which in many ways and at many times he was—the secretary was expected to get it all down exactly as he said it, even though he would often correct himself by going back several paragraphs.

I asked Grace what sort of a person he was to work for. Very difficult, she said, and often short-tempered and very inconsiderate. When I asked why she had put up with it, she was very brief and to the point. "He was always truly sorry when he was rude. Besides, we all loved him and he was, after all, the greatest man alive."

Vera Lynn and an Unknown East Londoner

The night of May 8, 1995, the 50th anniversary of VE Day, Wendy and I went to Speakers' Corner in Hyde Park for the extravaganza to end all extravaganzas. Fortunately we had seats in the instant stands that had been erected, and sitting next to and behind us were a group of perhaps a dozen elderly people from the East End of London who had lived through the Blitz and were now having the time of their lives. The show was a revue of all the musicals over the years leading up to World War II and from the wartime as well, and our East Enders chomped their sandwiches and drank their wine as they sang "Knees Up, Mother Brown" and other classics along with the performers.

Periodically the songs were interrupted by more serious matters such as a song by Vera Lynn, "The Sweetheart of the Armed Forces," or the appearance of the Queen who lit a torch starting a similar process around the country. During one such moment, Robert Hardy of *All Creatures Great and Small* fame, who has played Churchill in films and television, gave us Churchill's May 8, 1945, speech to the crowd. "Never in our long history have we ever seen a day like this," proclaimed Hardy in an excellent copy of Churchill's voice. As he paused, you could have heard a pin drop, and an eighty-ish lady from our East End group stood up, clenched her fist and shouted, "And we stood alone!" It was an electric moment. Just writing about it sends shivers up my back! The show closed with Vera Lynn singing "We'll Meet Again," to the accompaniment of 250,000 voices. I'm sure there wasn't a dry eye in the house.

Some years later I had the great honour of interviewing Dame Vera and, as we played a couple of her songs in the intervals, I had the great fun of singing "We'll Meet Again" along with her. A wonderful moment.

Reverend Ian Paisley

I interviewed the Reverend Ian Paisley around 1982 when the "troubles" in Northern Ireland were heating up. He was in Vancouver to speak and raise money for the Protestant cause. When the interview started out, he was charming and almost laid-back as he chatted about affairs in the Belfast he loved, but then he slowly but surely warmed to his task. Bit by bit, without any interruption from me—I don't know how I could have done that if I'd wanted to—he began to lambaste the Catholics in general and the Pope in particular, referring to him as that "man in Rome with the funny leggings and the silly white beanie." By the end of the interview I was wringing wet just watching and listening.

I didn't care for him much but it was an experience worth having.

J.K. Rowling

The arrangements for my interview with J.K. Rowling were shrouded in mystery. So popular was the creator of *Harry Potter* that my studio would never do for the interview; we would have to set up a makeshift studio elsewhere. But where? I would only find that out on the morning of the interview. (It turned out to be a room in the Waterfront Hotel.)

I cursed this interview because I wasn't in the slightest bit interested in reading a kids' book called *Harry Potter and the Philosopher's Stone*. However, I left myself an hour or so on the Sunday prior to the interview to flip through it, and the next thing I knew I'd read the whole damned thing! I loved it. It mesmerized me!

J.K. Rowling, better looking by far than her pictures (in which she's still very pretty), is soft-spoken and modest, apparently genuinely so. One would expect that someone so recently a single mom on welfare would show some signs of exuberance at suddenly becoming a cagillionaire but no. She was calm and informative, her answers punctuated with a keen sense of fun.

The interview ended and I still wondered what all the fuss and secrecy had been about. But as I left the building, I was accosted by a small crowd of young people who indicated they were part of a larger crowd seeking her autograph, and I finally understood what it was all about.

Every so often a very nice, genuine person wins big—and that is the story of J.K. Rowling.

Salman Rushdie

I am not usually much awed by guests, but when the author of *The Satanic Verses* was to be my guest I was truly—for a moment anyway—overwhelmed. What could I ask him? I was told that he didn't want to talk about the million-dollar fatwa that had haunted him for so many years (you will remember that an Iranian ayotollah had offered all that money to anyone who would kill him) so what else was there to talk about? Like most of the world I'd read about 20 pages max of *Satanic Verses,* but he was with me to promote *Step Across These Lines,* a book of essays—always hard to interview on. I could just visualize the photos of him, those mysterious, piercing eyes, the visage of a mystic.

Well, he turned out to be thoroughly charming and quite willing to talk about his involvement on the Left with such luminaries as Sir Harold Pinter and his wife, Lady Antonia Fraser, Sir John Mortimer and so on and had no hesitation at all talking about what it was like to live in fear of the assassin's bullet. By all accounts it was one of my better interviews.

Sir John Mortimer

John Mortimer, creator of *Rumpole of the Bailey,* is an absolute delight whose books I have gobbled up over the years. The first time I interviewed him was on one of his autobiographical books, *Clinging to the Wreckage,* and I suppose I've interviewed him four or five times since. The last time it was in the bar of the

St. Georges Hotel at the top of Regent Street in London, which happened to be most convenient to Wendy and me since we had fallen in love there some six years earlier. John was gracious enough to pay for our celebratory drink of champagne.

As this was right after the O.J. Simpson trial, I asked him (a barrister by trade) what he thought, expecting him to dump all over the American justice system, and I was surprised to hear him say he expected Simpson to be acquitted. He reminded me that jurors are expected to bring their own life experiences into a case. Indeed, that is the reason many lawyers prefer a jury trial to one before a judge alone; judges come to trials with built-in prejudices, and many lawyers believe that these prejudices are a tad illiberal even for those from the upper strata of the Establishment. However, it was not Mortimer's belief that Simpson was innocent. To a barrister like Horace Rumpole or his creator, innocence or guilt is irrelevant. That particular jury, he said, by reason of its make-up, was bound to take a different view of police evidence than one from, say, Beverley Hills. "And who," asked John Mortimer, "is to say they're wrong?"

Leo McKern, the wonderful actor who played Rumpole on television, is now dead, and it seems that Mortimer has written his last Rumpole book. His books are, however, like the TV episodes, the sort of thing that one can indulge in over and over again and always get a great deal of pleasure from them.

Jeffrey Archer

I first met Jeffrey Archer in the early '90s in his sumptuous penthouse on the south side of the Thames overlooking the parliament buildings. The British Consulate had arranged for me to interview him about one of his books. After taping the interview, I went to Charing Cross station to catch the train to Chislehurst, where I was staying with the late Dick Lillico and his lovely wife, Joanna. While waiting, I decided to listen to the interview. Nothing! I'd buggered up the buttons again! I ran to the phone and got Diana, Archer's assistant, on the phone, and after a pause she said, "Mr. Archer understands. If you come back now, you can re-do the interview." He was charming.

That evening my wife wanted to hear the tape so I brought out the recorder. Goddammit! I'd done it again! Despite my wife's remonstrances, I got on the phone and called Diana again and told her what had happened and she laughed, checked with Archer, and I was booked back in for the following morning. This time Archer wasn't so kind and suggested a few failings he had noticed in me as a journalist. But all's well that end's well.

However, in this third interview we somehow got onto the subject of politics. He had, of course, been a Tory MP who had to resign because he went bankrupt in a Canadian mining share scheme. He had come back from bankruptcy with his book *Not a Penny More, Not A Penny Less*, written about this experience, and he was once again away to the races. His deep interest in politics established a new relationship between us—one political junkie to another—and thereafter I would interview Archer once a year on political matters as well as on his books. He was a delight because he was close to Margaret Thatcher and told me to watch a young man he was also close to, John Major. Archer also came to Vancouver on a couple of occasions so in those years I was able to interview him twice.

But Jeffrey Archer, now Lord Archer of Weston-Super-Mare, is a thorough-going scoundrel, and in 1987 the *Star* of London alleged that he had an affair with a hooker, which he obviously had. Archer, however, sued the paper for libel, and he somehow persuaded his spectacularly beautiful and brilliant wife, Mary, to take the stand on his behalf and provide him with an alibi. The judge swallowed the story and charged the jury that no one with so beautiful and accomplished a wife would ever cheat on her. As a result, Archer won and the damages were enormous, but in the years that followed the newspapers watched him like a hawk. It was, however, television producer Ted Francis who eventually "exposed" his friend Lord Archer because he wanted to stop him being elected mayor of London. In 2001 Archer was convicted of perjury arising out of this evidence and sent to jail, thus ensuring that he himself was one of his own best short stories.

But there is good in everyone. Some years ago Wendy came with me to the famous penthouse for my annual interview. Afterwards we walked over the Vauxhall Bridge and visited St. Margaret's Westminster Church where Sir Walter Raleigh was buried—that is, all but his severed head that went elsewhere—and where Churchill and Clemmie were married. It was in the church that Wendy discovered she had no purse. She was sure she had it on leaving Archer's pad but remembered that she had been jostled on the bridge. That was, as it turned out, where it was stolen. Just to be sure, we went back to the Archer flat. No, it wasn't there. Archer asked if we had any cash. We didn't. All our cash, credit cards plus passports were in that purse. Archer pulled out a wad of bills, gave me two fifties, then called his chauffeur and told him to drive Wendy and me to the police station to make out our reports then take us anywhere else we needed to go.

Jeffrey Archer: rogue, scoundrel, perjurer and friend in time of trouble.

Dylan Thomas

In the fall of 1953 the great Welsh poet Dylan Thomas, on the trip on which he would die, came to the University of British Columbia to give a reading of his grand and beautiful poetry. I would like to say I got to know the bard then, but I didn't. What I can say is that, accompanied by half the university, I drank with him in the old Georgia Hotel beer parlour and hung on every word he uttered. He died shortly afterwards in New York (drunkenly suffocating on his own vomit, it is rumoured, though that's not the official version) at the obscenely early age of 39, bringing to mind the final lines of one of my favourite poems, "Fern Hill":

> Oh as I was young and easy in the mercy of his means,
> Time held me green and dying
> Though I sang in my chains like the sea.

One of the books constantly on the table in our living room is a book of Thomas's poems.

Richard Attenborough

The movie was *Grey Owl* and the producer was the elder of the two famous Attenborough brothers, Richard, now Lord Attenborough. (Though a lifetime Labour supporter, like so many of his colleagues, he isn't averse to the trappings of the aristocracy.) I opened the interview with "Lord Attenborough, I remember you as a sniveling little coward!" He looked puzzled and I added, "In Which We Serve." This was the marvelous wartime movie that starred Noel Coward and had a very youthful Richard Attenborough as the young seaman who lost his nerve in battle for which he was forgiven, not shot, by Coward who played the captain. The film was based on the story of HMS *Kelly* and the captain in real life was Lord Louis Mountbatten who was always having ships under his command sunk, a fact that evidently qualified him to become an admiral of the fleet. Attenborough laughed.

The interview was great fun and at the end I thanked his

lordship for coming and he said, "Enjoyed it, Rafe. And please do call me Dick."

I said, "Goodbye, Dick," and I must admit it sounded better than m'lord by a long shot.

Good guy, my friend Dick.

Michael Moore

An ex-wife of mine, who is addicted to the quiz show *Jeopardy!*, often said that with my general knowledge I should seek to be a contestant on it. I knew, however, that I had an enormous gap in that general knowledge, namely, I seldom watched television and the only movies I ever saw were ones I watched under the duress of boredom on airplanes.

Thus it was that when one day I saw on my lineup the name Michael Moore, I asked Shiral Tobin, my esteemed producer and co-host on occasions, "Who's he?" She looked aghast. "You don't know who one of the most famous directors in the world is?"

I didn't, so I started reading the background material on him, but because I didn't recognize any names or productions, I was no better informed. Moore came into the studio, and I said, "Mr. Moore, we have something in common. Until a few moments ago you knew nothing about me and until a few moments ago I knew nothing about you. So I don't embarrass myself further, please tell me just who the hell your are!"

Fortunately, Moore has a neat sense of humour. He laughed and thus began one of the best interviews I've ever had! I later got to know him as a man who has very much the same views of George W. Bush and his entourage as I do.

Bob Hope

It was sometime in the fall of 1960, and I was an articled law student who, to make ends meet for my family of five with one more on the way, had become a teaching pro at the late Al Gleeson's Golflands Driving Range on Sea Island near the Vancouver International Airport. Four cars arrived and suddenly there were a dozen people wearing dark glasses in the small pro shop. They had a stopover in Vancouver on their way to Los Angeles. One of them was Patrice Wymore, the dashing Errol Flynn's then-current squeeze, another was Bob Hope who, as always, had his clubs with him. He had picked up a bit of a slice and wondered if the pro would have a look. I certainly would and I saw a smooth, almost languid swing that betrayed a lot of use. He was swaying somewhat on his backswing, not uncommon for those who swing rhythmically in the pattern of the days prior to Tiger. I got him hooking the ball a bit and he asked what my charge was. Three-fifty, I told him, and he gave me an American five and told me to keep the change. No hell as a tipper but I didn't care. The experience was worth that many times over.

Dr. Michael Smith

Dr. Michael Smith or "Mike," as he preferred to be called, was my guest shortly after he received his Nobel Prize for his work in genomics in 1993. I'm not usually afraid of guests, but I was terrified at the thought of interviewing one of the world's top scientists and, of course, the toast of my alma mater, the University of British Columbia. I imagined a sort of Ichabod Crane type, a toffee-nosed Englishman who didn't want to be here but was inveigled into it by a friend. How was I to question him, knowing absolutely nothing about his specialty?

(Not that this has stopped me before or even prevented me from expressing strong opinions on such matters.) But I could not have been more wrong about Mike. An avuncular, laid-back guy, he knew that I hadn't a clue about what he did and he patiently, but never for a second patronizingly, walked me through the fascinating study of genes.

He was my guest several times before his untimely death at 68 in 2000. In fact, I interviewed him shortly before he died and, although he knew how sick he was, no one else would have known it. What a man!

Ken Georgetti

Ken Georgetti became the youngest ever president of the British Columbia Federation of Labour at about the time we first met. Later he left the BC scene to become president of the Canadian Labour Congress, again the youngest to do so. At one time Ken and I did a weekly joust, and the blood spilling from it was great radio. Indeed, long after we'd stopped our duet, people would come up and say, "I sure love those shows you do with Georgetti!"

Ken is a modern trade unionist in the sense that he doesn't let philosophy dictate how he's going to deal with problems. That doesn't mean he isn't tough as Hell because he is. It does mean that he is going to be dealing with governments of various political hues. It also means that not only is the union movement well served by his involvement but we all are.

I remember doing one interview with him in which he got so angry that he stormed out of the studio without the suggestion of a "good-bye." When I got back to my desk, I sent him an email saying that I hoped he wasn't going to take what I said too seriously and that if he ever felt I had gone too far, why he should just let me know. He fired back, "I wish that sometimes I could write you and tell you that you haven't gone far enough!"

Since then we have been good friends, though when we do get together on air, the fur can still fly.

Christopher Gaze

Christopher Gaze, an Englishman by birth, a Canadian by choice, and a Vancouverite by conviction, is a Shakespearian in every sense of the word. He has acted in the Bard's plays, directed them, and most importantly for those of us lucky enough to live in Vancouver, produced them. Back in 1990 he took a gamble. With little evidence to back the proposition, Gaze decided that Vancouverites were dying to see more Shakespeare so badly that they would go in great numbers to a tent set up on Kitsilano Beach to see it. His gamble has been a huge success as the attendance numbers show. That first year 34 performances drew 6,000 people; in 2004 209 performances of *Much Ado about Nothing*, *The Merry Wives of Windsor* and *Macbeth* drew just a shade less than 70,000! It has become a great summer event for Vancouverites, and while Christopher Gaze would deny it, the credit is all his.

For me, the highlight of my broadcasting year—and I kid you not—is Christopher's pre-season appearance on my radio show when he does Henry V's speech on the eve of Agincourt. I don't know about my audience, but I'm ready to go to war, fight and die for my country by the time he has finished. An amazing man, an amazing talent. And the best part is that he belongs to us.

Dr. Malcolm MacIntyre

When I entered UBC law school in October 1952, Dr. Malcolm MacIntyre was the prof who taught torts (civil wrongs). A big man for his times, "Dr. Mac" had a shock of grey hair that tossed like the mane of a pony as he spoke and gesticulated, head forward, shoulders hunched. He loved the law and he loved his students in a general sense—he played no favourites but saw all of us as damp clay that with a bit of effort could be molded into something remarkable.

His was, I think, a variation of the Socratic method: He would throw out theories and, if we agreed with him, he would take the other side of the debate; if his theory was contested, he would hold his ground. In doing this he moved from student to student and the time went so fast the lecture seemed to have ended before it began. Attendance was always high for Dr Mac's lectures.

UBC had at that time a learned professor who, when a 55 percent average was needed to pass, gave such ridiculously low marks that, when I was in first year, half a dozen students in the third year class failed. Some actually received less than 10 for both of this brute's courses, making passing their year a near impossibility. I should explain that this was before the Law School Aptitude Tests (LSAT) were invented, and weeding out was done by attrition. It was expected that a quarter or more of first year students would fail their year, another handful would flunk second year, but by third year the students would be home free. There was no such thing as a supplemental examination available, so it looked as if these unlucky scholars would have to repeat third year.

The system, however, reckoned without Dr. Malcolm MacIntyre. He was a man of justice, and it so happened that the dean of the law school took off that summer for a sabbatical, leaving the acting dean, our friend Dr. Mac, in charge. He promptly permitted supplemental examinations, the failed students took them, duly passed them, and had their degrees before the dean could do anything about it.

By the time my class, devastated in first and second year and down to about 55 of its original 100, reached third year, most of us were scared stiff because we were facing two subjects with the evil professor. We also had two courses with Dr. Mac, and on day one he looked us over and said, "All of you have worked hard to get here, and I know you may be afraid of one or two subjects you will be taking. Well, I have two classes with you, and if you continue to work hard, what you lose on the swings you'll make up on the roundabouts." He then paused, looked hard at one student and said, "Except for you, Mr. L. I don't know how you made it this far, but if you don't mend your ways, you'll not be joining your mates on graduation day." Mr. L, as was his wont, snickered—and he didn't make it out of law school with us or any other time.

Dr. Mac had an enormous zest for life. A New Brunswicker by birth, he loved the sea and his small boat as much as he loved his students. I remember writing an article for what is now the *UBC Law Review* but was then called *Legal Notes* on the admissibility of illegally obtained evidence and he was my helper. It would not be too much an exaggeration to say that he, not I, should have been credited as author!

Dr. Mac used to pick up extra money lecturing business people in evening lectures. One night, as the lecture approached the end, Dr. Mac took out a package of tobacco and proceeded to roll himself a cigarette. As the bell rang, Vancouver's three-piece-suited best saw their prof in his baggy corduroys and old boating shoes bend over and scrape the tobacco droppings from the floor back into the package! Mac, if nothing else, was a man without pretensions. But he was more. *Reader's Digest* used to have a feature called "The Most Unforgettable Character I Ever Met" and for me at any rate that was Dr. Malcolm MacIntyre, a man beloved by all his students and a teacher who profoundly affected all of us, very much for the better.

(Malcolm MacIntyre had a son Jim who was in first year when I was, and he also went on to become a much loved prof in the University of British Columbia law school.)

Epilogue:
On Growing Old

When I was young, I learned and have never forgotten the lines of Dylan Thomas that are quoted earlier in this book in a different context:

> Oh as I was young and easy in the mercy of his means
> Time held me green and dying
> Though I sang in my chains like the sea.

I was 18 and in second year at UBC and taking Dylan Thomas amongst other British literary greats and, as I relate elsewhere, actually privileged to see him in the flesh and hear him recite those lines from "Fern Hill."

Also, as noted earlier, I have been a lifelong fan of the very funny American poet, Ogden Nash. He was famous for short snappers. He had this to say about women in slacks:

> Sure, deck your lower limbs in pants,
> Those are your limbs, my sweeting
> You look divine as you advance,
> Have you seen yourself retreating?"

And this on turtles:

> The turtle lives twixt plated decks
> That practically conceals his sex.
> I think it clever of the turtle
> In such a fix to be so fertile.

But Nash could be serious as well, and when I hit 50 and someone kindly gave me a book of Nash's work, I found this little poem in it. It's called "The Middle":

> When I remember bygone days
> I think how evening follows morn;
> So many I loved were not yet dead,
> So many I love were not yet born.

As I look back on my 50th birthday, I remember how melancholy I felt—I had just lost my lovely daughter Shawn—yet how strangely confident and ambitious I was at the same time. Looking ahead from that date I was to see the birth of seven more grandchildren to add to my namesake Kenneth Rafe Mair III and to have the love of my life, Wendy, become part of me. And a hell of a lot more has happened in the years since my 50th as well, including a pretty good political career and a new and final career in the media, both in radio and in print. Indeed, sometimes I must remind myself how much writing has become part of my life in the last quarter century.

But there was another poem in that book of Ogden Nash's work that I remember as well. It is called "Old Men":

> People expect old men to die,
> They don't really expect to mourn old men.
> Old men are different. People look
> At them with eyes that wonder when...
> People watch with unshocked eyes;
> But the old men know when an old man dies.

I have now reached that age, though happily I don't feel it and I'm told I don't look or act it. But when you pass your Biblical allotment there are some things that cross your mind fairly often, and every day when I read the obits, I remind myself I must just take it one day at a time. I tell Wendy, "Don't worry about the expense of going to London, love! As long as I can leave you our nice little nest and a few bob to add to pensions, let's enjoy ourselves together, go where we want to go, and leave the kids and grandkids to make their own way just as we did."

A few years ago I hit upon my own fountain of youth: I vowed to live—symbolically—from that moment on in the shoes of my oldest grandson, who is 25. That means I must worry in a constructive way about things that will happen long after I'm gone. It's not always easy to do this. For example, I will be in my 79th year when the Winter Olympics come to Vancouver/Whistler, and I feel I must worry about that one now. But this approach to life is too good just to let it slide every time I meet a severe test like that one.

None of us has the faintest idea when we're going to go. Even the terminally ill never know if there's a remission around the next corner. The robust, non-smoker can be gone tomorrow. I remember as a very young man having a full physical and the doctor saying I was in fine shape, but having said that, he couldn't guarantee that I would even make it to the elevator.

I have found that, considering the bad part—that is, that the party is coming to a close—there are some pretty good things about getting on a bit. (That's the nice way of saying becoming an old fart!) For one thing there are lots of freebees and cost reductions, though it always amazes me that when we are young and could use a pass or a price reduction here and there, we get zilch. When we have a bit of change in our pockets, people want to give us things! And you get more respect, too. For example, people call you "sir"…Nah, the hell with that one! Respect simply reminds you that you're doddering a bit!

But there are other good things. For instance, you don't usually have to do things you don't like anymore. You can become the revolutionary you wanted to be when you were younger without facing any consequences other than being laughed at behind your back.

Grandchildren, however, are both a joy and a burden. They are a joy because for idiotic reasons of pride we want to continue our genes. It's also kind of neat to be around kids again, especially when you don't have to deal with the sticky bits. But, dammit, as they grow up you age exponentially. It was fun when they were little scapers starting to walk and learning to say some reasonably understandable version of "Grandpa," but when they get older, it's a continuing reminder of your own mortality. As I said, my oldest grandchild is 25 and busy buying a house with his partner, so can it be long before I'm a great-grampa? That, folks, is scary.

At my age people find life is more precious than when they had a lifetime ahead of them, when they did crazy things that exposed their mortality at every turn—driving fast and doing nutty things like hang-gliding, jumping out of planes and scuba diving. Now I've become a slowpoke and even obey the speed signs on the curves in the road, my riskiest undertaking being to get my feet wet when I'm throwing tennis balls into the ocean for Chauncey.

Oddly enough, however, I've found that I've started to move to the Left rather than become more conservative as people generally do with age, but this may be because I'm becoming more conservative in the real meaning of the word. I see the environment crumbling around me and want to do something, even though there's not a hell of a lot I can do as an individual. I've watched the sea around me go from an abundance of fish to a complete absence of some species and the near extinction of others. I can see the effects of global warming and can sense extremely serious consequences of doing nothing—and doing nothing is what our politicians do best. I see the corporatization of my life. Corporations own everything around me including the government. I'm a free trader at heart yet I've come to know that there is no such thing as a good corporate citizen; some may be better than others but the duty of companies is not to do good but make money for their shareholders. I often pose this question to my listeners: Suppose the chairman of a large company came to an annual general meeting of shareholders and said, "Guess what, folks? There will be no dividend this year because your board has decided that, even though no one has forced us, we will put $100 million into new anti-pollution equipment." How long do you think he would stay chairman? My listeners know that he would be out of there tomorrow. But unions are no better. They sometimes talk a better game than Daddy Warbucks, but if it is a toss-up between a lousy little fish-bearing stream and another day's work on the trees surrounding it, they'll chop away every time.

And there is another paradox I'm having trouble handling. In middle age I was coming back to religion, and now, though I believe in a supreme being and the things Jesus taught us about loving God and our neighbours, I find that I have utterly rejected doctrine and can no longer get past the first line of the creed without feeling like an exposed hypocrite. However, I do draw some strength from a story about St. Francis of Assisi who, while hoeing his garden one day, was asked, "What would you do if you knew you were going to die tonight?"

"I'd go right on hoeing my garden," the great holy man replied.

And what else could he do? What can any of us do except go right on hoeing our gardens?

There is no satisfactory answer to old age—for me at any rate—other than to keep on doing what I love most, which is working and avoiding, at all cost, being driven to have coffee with the gang every morning, followed by a rousing game of checkers in the mall. And I keep in mind that growing old was never meant for the faint of heart.

INDEX